"Matthew S. Boone has provided experts in their respective fields that brings the reader up to date with recent developments in the emerging areas of mindfulness and acceptance practice. The authors draw upon their own practice and recent research to provide new concepts and interventions that can be integrated into any social worker's practice model. This is another example of the use of science (research) to enhance our practice artistry."

—**Lawrence Shulman, MSW, EdD**, emeritus professor and dean at the School of Social Work, University at Buffalo

"Matthew S. Boone's edited book on mindfulness and acceptance models for social work practice follows a rising movement in mental health and mind-body interventions. In his own introduction and first chapter, Boone anchors the underlying concepts in social work and evidence-based behavioral health practice, and provides clear examples of how these methods serve clients in great need. Written by social workers and their colleagues, the chapters cover a range of applications of mindfulness and acceptance treatments. The book's accessible and clear writing will be helpful for all who read it."

—**Gail Steketee, PhD**, dean and professor at Boston University School of Social Work

"Social workers: get ready for some brain yoga! This book is a refreshing compilation of articles by social workers for social workers in which ACT and other mindfulness-based interventions are comprehensively portrayed as flexible approaches to remediating many life transitions."

—**Claudia Dewane, DEd**, assistant chair and associate professor in the College of Health Professions and Social Work, Temple University

The Mindfulness & Acceptance Practica Series

As mindfulness and acceptance-based therapies gain momentum in the field of mental health, it is increasingly important for professionals to understand the full range of their applications. To keep up with the growing demand for authoritative resources on these treatments, *The Mindfulness and Acceptance Practica Series* was created. These edited books cover a range of evidence-based treatments, such as acceptance and commitment therapy (ACT), cognitive behavioral therapy (CBT), compassion-focused therapy (CFT), dialectical behavioral therapy (DBT), and mindfulness-based stress reduction (MBSR) therapy. Incorporating new research in the field of psychology, these books are powerful tools for mental health clinicians, researchers, advanced students, and anyone interested in the growth of mindfulness and acceptance strategies.

Visit www.newharbinger.com for more books in this series.

MINDFULNESS & ACCEPTANCE IN SOCIAL WORK

Evidence-Based Interventions & Emerging Applications

Edited by
MATTHEW S. BOONE, LCSW

CONTEXT PRESS
An Imprint of New Harbinger Publications, Inc.

Publisher's Note

This publication is designed to provide accurate and authoritative information in regard to the subject matter covered. It is sold with the understanding that the publisher is not engaged in rendering psychological, financial, legal, or other professional services. If expert assistance or counseling is needed, the services of a competent professional should be sought.

Chapter 5 of this volume is adapted and expanded from "Returning to Silence, Connecting to Wholeness: Contemplative Pedagogy for Critical Social Work Education," by Yuk-Lin Renita Wong, *Journal of Religion and Spirituality in Social Work*, reprinted by permission of Taylor & Francis (http://www.tandfonline.com).

Distributed in Canada by Raincoast Books

Copyright © 2014 by Matthew S. Boone
                New Harbinger Publications, Inc.
                5674 Shattuck Avenue
                Oakland, CA 94609
                www.newharbinger.com

Cover design by Amy Shoup
Acquired by Catharine Meyers
Edited by Melanie Bell
Indexed by James Minkin

All Rights Reserved

Library of Congress Cataloging-in-Publication Data on file

Printed in the United States of America

16   15   14

10 9 8 7 6 5 4 3 2 1   First printing

For Toni

Contents

Preface   ix

Acknowledgments   xv

Introduction: Mindfulness and Acceptance
in Social Work   1
Matthew S. Boone, LCSW, *University of Arkansas at Little Rock*

PART I
The Present Moment: Mindfulness and Acceptance in Direct Practice

1   Acceptance and Commitment Therapy
in Social Work   21
Matthew S. Boone, LCSW, *University of Arkansas at Little Rock*

2   Social Work and Dialectical Behavior Therapy   49
Felicia Marohn, LMSW, *Private Practice, Santa Fe DBT;*
Cedar Koons, MSW, LISW, *Private Practice, Santa Fe DBT,
Behavioral Tech, Seattle, WA*

3   Mindfulness-Based Stress Reduction
    and Social Work   75
    Elana Rosenbaum, LICSW, *Center for Mindfulness in Medicine,
    Health Care, and Society, Worcester, Massachusetts*

4   Social Work and Behavioral Activation   101
    Jonathan W. Kanter, PhD; Ajeng Puspitassari, MA;
    Maria Santos, MA; Gabriela Nagy, BA; *University of
    Wisconsin—Milwaukee*

PART 2
New Directions: Emerging Applications of Mindfulness and Acceptance in Social Work

5   Radical Acceptance: Mindfulness and Critical
    Reflection in Social Work Education   125
    Yuk-Lin Renita Wong, PhD, *York University*

6   Facilitating Mindfulness Using Arts-Based Methods
    and a Holistic Strengths-Based Perspective   145
    Diana Coholic, PhD, *Laurentian University*

7   Doing ACT Briefly: The Practice of Focused
    Acceptance and Commitment Therapy   163
    Tom Linde, MSW, *Private Practice, Group Health Cooperative
    Family Medicine Residency, Seattle, Washington;*
    Kirk Strosahl, PhD, *Mountainview Consulting Group, Central
    Washington Family Medicine, Family Medicine Residency, Yakima,
    Washington*

8   In Pursuit of Excellence: Developing Competencies
    for Delivery of Brief Interventions   187
    Patricia J. Robinson, PhD, *Mountainview Consulting Group,
    Inc., Zillah, WA;* Brian Mundy, LCSW, *Institute for Community
    Living, New York, NY*

PART III
The Client in Context: Addressing Broader Systems

9 Mindfulness and Engaged Buddhism: Implications for a Generalist Macro Social Work Practice   215
Michael Uebel, PhD, LCSW; Clayton Shorkey, PhD, LCSW, *University of Texas at Austin*

10 Thinking Functionally and Contextually About Cultural Diversity in Mindfulness-Based Treatments   235
Akihiko Masuda, PhD, *Georgia State University*; Matthew S. Boone, LCSW, *University of Arkansas at Little Rock*; Mary L. Hill, MA, *Georgia State University*; Rebecca M. Pasillas, PhD, *Texas Tech University Health Sciences Center, Paul L. Foster School of Medicine*

11 Contextual Behavioral Science and Social Work: A Natural and Effective Partnership?   257
Joanne Steinwachs, LCSW, *Private Practice, Denver, Colorado*; Matthew S. Boone, LCSW, *University of Arkansas at Little Rock*

Index   281

Preface

It is not often that you have a genuine epiphany, but I had one when I was twenty-four. It was a modest epiphany—a brief moment when I stumbled onto something simple and striking. And it has shaped my personal and professional lives in the years since.

When I was twenty-two, I developed a puzzling pain condition in both of my arms. I was a musician—a guitarist—and was devoted enough to music that I took two years off from college to pursue a career in Los Angeles. By twenty-two I had returned to school but was still playing as much as possible: performing solo singer-songwriter gigs around town, leading a youth choir, playing an occasional studio session, taking a jazz class, and writing and recording in my home studio. One April day, the morning after hauling my own sound system to a gig and playing for three hours straight, I woke up with pain in my right wrist. This sort of thing happened from time to time when I overdid it. But this time it was different. No matter what I did, the pain would not go away. By the end of that summer, both of my arms hurt whenever I did almost anything. Not only was I unable to play guitar for any length of time, I could not handwrite or type. I was an English major in college, and taking notes and writing papers were my bread and butter. The two things I spent most my time doing, playing and writing, were incredibly painful.

Over the next two years, I went from doctor to doctor, treatment to treatment, accumulating diagnoses along the way: tendinitis, radial tunnel syndrome, myofascial pain syndrome, early reflex sympathetic dystrophy, thoracic outlet syndrome. No diagnosis stuck, and no treatment made much difference. To help me get through my classes, the student disability services at school paid for notetakers. At the time, dictation software was in its infancy, so I wrote my papers looking over the shoulders of the many generous friends who volunteered to type for me. Anyone who writes can probably imagine how excruciating it was to go from rough draft to finished product with an audience every step of the way. In addition to being in daily pain, I was constantly anxious about the lack of control I had over my life. I worried about not knowing what was wrong with me and about how on earth I was going to get through life without the use of my hands. My life narrowed considerably as I spent most of my time trying to stay pain-free. (Readers will notice echoes of my experience in the story of Valerie in chapter 1.)

In the midst of all of this, the two things that actually helped were mindfulness and acceptance, the subjects of this book. My therapist taught me to meditate and encouraged me to read Thich Nhat Hanh, the Vietnamese Zen master and author. Meditation offered me a new relationship to my experience, one in which I was more aware and more patient. Through therapy and meditation, as well as yoga, I learned to come out of my mind and into the present (to be mindful) and to let go of struggling with my circumstances and feelings (to be accepting). When I say I "learned" to do these things, I mean that I discovered them over and over again, little by little. There was no final endpoint; mindfulness and acceptance are orientations toward life we can return to in any given moment. We never "perfect" them. The pain did not go away, but over time I became a little steadier in the face of it. And so I was primed for this small epiphany when it occurred.

I was driving down Highway 880 in Northern California on the way to have lunch with friends. I was in a lot of pain, having played guitar earlier in the day in an effort to finish a song I was writing. I usually avoided playing for more than a few minutes, but that day I had pushed myself, which I occasionally did when I got frustrated with being careful all the time. As a result, just holding the steering wheel hurt. As was my habit in these moments, I was angry and anxious, ruminating about how stupid I was for doing *anything* that would incur pain.

For some reason, in the midst of all this thinking my mind drifted to something my yoga teacher had observed a few weeks earlier. I had expressed reluctance to go deeper into a pose, and she had remarked, "You are really afraid of pain, aren't you?" At the time I had thought, "Of course I am!" as if fear were the only reasonable response to pain. But in that moment in the car, instead of staying wrapped up in my fear, I simply noticed my pain as I had learned to notice my breathing during meditation. I did my best to experience it as it really was. From this perspective, it was really just a feeling, no more intense than a muscle pull or a bad sunburn. I also noticed something else: the fear and the pain were different from one another. The fear was one thing; the pain was another. Everything that followed the fear—the self-criticism, the worry about the future, the desperate need to escape—was just something I added to the pain. I thought to myself, "It's just pain. It's just a sensation." Right then I felt a small sense of peace and a spark of joy. I may have even laughed—my memory is a bit fuzzy.

It is not like everything changed overnight, but this moment set the stage for the next phase of my life. Seeing my pain in this new way allowed me to look up and see the life I was missing. I eventually decided I no longer wanted to be a professional patient, and I stopped seeing doctors all the time. I asked my neurologist if I was in any danger of making my arms worse by occasionally choosing to do things that caused me pain. He said, "Probably not," and I let that be good enough for me. I decided to put my energy into living my life instead of desperately trying to protect myself from discomfort. Despite how difficult finishing my undergraduate degree had been, I eventually went to graduate school and pursued a career in social work. I discovered a new love, one just as strong as my love of music: helping people through psychotherapy.

I am not just any kind of psychotherapist, however—I am a social worker. "Psychotherapist" is just one role social workers inhabit. Social workers are also caseworkers, school counselors, resource brokers, educators, agency managers, advocates, social activists, community organizers, researchers, and political leaders, and they work in just about any setting where people seek help. What ties these disparate roles together is a commitment to viewing human problems as nested within a greater context. Problems like pain or poverty do not just exist inside a person, and neither do their solutions. Both problems and solutions emerge in the dynamic interaction between a person and his or her environment. This is why the profession of social work has always focused, to greater and lesser degrees, on social change. And this is why it is important for me to consider broader contexts when working with individuals and groups, even when we are just talking about thoughts and feelings. For example, though I may never really know the answer, I always question, either out loud or silently to myself, how dynamics that are bigger than us, like race, class, culture, and gender, are influencing our relationship. And I do my best to undermine the inevitable power asymmetry that emerges between the helper and the person being helped so that dynamics that oppress others outside of my office do not find their way into my office. And therefore, more than anything, I try to be a real human being in the face of real human suffering.

It is my desire to truly be present to the suffering of others, as well as my experience as a person who has suffered himself, that draws me to mindfulness and acceptance as tools in the helping process. Mindfulness and acceptance connect me to others in a way that simply sitting and listening does not. They open up space for all of my reactions, even the ones that are not pretty, so that I can face the pain of my clients the way I have learned to face my own. At the same time, practicing mindfulness and acceptance creates new possibilities for my clients and helps facilitate change that is both compassionate and enduring. Mindfulness-based stress reduction, acceptance and commitment therapy, dialectical behavior therapy, and the other models described in this book have offered me comprehensive, well-realized approaches for bringing mindfulness and acceptance to bear in my practice, and I hope readers will be as inspired by them as I have been.

Almost twenty years to the day after I woke up with pain in my right wrist, I still have the same problem: my arms hurt whenever I do most things. Though there is still no explanation, I have found medications that make it less intense, and mindfulness continues to help me experience it for what it is: merely another sensation in my body. Despite daily pain, I think I can say I lead a fulfilling life. And the pain has been an integral part of shaping that fulfillment. If someone were to offer to take it away tomorrow, I would not hesitate. But I would not change the last twenty years for anything.

—Matthew S. Boone
July 2013

Acknowledgments

This book would not be possible without the encouragement and support of many people.

First, I would like to thank this book's chapter authors, who trusted me as a first-time editor, devoted a great deal of time and heart to their efforts, and submitted lovely representations of the best of our field. I cannot thank them enough.

I would also like to thank Steven C. Hayes, who suggested I propose this book. Steve introduced me to acceptance and commitment therapy in a talk he gave at a conference in Boston in 2007, which changed the course of my professional life.

I would also like to acknowledge others in the ACT community with whom I have trained, especially Robyn Walser and Kelly Wilson. I am indebted to their wisdom, compassion, and humor.

Jacqueline Pistorello and Aki Masuda gave me my first opportunities to write about mindfulness and acceptance and were enthusiastic cheerleaders and collaborators despite my tendency to rewrite *their* revisions of my text. Over the last six years, the Association for Contextual Behavioral Science (ACBS) has provided what amounts to a second graduate education in the social sciences, and the Social Work Special Interest Group has become my new home inside ACBS.

Catharine Meyers and Melissa Valentine at New Harbinger walked me through the book development process from start to finish and were forever patient with my rookie questions.

Randy Patterson, Suki Montgomery, and Ken Cohen did not blink when I "came out" as a behaviorist and provided, without question, the strongest influence on my development as a psychotherapist.

Greg Eells, Robin Hamlisch, Sonya Shropshire, Sharon Mier, Cory Myler, the CBS team (my brothers and sisters in social justice), the CHEP Team, and the rest of my colleagues at Cornell University were consistently supportive and rarely yawned at my incessant nattering about acceptance. Jerry Gabriel, Karen Anderson, and Theo Hummer inspired me to make writing a part of my daily life and also made me fancy dinners and cocktails.

The Boston University School of Social Work taught me what it means to be a social worker and made sure I never forgot the bigger, macro picture. (The loans will be paid off next year, in case anyone is wondering.) The CAVHS DBT team warmly embraced me when I relocated to Little Rock and continues to school me in compassionate behavior change every Monday at noon.

Dave Gattey introduced me to mindfulness and acceptance, for which I will forever be grateful. Jim Crofut was my partner in mindfulness early on and remains one of my models of integrity and values-based living. In the early days of my chronic pain, Jenny and Steve Riester Graham demonstrated repeatedly what it looks like to willingly and graciously be of help, an example I do my best to follow in my life and work. Valerie and Jeptha Boone, my parents, taught me more about love, values, and service to others than anyone else, and my four siblings continue to provide me with opportunities to practice noticing my feelings without giving in to the urge to instigate intrafamilial mayhem.

Most importantly, I would like to thank Toni Wall Jaudon, my partner and in-house editor, for her love, patience, and grace every day.

INTRODUCTION

Mindfulness and Acceptance in Social Work

Matthew S. Boone, LCSW

University of Arkansas at Little Rock

> The curious paradox is that when I accept myself just as I am, then I change.
>
> —Carl Rogers (1961, p. 17)

In a conference room in a county hospital, eight patients with chronic illnesses are lying on mats on the floor as a social worker instructs them to imagine breathing in and out of different parts of their bodies. The patients are participants in a mindfulness-based stress reduction (MBSR) program, and they have spent the last five weeks practicing this exercise, called the "body scan," as well as other breathing and yoga exercises, to help them cultivate an open, aware, and nonjudgmental relationship with their bodies. Some of them are beginning to feel a noticeable difference, if not in the level of their daily discomfort, then in their emotional reactions to their discomfort and their willingness to engage in the activities of daily living.

In an urban community mental health center, a social worker is talking with a young man who is facing eviction. He is desperate to find anything to quell the panic and dread he feels at the thought of losing his apartment, and he is worried about relapsing into substance abuse after a year of sobriety. The social worker is helping him name and describe his feelings without trying to change them, "radically accept" his circumstances, and engage in a problem-solving conversation about finding a lawyer. This approach is very different from his usual response to a crisis. Left to his own devices, he might leave harassing messages for his landlord and return to using heroin. Fighting and fleeing are the only ways he has learned to cope. The young man is engaged in a year-long dialectical behavior therapy (DBT) program that combines individual therapy, skills-building groups, and telephone crisis coaching to teach him to navigate his erratic emotions and find alternatives to the self-defeating behaviors with which he usually responds to them.

At a rural Veterans Affairs clinic, a combat veteran who lives with daily flashbacks and a powerful sense of fear is exploring what matters most to him. Because he wants to be the best father he can be, he decides that taking his son to a baseball game will be worth the spike of anxiety he will inevitably experience when he leaves his house. His social worker, a practitioner of acceptance and commitment therapy (ACT, said as one word), reminds him of the compassionate relationship he has begun to build with his fear, noting that welcoming it, rather than gritting his teeth through it, will open up more space to be present with his son, as well as with the game.

MBSR (Kabat-Zinn, 1990), DBT (Linehan, 1993), and ACT (Hayes, Strosahl, & Wilson, 1999) are part of a wave of mindfulness- and acceptance-based interventions which have emerged in the last thirty years to address a variety of health and mental health problems. The list also includes integrative behavioral couple therapy (Jacobson & Christensen, 1998), mindfulness-based cognitive therapy (Segal, Williams, & Teasdale, 2002), mindfulness-based relapse prevention (Bowen, Chawla, & Marlatt, 2011), and others. Though many have come from the cognitive and behavioral traditions in clinical psychology, they all mark, to varying degrees, a shift away from the familiar targets of traditional cognitive behavioral therapy, or CBT (e.g., Beck, Rush, Shaw, & Emery, 1979). Strategies for directly changing painful thoughts and feelings are de-emphasized, though not necessarily abandoned, in favor of reducing unnecessary struggle and allowing pain, whatever form it takes, to simply *be*.

The terms "mindfulness" and "acceptance" have become increasingly common in both the language of health care and the popular vernacular. Mindfulness, especially, has become something of a buzzword, with a host of books, blogs, and self-help programs promising to harness its power in the service of greater peace and contentment. It quickly brings to mind the image of a serene, young, well-dressed, and clear-skinned meditation practitioner, with eyes closed and back straight, sitting attractively on a cushion—the contemporary analogue to the blissful mountaintop guru of years past. Watered down like this, mindfulness risks becoming yet another superficial salve residing in our self-care medicine cabinets, something to be taken out when times are tough, but not something that fundamentally influences the way we live our lives.

Like the practice of mindfulness, the practice of social work is about something more than Band-Aids and easy solutions. Practicing social work is about helping people and communities overcome oppressive circumstances—whether internal or external—and shape their contexts to be more just and attuned to their needs. This book, *Mindfulness and Acceptance in Social Work*, offers a small but important part of the conversation about what happens when we bring together mindfulness and acceptance with the theory and practice of social work—about what happens when individuals, groups, and communities slow down, let go of judgment, and open up to experience. Woven through this text is a gentle encouragement to helping professionals, one which is grounded in social work values, to think about something bigger than the individual's relationship with him- or herself when we think about mindfulness and acceptance. Social work has always been about the ongoing interaction of individuals, groups, families, and communities with their social and physical environments, and mindfulness and acceptance offer a flexible and compassionate context for this interaction.

Awareness, Clarity, and Acceptance

Mindfulness practice comes from Buddhist meditation traditions, but resonances of mindfulness can be found, in one form or another, in many other religious and cultural traditions (e.g., Christian contemplative practices). Mindfulness practice as a psychosocial intervention arguably first gained popularity through the work of Jon Kabat-Zinn at the Stress Reduction Clinic of the University of Massachusetts Medical Center (Kabat-Zinn, 1990). There, Kabat-Zinn and his colleagues developed MBSR to help patients with chronic health conditions. Kabat-Zinn's simple and often quoted definition provides a good introduction to mindfulness: "Mindfulness means paying attention in a particular way: on purpose, in the present moment, and nonjudgmentally" (1994, p. 4). But what follows this definition in his practical introduction to mindfulness, *Wherever You Go, There You Are: Mindfulness Meditation in Everyday Life* (1994), is equally illuminating:

> This kind of attention nurtures greater awareness, clarity, and acceptance of present-moment reality. It wakes us up to the fact that our lives unfold only in moments. If we are not fully present for many of those moments, we may not only miss what is most valuable in our lives but also fail to realize the richness and depth of our possibilities for growth and transformation. (p. 4)

Notice that this passage includes words such as "awareness," "clarity," and "acceptance," not "relaxation," "peacefulness," or "happiness." The latter experiences might show up during a mindfulness exercise, but for the purposes of MBSR and the other models of helping described in the chapters that follow, they would be pleasant by-products. Mindfulness, whether practiced formally as sitting meditation or informally as washing the dishes with intentionality, is simply the practice of noticing, over and over again, what is going on in the continuous present. As a result, the growth and transformation Kabat-Zinn describes may hinge not on *working* to grow and transform, but rather on *slowing down* and *noticing* that nothing inside us really needs to change.

The Theory and Practice of Social Work

The practice of social work overlaps considerably with other helping professions such as psychology, nursing, and medicine. However, social work has a distinctive focus on serving the needs of people who are vulnerable, oppressed, and living in poverty. Social work values (Reamer, 2006) encourage practitioners to understand and address the contextual forces that contribute to human problems. As a result, social workers not only provide services to individuals, couples, families, and groups—"micro" and "mezzo" practice, in social work parlance—but also participate in organizational development, community organizing, large-scale advocacy, and social justice work, all of which are known as "macro" practice.

The spectrum of micro to macro practice, and the occasional distance between them, reflects the multifaceted origins of the field of social work, at least as it came to be in the United States. Social work began, in part, with two responses to poverty borrowed from Britain in the late 19th century, which eventually intersected to create the field as we know it (Farley, Smith, & Boyle, 2012; Glicken, 2011; Howe, 2009; Specht & Courtney, 1994). Charity organization societies helped charities target their resources by assessing the suitability of poor people for receiving support. A system of assessment was created—the precursor to modern social work assessment—to reduce indiscriminate giving and determine the needs of those who sought help. At around the same time, the settlement house movement, spearheaded by Jane Addams in the US, established settlements in poor neighborhoods where local people could be exposed to culture, education, and ideas. Charity organization societies are often given credit for the origins of social casework—later called "clinical" or micro and mezzo social work—and the settlement houses are often cited as the origins of macro, or more systems level, social work, though the distinction between "clinical" and "macro" is not always as robust as the terminology suggests.

These different strands point to an ongoing tension embedded in the history of social work, a tension between addressing suffering at the individual level versus the level of community or society. This tension has inevitably shaped the theoretical and research base of social work. On one end, social work has drawn heavily from psychology, medicine, and related fields; on the other, it has drawn from sociology, anthropology, political science, and others (Howe, 2009; Sheldon & MacDonald, 2009). This helps to explain why pinning down what "social work theory" is can be a daunting task.

However, if cultivating mindfulness and acceptance is about building awareness in the service of compassionate change, then mindfulness and acceptance mesh nicely with most of the major theoretical traditions within social work. These traditions all attempt to understand the human experience in order to reduce human suffering, but do so with relatively finer- and coarser-grained perspectives on the individual within his or her context. For instance, psychodynamic approaches, which had a great influence on casework starting in the 1930s and still thrive within social work in contemporary forms (e.g., Perlman & Brandell, 2011), focus the social worker's attention on the dynamics, both conscious and outside of awareness, that influence behavior. The same could be said for the various behavioral and cognitive approaches (e.g., Thyer & Myers, 2011), though the theory, vocabulary, and interventions might look and sound quite different. Family therapy approaches (e.g., McGoldrick and Hardy, 2008)—which unravel complex interactions between family members that generate and maintain problems—seek awareness and change through interventions at the group level. Comprehensive, higher-order perspectives such as systems and ecological theories (Friedman & Allen, 2011; Payne, 2005), which attempt to provide a unified theoretical model for social work, take an even wider view, noting how institutions, communities, and culture interact with the interpersonal and intrapsychic. Contemporary social work weaves into these perspectives many other threads, such as encouragements to mobilize the strengths of the client or client system (e.g., Saleebey, 2012), critical analyses of the influence of ideologies and institutions on social problems and social work (e.g., Allan, Briskman, & Pease, 2009), feminist perspectives on power dynamics in the therapeutic relationship (e.g., Miller & Stiver, 1997), and solution-focused (e.g., De Shazer, 1985) and social constructivist interventions for client problems (e.g., White & Epston, 1990). On the ground, this leads to a practice of social work that is pragmatic, client-focused, and social justice–oriented—a practice where mindfulness and acceptance rightly belong. (For extensive discussions of social work theories, see Payne, 2005 and Turner, 2011.)

Mindfulness and Acceptance in Contemporary Social Work

The last decade has seen an outpouring of social work scholarship on mindfulness as a treatment intervention, self-care strategy, pedagogical tool, and general framework for social work practice. Social work scholars have proposed using mindfulness to navigate powerful emotions in community work (Todd, 2009), adapting mindfulness principles into a framework for collaboration in international HIV/AIDS research and service (Abell & Rutledge, 2010), and incorporating mindfulness into social justice approaches (Hick & Furlotte, 2009). Others (e.g., Lynn, 2010) have proposed integrating mindfulness into social work education by adapting it as an "accompanying place" for the thoughts and feelings of social work students (Birnbaum, 2008) and using it to foster essential skills, increase self-care, and reduce the impact of occupational stress (Gockel, 2010). Social workers have also reviewed the use of mindfulness techniques in CBT (Koons, 2007), argued convincingly for the fit between DBT and social work (Stone, 2007), presented case studies (Beckerman & Corbett, 2010), and reviewed the research base (Montgomery, Kim, & Franklin, 2011) of established mindfulness-based treatment models, and explored the integration of mindfulness and psychotherapy (Lord, 2010; Turner, 2009). They have also explored mindfulness and the therapeutic relationship (Hick & Bien, 2008) and noted the emergence of mindfulness as a central practice in the implementation of spiritually-oriented techniques in social work (Birnbaum & Birnbaum, 2008). Hick's *Mindfulness and Social Work* (2009a) draws this emerging scholarship into a single volume, which includes reviews of the mindfulness literature, instructions on conducting mindfulness exercises, descriptions of emerging mindfulness-based social work interventions, and discussions of the application of mindfulness to specific practice areas such as family work, work with immigrant populations, community work, and activism.

In recent quantitative and mixed methods research, social work scholars have conducted studies on mindfulness-based arts interventions with children and adolescents (Coholic, Lougheed, & LeBreton, 2009), mindfulness as a pedagogical strategy in social work education (Gockel, Cain, Malove, & James, 2013; Napoli & Bonifas, 2011; Wong, 2004), and mindfulness for self-care in human service workers (McGarrigle & Walsh, 2011), among others. Social workers have adapted MBSR for severely economically disadvantaged people (Hick & Furlotte, 2010), caregivers of children with chronic conditions (Minor, Carlson, Mackenzie, Zernicke, & Jones, 2006), and nursing home residents (McBee, Westreich, & Likourezos, 2004). Using qualitative methods, social workers have studied the experience of mindfulness interventions for stress management in college students (Margolin, Pierce, & Wiley, 2011), recovery in people with addictions (Garland, Schwartz, Kelly, Whitt, & Howard, 2012), and skill-building in clinical social workers (Brenner, 2009), as well as the challenges of implementing mindfulness programs in treatment agencies (Larkin, Hardiman, Weldon, & Kim, 2012). In other research, social workers have examined the relationship between mindfulness and other psychological phenomena, such as compassion satisfaction, compassion fatigue, and burnout in clinical social workers (Thomas & Otis, 2010), and depression and anxiety in Masters level students (Ying, 2009). At the same time, some social work scholars (e.g., Gause & Coholic, 2010) have suggested that something essential may be lost when mindfulness is abstracted from its original spiritual context and have argued against allowing mindfulness to be marginalized as merely a technique within a given treatment. Others have noted the elusiveness of researching mindfulness with methods commonly used in the social sciences (e.g., Hick, 2009b).

Understanding Mindfulness and Acceptance Intellectually and Experientially

Kabat-Zinn's brief definition of mindfulness—"paying attention in a particular way: on purpose, in the present moment, and nonjudgmentally" (1994, p. 4)—is not the only one. Mindfulness's varied definitions may reflect the difficulty of capturing in words an experience that lies primarily outside of thinking and meaning making. Like Kabat-Zinn's, most definitions describe a "what" and a "how" of mindfulness (e.g., Linehan, 1993). Bishop and colleagues (2004) have proposed a two-component conception of mindfulness that provides a good example. The first component is self-regulation of attention to the "changing field of thoughts, feelings, and sensations from moment to moment" (p. 232)—the "what." The second is adopting an orientation to these experiences that is curious, open, and accepting—the "how." This attention is flexible, meaning it can move lightly but intentionally from one thing to another, and not elaborative, meaning it captures what is going on in the moment without being pulled away by the thoughts one might have about the moment.

To better understand this distinction between experiencing the moment and thinking about the moment, a simple exercise is helpful. If you are willing, read the next few sentences in the block that follows slowly, pausing briefly with each ellipsis.

> *Bring your attention to the places where your body makes contact with the chair in which you are sitting.... Notice your legs.... Notice your back.... Notice the borders between where your body makes contact and stops making contact.... Hold that awareness for a few moments.... Now, have some thoughts about chairs.... Think about your favorite chair. What is it like?... Remember some of the worst chairs you have had the displeasure of sitting in.... What were they like?... How would you describe the chair you are sitting in right now? What do you think of it?*

Notice the difference between these two ways of experiencing. The first "unfolds in moments," as Kabat-Zinn says. It is what is actually happening *right now*. The second is where we usually spend our time: in our "heads" as we think, remember, predict, compare, and evaluate.

Acceptance: Letting Go of Struggle

The word "acceptance" usually shows up in definitions of mindfulness; it can be found in the "how" of both the Kabat-Zinn and Bishop et al. definitions. Despite its greater presence in everyday speech, acceptance, like mindfulness, can be quite tricky to describe or put into practice through words. If I say that I must accept myself as I am, does this actually change me in any meaningful way? If I tell a child to accept that life is not always fair, does she suddenly let go of sadness in the face of disappointment? Maybe. Mindfulness, however, is acceptance in *practice*. Rather than simply saying, "You've got to accept," mindfulness, and the interventions described in this volume, model what acceptance looks like on the ground. Whether it is imagining holding a painful feeling delicately like a dried flower in ACT, dispassionately observing thoughts that usually lead to depressive relapse in mindfulness-based cognitive therapy, or bravely exposing oneself to shame without escaping through self-injury in DBT, clients in these treatments learn to practice acceptance rather than just talk about it.

Practicing acceptance draws on counterintuitive approaches to thoughts, feelings, and circumstances that are usually deemed "bad" or unwanted. For example, DBT skills training educates clients about the function of emotions, noting how important sadness, anger, and guilt can be when they are not complicated by secondary responses (such as self-criticism) or self-defeating behaviors (such as abusing alcohol). Anger is necessary for mobilizing against a threat, and sadness marks what we care about through loss or merely the possibility of loss. ACT divides acceptance into behavioral willingness and psychological acceptance. Willingness involves voluntarily sticking with thoughts and feelings, as well as the circumstances that give rise to them, if doing so serves something meaningful. This might mean sometimes consciously moving toward thoughts, feelings, and circumstances that are painful. Psychological acceptance involves adopting a posture that is "intentionally open, receptive, flexible, and nonjudgmental" (Hayes, Strosahl, & Wilson, 2012, p. 77) to experience as it occurs from moment to moment. In conjunction with psychological acceptance, willingness is not a teeth-gritting, "no-pain, no-gain" choice, but rather something softer, more connected. Notice how these conceptions of acceptance rely heavily on metaphor (e.g., "let go of struggling," "be flexible," "stay open"). Acceptance, like mindfulness, is not a *thing*. It is fluid, active, and embodied.

Overview

Part I, "The Present Moment: Mindfulness and Acceptance in Direct Practice," features ACT, DBT, and MBSR with a focus on their relevance to the practice of clinical social work. Each chapter is written or cowritten by a social worker who has extensive experience in the model being described. Part I ends with behavioral activation (BA; Martell, Addis, and Jacobson, 2001), which may seem like an odd fit given that it has no explicit focus on acceptance or mindfulness. However, BA has much in common with these other treatments. Like ACT and DBT, it is grounded in basic behavioral principles and, like all the treatments described in part I, it is well researched. Moreover, it can be argued that BA is implicitly accepting. BA is a treatment for depression that eschews attempts to directly change depressive thoughts and feelings in favor of encouraging the client to simply get moving. At first in small ways, then more globally, the client engages in actions that bring him or her in contact with the naturally reinforcing contingencies in the environment: relationships, meaningful work, fun—whatever is salient for the client. And without challenging cognitive distortions or unearthing depressive schemas, thoughts and feelings tend to change. Research on behavior activation conducted in the mid-90s (Jacobson et al., 1996) provided some of the strongest evidence that directly targeting thoughts and feelings was not necessarily the active ingredient in cognitive behavioral therapy (Longmore and Worrell, 2007).

Part II, "New Directions: Emerging Applications of Mindfulness and Acceptance in Social Work," provides an introduction to emerging interventions within social work and psychology that complement these treatments and offer a broader application of mindfulness and acceptance. Chapters 5 and 6 describe interventions developed by social workers. In chapter 5, Yuk-Lin Renita Wong describes using mindfulness as a pedagogical tool for facilitating students' critical reflection on issues that are central to social work, such as the social determinants of client problems, asymmetrical power relationships between practitioners and clients, and social workers' inadvertent role in reproducing oppression. In chapter 6, Diana Coholic describes the Holistic Arts-Based Group Program (HAP), a group intervention for children facing multiple challenges that attempts to both adapt mindfulness-based interventions to be more attuned to this population and reconnect the practice of mindfulness to its roots in spiritual practice. Chapters 7 and 8 move from groups and classrooms to very brief interventions, the bread and butter of the vast number of social workers who do not necessarily provide mental health treatment, such as case managers, primary care social workers, school social workers, and others. Both draw on the work of Kirk Strosahl and Patricia Robinson, who have adapted ACT as a model for brief interventions.

Part III, "The Client in Context: Addressing Broader Systems," explores the intersection of mindfulness and acceptance with the culture at large, as well as the cultures of social work and other helping professions. In chapter 9, Michael Uebel and Clayton Shorkey argue that the practice of engaged Buddhism, which emphasizes the dynamic interdependence of all things, is a worthy framework for generalist macro social work practice. In chapter 10, Akihiko Masuda, Mary Hill, Rebecca Pasillas, and I address cultural diversity and cultural competence through the perspective of functional contextualism, a philosophy of science that is new to social work, but which provides a frame for understanding how mindfulness- and acceptance-based approaches can be adapted to suit the needs of diverse populations. And in chapter 11, Joanne Steinwachs and I make an argument for approaching the science of mindfulness, acceptance, and social work in a more comprehensive way by drawing on an emerging tradition in the behavioral sciences called contextual behavioral science (CBS). CBS encourages us to articulate our starting assumptions, connect interventions to basic principles, and bring together researchers and practitioners in the service of better helping people.

Finally, for those interested in further exploring mindfulness and integrating it in their work with clients, I have prepared mindfulness exercises that provide an introduction to the practice. You can download MP3s of these exercises, along with a brief guide for their use, from the publisher's website for this book: http://www.newharbinger.com/28906. (See the back of the book for more information.)

Final Thoughts: Why Mindfulness and Acceptance?

People practicing mindfulness for the first time will often complain that it does not "work" for them because they cannot maintain their focus. They notice that trying to corral their concentration is a bit like trying to get a group of cats to pose for a picture: their minds will just as likely end up chasing an imagined mouse or taking a nap as sitting still. When they are supposed to be observing their breath or something else, they find that they are instead making grocery lists, rehashing old arguments with significant others, or worrying about what their bosses think of them. They believe this is evidence that they are doing it wrong. But this is exactly what mindfulness practice is like. It is certainly not a constant stream of serenity. Even for experienced meditators, the mind stays anchored for only a few moments before it starts congratulating itself for being in the present—which is precisely the moment it is no longer *in* the present. At times, mindfulness practice can even be painful: though peace and calm can be found in the present moment, so can anxiety and sadness. The "automatic pilot" we undermine with mindfulness often masks the pain we are avoiding. Furthermore, when the mind *does* focus, it does not always rest in pleasant places, and many a person practicing mindfulness has stumbled into a thicket of self-criticism and worry. As a speaker at a conference on meditation and psychotherapy I once attended observed, mindfulness practice can be like being "trapped in a phone booth with a madman."

So why practice mindfulness and acceptance, and, more importantly for this volume, why incorporate them into the practice of social work? Each of the following chapters answers this question in its own way. But one answer could be that by slowing down and simply noticing, if only for a moment, we begin to experience the world, both inside and outside of us, in a more viable way. Troublesome thoughts become just thoughts. Physical discomfort becomes just discomfort. Painful emotions still sting but come and go without overwhelming us. And from this place, new possibilities can emerge. Maybe we pause for a moment before saying the first thing that comes to our minds. Maybe we finally acknowledge the pain we run away from by working all the time. Maybe we begin to notice what actually matters to us rather than what we have been taught to care about. And especially for those who seek the help of social workers, maybe the depression, marital conflict, poverty, cancer, or drinking (or whatever else) begins to look like something we can move *toward*—not necessarily in order to overpower or combat it, but to embrace it in a way that diffuses its power over our lives. This is where the "possibilities for growth and transformation" that Kabat-Zinn describes lie: right here, right now, in the present.

References

Abell, N., & Rutledge, S. E. (2010). Awareness, acceptance, and action: Developing mindful collaborations in international HIV/AIDS research and service. *British Journal of Social Work, 40*, 656-675.

Allan, J., Briskman, L., & Pease, B. (2009). *Critical social work: An introduction to theories and practices* (2nd ed.). Crows Nest, NSW, Australia: Allen & Unwin.

Beck, A. T., Rush, A. J., Shaw, B. F., & Emery, G. (1979). *Cognitive therapy of depression*. New York: Guilford Press.

Beckerman, N. L., & Corbett, L. (2010). Mindfulness and cognitive therapy in depression relapse prevention: A case study. *Clinical Social Work Journal, 38*, 217-225.

Birnbaum, L. (2008). The use of mindfulness training to create an 'accompanying place' for social work students. *Social Work Education, 27*, 837-852.

Birnbaum, L., & Birnbaum, A. (2008). Mindful social work: From theory to practice. *Journal of Religion & Spirituality in Social Work: Social Thought, 27*, 87-104.

Bishop, S. R., Lau, M., Shapiro, S., Carlson, L., Anderson, N. D., Carmody, J., et al. (2004). Mindfulness: A proposed operational definition. *Clinical Psychology: Science and Practice, 11*, 230–241.

Bowen, S., Chawla, N., & Marlatt, G. A. (2011). *Mindfulness-based relapse prevention for addictive behaviors: A clinician's guide*. New York: Guilford Press.

Brenner, M. J. (2009). Zen practice: A training method to enhance the skills of clinical social workers. *Social Work in Health Care 48*, 462-470.

Coholic, D., Lougheed, S., & LeBreton, J. (2009). The helpfulness of holistic arts-based group work with children living in foster care. *Social Work with Groups, 32*, 29-46.

De Shazer, S. (1985). *Keys to solution in brief therapy*. New York: W.W. Norton.

Farley, O. W., Smith, L. L., & Boyle, S. W. (2012). *Introduction to social work* (12th ed.). Boston: Pearson.

Friedman, B. D., & Allen, K. N. (2011). Systems theory. In J. R. Brandell (Ed.), *Theory & practice in clinical social work* (pp. 3-20). Thousand Oaks, CA: Sage Publications.

Garland, E. L., Schwarz, N. M., Kelly, A., Whitt, A., & Howard, M. O. (2012). Mindfulness-oriented recovery enhancement for alcohol dependence: Therapeutic mechanisms and intervention acceptability. *Journal of Social Work Practice in the Addictions, 12*, 242-263.

Gause, R., & Coholic, D. (2010). Mindfulness-based practices as a holistic philosophy and method. *Currents: New Scholarship in the Human Services, 9*.

Glicken, M. D. (2011). *Social work in the 21st century: An introduction to social welfare, social issues, and the profession*. Thousand Oaks, CA: Sage Publications.

Gockel, A. (2010). The promise of mindfulness for clinical practice education. *Smith College Studies in Social Work, 80*, 248-268.

Gockel, A., Cain, T., Malove, S., & James, S. (2013). Mindfulness as clinical training: Student perspectives on the utility of mindfulness training in fostering clinical intervention skills. *Journal of Religion & Spirituality in Social Work: Social Thought, 32,* 36-59.

Hayes, S. C., Strosahl, K., & Wilson, K. G. (1999). *Acceptance and commitment therapy: An experiential approach to behavior change.* New York: Guilford Press.

Hayes, S. C., Strosahl, K., & Wilson, K. G. (2012). *Acceptance and commitment therapy: The process and practice of mindful change* (2nd ed.). New York: Guilford Press.

Hick, S. F. (2009a). *Mindfulness and social work.* Chicago: Lyceum Books.

Hick, S. F. (2009b). Mindfulness and social work: Paying attention to ourselves, our clients, and society. In S. F. Hick (Ed.), *Mindfulness and social work* (pp. 1-30). Chicago: Lyceum Books.

Hick, S. F., & Bien, T. (2008). *Mindfulness and the therapeutic relationship.* New York: Guilford Press.

Hick, S. F., & Furlotte, C. (2009). Mindfulness and social justice approaches: Bridging the mind and society in social work practice. *Canadian Social Work Review, 26,* 5-24.

Hick, S. F., & Furlotte, C. (2010). An exploratory study of radical mindfulness training with severely economically disadvantaged people: Findings of a Canadian study. *Australian Social Work, 63,* 281-298.

Howe, D. (2009). *A brief introduction to social work theory.* Basingstoke, UK: Palgrave Macmillan.

Jacobson, N. S., & Christensen, A. (1998). *Acceptance and change in couple therapy: A therapist's guide to transforming relationships.* New York: Norton.

Jacobson, N. S., Dobson, K. S., Truax, P. A., Addis M. E., Koerner, K., Gollan, J. K., et al. (1996). A component analysis of cognitive behavioral treatment for depression. *Journal of Consulting and Clinical Psychology, 64,* 295-304.

Kabat-Zinn, J. (1990). *Full catastrophe living: Using the wisdom of your body and mind to face stress, pain, and illness.* New York: Delacorte.

Kabat-Zinn, J. (1994). *Wherever you go, there you are: Mindfulness meditation in everyday life.* New York: Hyperion.

Koons, C. R. (2007). The use of mindfulness interventions in cognitive behavior therapies. In T. Ronen & A. Freeman (Eds.), *Cognitive behavior therapy in clinical social work practice* (pp. 167-186). New York: Springer.

Larkin, H., Hardiman, E., Weldon, T., & Kim, H. (2012). Program characteristics as factors influencing the implementation of mindfulness meditation in substance abuse treatment agencies. *Journal of Religion & Spirituality in Social Work: Social Thought, 31,* 311-327.

Linehan, M. M. (1993). *Cognitive-behavioral treatment of borderline personality disorder.* New York: Guilford Press.

Longmore, R., & Worrell, M. (2007). Do we need to challenge thoughts in cognitive behavior therapy? *Clinical Psychology Review, 27,* 173–187.

Lord, S. A. (2010). Meditative dialogue: Cultivating sacred space in psychotherapy—an intersubjective fourth? *Smith College Studies in Social Work, 80*, 269-285.

Lynn, R. (2010). Mindfulness in social work education. *Social Work Education, 29*, 289-304.

Margolin, I., Pierce, J., & Wiley, A. (2011). Wellness through a creative lens: Meditation and visualization. *Journal of Religion & Spirituality in Social Work: Social Thought, 30*, 234-252.

Martell, C. R., Addis, M. E., & Jacobson, N. S. (2001). *Depression in context: Strategies for guided action.* New York: Norton.

McBee, L., Westreich, L., & Likourezos, A. (2004). A psychoeducational relaxation group for pain and stress management in the nursing home. *Journal of Social Work in Long-Term Care, 3*, 15-28.

McGarrigle, T., & Walsh, C. A. (2011). Mindfulness, self-care, and wellness in social work: Effects of contemplative training. *Journal of Religion & Spirituality in Social Work: Social Thought, 30*, 212-233.

McGoldrick, M., & Hardy, K. V. (2008). *Re-visioning family therapy: Race, culture, and gender in clinical practice.* New York: Guilford Press.

Miller, J. B., & Stiver, I. P. (1997). *The healing connection: How women form relationships in therapy and in life.* Boston: Beacon Press.

Minor, H. G., Carlson, L. E., Mackenzie, M. J., Zernicke, K., & Jones, L. (2006). Evaluation of a Mindfulness-Based Stress Reduction (MBSR) program for caregivers of children with chronic conditions. *Social Work in Health Care, 43*, 91–109.

Montgomery, K. L., Kim, J. S., & Franklin, C. (2011). Acceptance and commitment therapy for psychological and physiological illnesses: A systematic review for social workers. *Health & Social Work, 36*, 169-181.

Napoli, M., & Bonifas, R. (2011). From theory toward empathic self-care: Creating a mindful classroom for social work students. *Social Work Education 30*, 635-649.

Payne, M. (2005). *Modern social work theory* (3rd ed.). Chicago: Lyceum.

Perlman, F. T., & Brandell, J. R. (2011). Psychoanalytic theory. In J. R. Brandell (Ed.), *Theory & practice in clinical social work* (pp. 41-80). Thousand Oaks, CA: SAGE.

Reamer, F. G. (2006). *Social work values and ethics* (3rd ed.). New York: Columbia University Press.

Rogers, C. R. (1961). *On becoming a person: A therapist's view of psychotherapy.* New York: Houghton Mifflin.

Saleebey, D. (2012). *The strengths perspective in social work practice* (6th ed.). Boston: Pearson.

Segal, Z. V., Williams, J. M.G., & Teasdale, J. D. (2002). *Mindfulness-based cognitive therapy for depression.* New York: Guilford Press.

Sheldon, B., & Macdonald, G. M. (2009). *A textbook of social work.* New York: Routledge.

Specht, H., & Courtney, M. E. (1994). *Unfaithful angels: How social work has abandoned its mission*. New York: Free Press.

Stone, S. D. (2007). Using dialectical behavior therapy in clinical practice: Client empowerment, social work values. In T. Ronen & A. Freeman (Eds.), *Cognitive behavior therapy in clinical social work practice* (pp. 147-165). New York: Springer.

Thomas, J. T., & Otis, M. D. (2010). Intrapsychic correlates of professional quality of life: Mindfulness, empathy, and emotional separation. *Journal of the Society for Social Work and Research, 1*, 83-98.

Thyer, B. A., & Myers, L. L. (2011). Behavioral and cognitive theories. In J. R. Brandell (Ed.), *Theory & practice in clinical social work* (pp. 21-40). Thousand Oaks, CA: SAGE.

Todd, S. (2009). Mobilizing communities for social change: Integrating mindfulness and passionate politics. In S. F. Hick (Ed.), *Mindfulness and social work* (pp. 171-185). Chicago: Lyceum Books.

Turner, F. J. (Ed.) (2011). *Social work treatment: interlocking theoretical approaches* (5th ed.). New York: Oxford University Press. [Kindle for PC edition]. Retrieved from Amazon.com.

Turner, K. (2009). Mindfulness: The present moment in clinical social work. *Clinical Social Work Journal, 37*, 95-103.

White, M., & Epston, D. (1990). *Narrative means to therapeutic ends*. New York: Norton.

Wong, Y. R. (2004). Knowing through discomfort: A mindfulness-based critical social work pedagogy. *Critical Social Work, 5*. Retrieved from http://www1.uwindsor.ca/criticalsocialwork/knowing-through-discomfort-a-mindfulness-based-critical-social-work-pedagogy

Ying, Y. (2009). Religiosity, spirituality, mindfulness, and mental health in social work students. *Critical Social Work 10*(1). Retrieved from http://www1.uwindsor.ca/criticalsocialwork/religiosity-spirituality-mindfulness-and-mental-health-in-social-work-students

PART I

The Present Moment: Mindfulness and Acceptance in Direct Practice

CHAPTER 1

Acceptance and Commitment Therapy in Social Work

Matthew S. Boone, LCSW

University of Arkansas at Little Rock

Imagine a young mother suffering with chronic back pain and persistent depression. On days when she wakes up hurting, the last thing she wants to do is drag herself out of bed to get her daughter off to school. She feels a pit of anxiety in her stomach. She worries about what she will feel when she gets up. She also worries about neglecting her daughter if she stays in bed. She criticizes herself for being weak, then criticizes herself for being so hard on herself. None of her thoughts motivate her to get out of bed. The urge to go back to sleep tugs at her, promising a respite from the pain in her back, the burning in her stomach, and the war in her head. Meanwhile, what she really cares about—being an attentive and loving parent—slips quietly into the background.

Popular conceptions of health and wellness suggest that the solution to her problem lies in alleviating her pain, both physical and emotional, so that she can live a better life. And indeed, this is sometimes possible: with the right medicine or treatment, pain can go away. But a lot of pain is not so easy to alleviate—not only the kind of chronic back pain and depression she experiences, but also the normal pain of living, like sadness and anger. And preventing pain from showing up is next to impossible. If we are going to live, we are going to hurt. If we try to succeed at something, we will risk failing. If we build loving relationships, we will risk losing them. No treatment in the world can prevent life from hurting.

Furthermore, if we try too hard to minimize the possibility of pain, we risk draining the vitality from our lives. This is especially true for the people who show up in the offices of social workers and other professionals. A person with severe social anxiety can avoid feeling anxious much of the time; all he needs to do is stay away from engaging with people. But he loses the possibility of meaningful relationships, and he adds loneliness and isolation to his anxiety. A person struggling with alcohol dependence can easily prevent feeling the craving and dread that being sober brings. But she loses the possibility of a life in which she is not beholden to her desire for alcohol. And the young mother described above can readily escape the agony of waking up: all she needs to do is go back to sleep. But the cost of escape is missing out on being the parent she wants to be. In each of these examples, pain is held at bay, but suffering arrives to take its place.

Acceptance and commitment therapy (ACT, said as one word) is a mindfulness-based cognitive behavioral therapy that draws on this understanding of human experience. ACT normalizes pain, even the pain that shows up as part of what we call psychopathology, and teaches clients to respond differently to it. Where there is unnecessary avoidance, ACT teaches approach. Where there is unnecessary attachment, ACT teaches letting go. Clients learn to open up to their pain, welcoming it as an invited guest (i.e., acceptance) when doing so facilitates pursuing what truly matters to them (i.e., commitment). Using a variety of tools, including mindfulness, metaphors, experiential exercises, and the therapeutic relationship itself, ACT encourages clients—as well as social workers—to articulate what matters to them most and move in that direction, bringing their thoughts and feelings along for the journey.

ACT: Responding Flexibly to What Life Offers

ACT seeks to increase *psychological flexibility*, "the ability to contact the present moment more fully as a conscious human being, and to either change or persist when doing so serves valued ends" (Hayes, Strosahl, Bunting, Twohig, & Wilson, 2004, p. 5). Put more simply, psychological flexibility means responding effectively to what life offers. When faced with difficult circumstances, a person acting in a psychologically flexible way forgoes ineffective or unnecessary attempts at controlling thoughts and feelings and acts in the service of what is personally defined as important.

In more technical language, psychological flexibility involves bringing a broad and flexible repertoire of behavioral responses to any given circumstance (Wilson and Dufrene, 2008). Imagine a man who loses his job. The day after he is fired, all he wants to do is numb himself by surfing the web. Instead he sits at his computer and updates his resume, even though it brings him closer to his worries and the heaviness in his chest. And though it is painful, he opens up about his sense of humiliation to his spouse, while leaving room to support her in her concerns as well. He often has the urge to shut down, sensing that everything would be easier if he could just hide under the covers. Rather than rejecting this urge in the service of "pushing through" the pain, however, he acknowledges it as a natural part of himself. He gives in to it once in a while, repeatedly checking his favorite social networking site or taking naps that are just a little too long. Yet he gets moving when the situation calls for it, even if this means feeling more anxiety as he cold calls potential business contacts or goes to dinner with friends who inevitably ask uncomfortable questions about how he is doing. His repertoire of responding is *broad* in that he enlists a variety of responses, some ineffective, but most more or less effective given the situation. His repertoire is also *flexible* in that he does not get stuck in any one pattern of responding, especially when it takes him away from what matters to him: finding a job and moving on with his life. This is psychological flexibility.

Note that psychological flexibility is not an action or feeling state, but rather a *quality* of responding, one that is dimensional rather than "all-or-nothing." A person can be thought of as more or less psychologically flexible in any given situation, and behavior can be imagined to lie on a continuum from inflexible to flexible depending on the context.

The ACT Model of Psychopathology and Human Suffering

The psychological flexibility model on which ACT is based rejects the *assumption of healthy normality* (Hayes, Strosahl, & Wilson, 2012), or the perspective that emotional well-being is marked by an absence of pain and a surfeit of pleasure. One needs only to watch television through a single commercial break, or visit a great many health professionals, to encounter this perspective. Instead, ACT assumes that a person will naturally encounter a continuous stream of thoughts, feelings, emotions, physical sensations, and memories—some sweet, some sad, some neutral—throughout his or her life. These "private experiences," in ACT terminology, are neither bad nor good. Problems emerge when normal, evolutionarily shaped behavioral processes are inflexibly applied in response to uncomfortable private experiences. And so, the inevitable pain of living, such as the grief one feels at the loss of a loved one, becomes entrenched and calcified into something different: *suffering*. In ACT, this is called the *assumption of destructive normality* (Hayes, Strosahl, & Wilson, 2012).

Experiential Avoidance

One of these processes is *experiential avoidance*, or excessive efforts to avoid and control private experiences or the situations that give rise to them. The behaviors described in the introduction—sleeping to escape physical pain, isolating to prevent feeling anxious, and drinking to quell craving and dread—are all examples of experiential avoidance. Each behavior is more or less effective in the short term. But the consequences of these behaviors, accumulated over time, create and reinforce the very problems they are intended to manage.

To be sure, behaviors like avoidance and escape are not always problematic. Our ancestors would not have survived without the ability to stay far afield of predators by avoiding them or running away. But when experiential avoidance becomes a generalized pattern—one in which *all* discomfort must be controlled, and one which leads to problems like depression, social phobia, and alcoholism—it becomes psychological inflexibility.

Social workers, being human, are not immune to experiential avoidance, even in their work. It is quite easy for any social worker, when not at his or her best, to direct a client away from the painful memory she is discussing and onto a safer topic, either because what she is sharing is too close to the social worker's experience or because the new topic is something the social worker feels more capable of handling. This is not an empathic lapse about which the social worker should be ashamed; it is the inevitable action of a real human being, one who has a built-in propensity to run away.

Fusion

Another process that can contribute to inflexibility and suffering is *fusion*. Fusion is the propensity to allow the products of one's mind—thoughts, images, memories, and meaning making generally—to have a dominating influence over one's actions. A person with a history of trauma experiences a flashback and tries to escape the "danger" by drinking or injuring herself. A person with a history of failed relationships thinks, "I can't trust anyone," and repeatedly accuses his partner of infidelity. In a state of fusion, rules, predictions, evaluations, judgments, comparisons, and whatever else the mind can create crowd out other sources of influence, such as lived experience and personal values.

The word "fusion" is grounded in a metaphor of being stuck—that is, "fused"—to a thought. In many situations, this propensity to be led by our minds is quite useful. Without it, we could not do any of the tasks that require thinking, big or small, from deciding what to wear to building a skyscraper. But there is a dark side to fusion. Humans have the propensity to treat thoughts as literal truths. Think of a depressed person who has the thought "I'm hopeless." There is no reasonable way to measure the "hopelessness" of a person, and predicting the future is impossible; but in the throes of depression, this hopelessness can feel palpably, overwhelmingly real. And he or she can respond accordingly by withdrawing from life.

Just as social workers are prone to experiential avoidance, they are also prone to fusion. A therapist thinks, "He's so borderline," and interprets every action of a client as a manipulation. A case manager thinks, "I'm working harder than this client," and fails to notice the variety of contingencies other than the client's motivation, like poverty and racism, preventing her from helping herself. Again, these are not the actions of bad social workers; these are the actions of normal people who are just as likely to be wrapped up in thoughts as their clients are.

Workability

Because experiential avoidance and fusion are not necessarily problematic, but only become so when rigidly applied, ACT encourages social workers and clients to consider whether a given behavior is "workable," both in terms of what it is intended to achieve and in the service of building a vital and meaningful life. Building such a life is at the heart of the emphasis on personal values in ACT, which will be discussed later in the chapter.

ACT and Social Work

The wide and varied scope of social work, as well as its mission to serve those in greatest need, demands that its interventions be applicable to a wide variety of problems, grounded in research, and consonant with core social work values.

ACT Is Evidence Based for a Broad Spectrum of Problems

Consistent with the assumption that psychological inflexibility plays a role in the broad spectrum of human suffering, ACT has shown promise for treating an impressive array of both clinical and nonclinical problems. In over seventy randomized controlled trials of various sizes, ACT has demonstrated its efficacy not just with mental health problems such as depression, anxiety, OCD, trichotillomania, substance abuse, body image dissatisfaction, and psychosis, but also with health problems such as chronic pain, nicotine addiction, epilepsy, diabetes, cancer, chronic headache, and tinnitus distress. ACT has also proven to be useful with nonclinical problems such as worksite stress, stigma, burnout, and the reluctance of practitioners to use evidence-based treatment. Furthermore, ACT studies often demonstrate that ACT works, at least in part, by its theorized mechanism of change: increasing psychological flexibility. This is important because we rarely know what makes a therapy work beyond factors that are common to all therapies such as the therapeutic alliance. For recent summaries of ACT research, see Ruiz (2010), Montgomery, Kim, and Franklin (2011), and the continually updated list of randomized controlled trials on the Association for Contextual Behavioral Science website (http://contextualpsychology.org/ACT_Randomized_Controlled_Trials).

ACT Can Be Flexibly Applied

Though there are a number of treatment manuals for specific problems that provide session-by-session guidelines for implementing ACT (e.g., Eifert & Forsyth, 2005), the ACT and psychological flexibility model on which it is based can be adapted to a variety of formats, modalities, and presenting problems (Ruiz, 2010). ACT can be facilitated in individual meetings, single-session workshops, and groups of varying lengths. ACT has been adapted as a self-help intervention (e.g., Fledderus, Bohlmeijer, Fox, Schreurs, & Spinhoven, 2013), a web-based application (e.g., Bricker, Wyszynski, Comstock, & Heffner, in press), and, under the name "Acceptance and Commitment Training," a worksite stress-management intervention (Flaxman and Bond, 2010). ACT has also been adapted as a very brief intervention model (see chapter 7 in this volume), which makes it suited for the great variety of practice roles (e.g., case manager, discharge planner, mediator) and settings (e.g., hospitals, social service agencies) in which social workers may not necessarily provide mental health treatment. And though the majority of ACT studies have been conducted with adults, a growing body of research supports its efficacy with children (e.g., Wicksell, Melin, Lekander, & Olsson, 2009).

ACT Fits with Social Work Values

ACT is consonant with the core social work values described in the ethics code of the US National Association of Social Workers (NASW, 2008). Three of them—dignity and worth of the person, importance of human relationships, and social justice—are explored here.

ACT recognizes the *dignity and worth of the person* by offering an effective model for change that does not position the social worker as different from the client. ACT assumes that social workers and clients are both subject to the same psychological processes and prone to responding in more or less flexible ways in different circumstances. The social worker is distinguished from the client only by the perspective he or she has. A helpful ACT rubric for this perspective is the "Two Mountains" metaphor (Hayes, Strosahl, & Wilson, 1999): The social worker and client are climbing two separate mountains. The social worker, viewing the client from his or her vantage point, can point out useful footholds, ledges on which to rest, and safer routes to climb, all of which the client may not be able to see. At the same time, the social worker is on his or her own mountain and will encounter similar trials and challenges.

ACT privileges the *importance of human relationships*, in part, by identifying the therapeutic relationship as a locus of change. The ACT practitioner models ACT processes such as acceptance and mindfulness and makes his or her commitment to both the work and the client explicit (e.g., "I will do my best to be present and engaged whenever we meet"). Practitioners also thoughtfully self-disclose about their own tendencies toward avoidance and control and getting wrapped up in thinking (e.g., "I noticed just then that I was trying to fix the sadness you were feeling"). ACT also stresses human relationships in its focus on values: conversations about meaningful living inevitably arrive at relationships. It is rare to encounter a person who does not value relationships on some level, even if that value only manifests in the pain of relationships' absence. For example, an isolated person suffering with depression and social anxiety likely feels these feelings because connection to others is important.

Threads of *social justice* are woven throughout ACT, despite its relative emphasis on psychological flexibility at the individual level. First, the explicit stance that both the social worker and client are in the same boat can help to undermine the inherent power differential in the therapeutic relationship, preventing the varieties of oppression that exist outside the therapeutic relationship (e.g., sexism, racism, homophobia) from manifesting themselves inside it. Second, the psychological flexibility model suggests that ACT, and other interventions like it, can be applied to issues of stigma and prejudice, and indeed it has (e.g., Masuda et al., 2007; Lillis & Hayes, 2007). Third, ACT has been applied to people of varying cultures, nationalities, and languages, which supports its interface with culturally competent practice. However, like most psychotherapy modalities, much more work needs to be done to explore its relevance and effectiveness across different populations (see chapter 10 for further discussion).

ACT in Practice

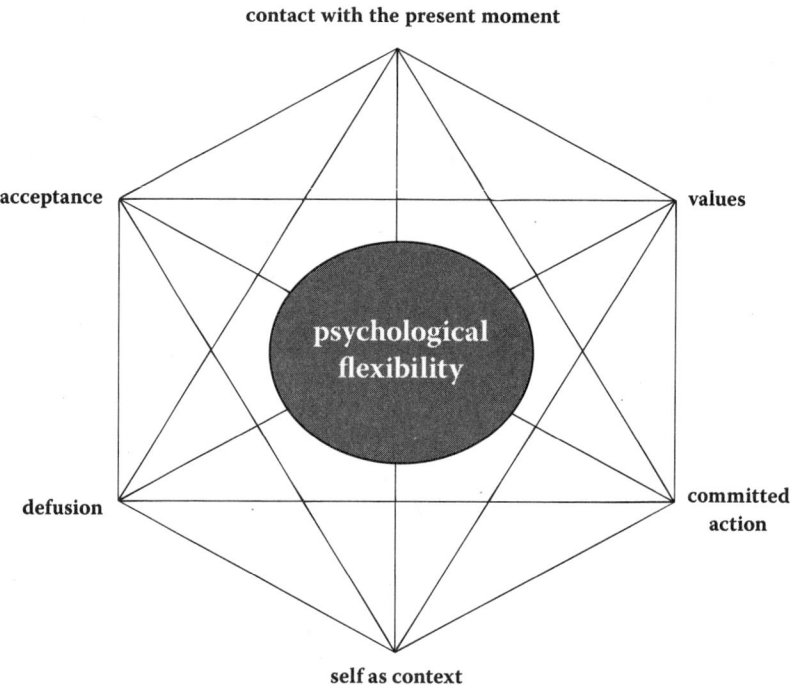

Figure 1.1   The hexaflex.

In ACT, psychological flexibility is broken down into six interrelated behavioral processes, which the social worker helps the client bring to bear in the session and in his or her life. For heuristic purposes, these processes are arranged in a diagram informally referred to as the *hexaflex* (figure 1.1). The processes are acceptance (willingly encountering thoughts and feelings, whether painful or pleasant), defusion (noticing thinking for what it is, nothing more), contact with the present moment (mindfully observing experience as it happens), self as context (making a distinction between one's *self* and the thoughts and feelings one *experiences*), values (identifying what matters), and committed action (acting in the service of what matters). The first four of these—acceptance, defusion, contact with the present moment, and self as context—are considered four components of mindfulness. The full six are best thought of as facets of psychological flexibility, not wholly independent processes. The intersecting lines of the hexaflex, which connect every process to the others, illustrate that one can see echoes of the others in each of the processes. For example, encountering thoughts and feelings mindfully as they occur (i.e., contact with the present moment) is an inherently accepting posture.

ACT Interventions

Though social workers can help facilitate acceptance, defusion, and the other processes with familiar strategies such as Socratic questioning and reflective listening, ACT emphasizes learning that is less verbal and more experiential. To do so, ACT enlists metaphors, mindfulness exercises, and experiential exercises.

Metaphors, which are often delivered in story form, illustrate concepts by borrowing the characteristics of the things they describe. It is one thing to tell a client that avoiding thoughts and feelings can be problematic; it is quite another to say, "Trying to stay away from thoughts and feelings is like feeding a hungry tiger: over time, the tiger gets bigger and bigger until it is capable of eating you." *Mindfulness exercises* help clients slow down and nonjudgmentally observe their private experiences. Clients learn to literally "sit with" their feelings, something social workers often encourage but that can be confusing and out of reach for clients who don't have the necessary skills. *Experiential exercises*, which often incorporate metaphors and mindfulness, help clients understand at an intuitive, "gut" level what it means to respond flexibly. For example, rather than merely describing controlling thoughts and feelings as a "tug-of-war with a monster," a common ACT metaphor (Hayes, Strosahl, & Wilson, 2012), the social worker might actually enact this tug-of-war with the client using a rope or something suitably ropelike. Thus the client actually feels the struggle in his or her body and experiences a sense of relief when the rope is dropped.

Scripts and descriptions of these interventions are available throughout the ACT literature (e.g., Hayes, Strosahl, & Wilson, 2012; Harris, 2010; Luoma, Hayes, & Walser, 2007), and social workers are encouraged to create their own. Whatever fits the psychological flexibility model is ACT.

• *Case Example: Valerie*

The six processes and the interventions that help facilitate them are best illustrated in a case example. Valerie, a fictional client introduced briefly in the introduction, is a twenty-three-year-old Filipino-American woman with chronic depression and back pain. She is a single mother living in a housing project in a medium-sized city in Northern California. Her daughter, Pia, attends first grade at a nearby elementary school.

Valerie first hurt her back while pregnant with Pia. Since then, she has experienced daily pain without much relief. Her pain and depressed moods make it hard for her to maintain a job, and she was fired from the department store at which she worked a year ago due to her repeated absences. She is now working as a checker at a grocery store, but her boss has warned her that she will be let go if she continues to come in late or miss work. She often worries about losing her job, being a bad mother, and being in pain for the rest of her life. After an evening out with friends, when she got visibly drunk and tearfully confessed her depression, one of her friends recommended she see a social worker at the local community mental health center.

Assessment: Drawing Out Patterns of Avoidance and Control

Assessment in ACT involves exploring the ways experiential avoidance, fusion, and other inflexible responses play out in a client's life. The following vignette occurs in Valerie's second session, after the social worker has completed the agency's formal intake interview and diagnostic assessment. The social worker begins by asking Valerie to identify the thoughts and feelings she most wants to get rid of. Valerie readily identifies the pain in her back, her worries, and her persistent sad moods. The worker then explores what she customarily does in response to these thoughts and feelings, with an emphasis on workability.

Social Worker: What sort of things do you do to keep these feelings from getting to you? If you don't mind, I'll make a list as we talk.

Valerie: Most of the time I try not to think about it. If my back is hurting, I just ignore it. If I'm feeling depressed, I tell myself to think positively.

Social Worker: (*Writing.*) Positive thinking. Ignoring. What else?

Valerie: Well, I can't always ignore it. Sometimes I just think and think about it. It drives me crazy.

Social Worker: Could we consider "thinking" another kind of strategy for solving your feelings?

Valerie: I guess so. But sometimes I feel like if I don't stay on top of it, it's going to get worse.

Social Worker: Interesting. What else do you do?

Valerie: I told you about how I drink too much sometimes. It really feels good to let loose.

Social Worker: It sounds like you can use some relief.

Valerie: Yes, very much so.

With the help of the social worker, Valerie goes on to list everything she tries, from watching television all day, to playing with her daughter, to just pushing on and getting things done.

Social Worker: Take a look at this list. (*She hands it to Valerie.*)

Valerie:	(*Laughing ruefully.*) I'm not sure much of this makes any difference.
Social Worker:	Really?
Valerie:	(*Tears begin to appear at the corners of her eyes.*) My back still hurts. I'm still depressed. I still worry all the time. What's wrong with me?
Social Worker:	These strategies make sense. They help in the short term. Like drinking: you get to escape for a little while. Or playing with your daughter: I'm sure you forget about the pain and your sadness sometimes. But they don't really work in the long term. And I bet they cost you something.
Valerie:	They do. I get so mad at myself on Sunday mornings when I'm lying in bed, hung over, and I can hear Pia running around the house. I should be with her. But all I really want to do is lie there. And then I feel bad about myself.
Social Worker:	Trying to get away from the pain and sadness leads to other kinds of pain.
Valerie:	Yeah. But I don't know what else to do.

Focusing on this lack of workability in controlling thoughts and feelings opens up a space, called *creative hopelessness*, in which the worker can introduce acceptance. This space is "hopeless" in that continuing to avoid and control seems less and less viable; it is "creative" in that room is cleared in which something new can emerge.

Acceptance

In ACT, *acceptance* means willingly encountering *all* private experiences, as well as external circumstances, without unnecessary struggle. This kind of acceptance is different from resigning oneself to a barren life, and it does not require liking or wanting what shows up. It simply means being willing to have what is already there. The following vignette shows the social worker weaving a common ACT metaphor—of holding a thought or feeling as one would a butterfly—into an experiential exercise that embodies the difference between control and acceptance. The social worker introduces the exercise, called the "Butterfly" (Boone & Canicci, 2013), at the point where the last vignette left off:

Social Worker: Maybe "doing" is part of the problem.

Valerie: What do you mean?

Social Worker: It seems like you've *done* just about everything you can to make this stuff go away. But it's still here. Would you be willing to try something playful to help me illustrate a point?

Valerie: Sure.

Social Worker: I don't want to give it away, but this exercise involves me coming into your personal space a little bit and you pushing against my hand. Is that okay?

Valerie: No problem. My back feels okay today.

Social Worker: Great. Choose a difficult feeling, one you are willing to do some work with.

Valerie: How about sadness?

Social Worker: (*Taking out a 3 by 5 card and a black permanent marker.*) Okay. I'm going to write "sadness" on this card. (*Writes the word and holds it up so Valerie can see it.*) Imagine that your sadness is somehow embodied by the card—however you make sense of that.

Valerie: Ugh. I feel kind of sick just looking at it.

Social Worker: You still willing?

Valerie: Yeah. What's next?

Social Worker: I'm going to bring the card toward you. (*Holding the card facing outward, the social worker slowly rolls her chair forward.*) As I get closer, I want you to put your hand up to mine and try to push it away. (*Their hands meet with the card in between them.*) Just push gently at first… Then push a little bit harder. (*A slight strain in their arms is visible.*) Don't think about it too much, but notice what this is like in your body.… Have you got it? (*Valerie nods.*) Now release, maintaining enough pressure to keep the card between our hands.… Take the card and hold it in your hand.… Tell me: Is it gone?

Valerie: No.

Social Worker: Notice that. Now we're going to try something different. Hold the card with both hands. (*Valerie holds the card at its edges.*) I want you to squeeze the card as hard as you can without hurting yourself. (*Valerie closes her eyes and squeezes the card. Her upper arms shake a bit as she does.*) Don't think about it too much, just notice what this is like in your body.… Got it? (*Valerie nods.*) Okay, stop squeezing.… Is the card gone?

Valerie: It's all crushed up.

Social Worker: But is it gone?

Valerie: No, I guess it's still here.

Social Worker: Notice that. Finally, we're going to do something different. I want you to hold both hands in front of you with your palms together and facing up. (*The social worker slowly moves the card, face up, toward Valerie's hands.*) And as the card comes your way, I want you to catch it like a butterfly landing on your

	hands… (*The social worker delicately rests the card on Valerie's open hands.*) See if you can hold it gently like something precious…and bring it close to you, like it's not your enemy, like it's something you could take care of. (*Valerie brings it close to her chest and stares down at it.*) …Is it gone?
Valerie:	(*In a quiet voice.*) No.
Social Worker:	What's different?
Valerie:	I'm different. I'm more relaxed.
Social Worker:	So the card is the same, but *you* are different. We might say that you have changed your *relationship* to the card.
Valerie:	Yeah, it's like I'm softer now. But I still have this sadness.
Social Worker:	If it were a real butterfly, what might happen next?
Valerie:	It might fly away.
Social Worker:	Or it might stick around for a while. But it would leave when it leaves, not when you make it leave. If you were feeling this sadness and playing with your daughter at the same time, what would be easier: holding it like a butterfly or squeezing and pushing it away?
Valerie:	Definitely holding it like a butterfly.

The social worker introduces Valerie to acceptance by helping her experience it rather than simply telling her about it. She also ties acceptance to what Valerie cares about: being a good mother to her daughter. For homework, the social worker asks Valerie to make a more extensive list of the thoughts and feelings she struggles with and the strategies she uses to keep them at bay. Afterward, Valerie is asked to identify which strategies work in the short term and long term and which ones take her away from what she cares about in life.

Defusion

Defusion, the antithesis of fusion, means recognizing thoughts as thoughts—nothing more, nothing less. Whereas a person responding in a fused way would treat the words, images, and memories that the mind produces as literal representations and empirical "truths," a person responding in a defused way would recognize these as merely the latest examples in a continuous, lifelong stream of mental products. A useful ACT metaphor for defusion envisions the mind as a "word machine," one that cannot be turned off; defusion involves standing at a distance from this machine, watching it work, and making thoughtful choices about which words are worth listening to. Thoughts are allowed to influence one's behavior only when doing so takes one in the direction of a workable, values-driven life. Note that fusion and defusion are not about "true or false"; in fact, ACT, unlike other forms of cognitive behavioral therapy, takes no position on which thoughts are more true than others, and makes no effort to identify "rational" thoughts. Instead, ACT encourages social workers and clients to focus on which thoughts are useful in the service of pursuing a meaningful life. Thus, a painful thought like "Nobody loves me" is put to the workability test: true or not, is "Nobody loves me" a thought worth following if building relationships is important?

Defusion is facilitated in a variety of ways. At the most basic level, the social worker can encourage a practice of framing thoughts, both privately to oneself and in conversation with the social worker, with statements such as "My mind is saying…" and "I'm having the thought…" The social worker can refer to the mind metaphorically as a great storyteller or a radio with the power switch stuck in the "on" position; the client can choose whether to listen to the old, worn-out stories or the latest disaster-filled broadcast. Or the social worker can facilitate a mindfulness exercise in which the client imagines each thought as a leaf floating on a passing stream.

The next vignette occurs in the third session, after acceptance and letting go of control have been introduced in the session before. The social worker introduces the metaphor of the mind as a great storyteller and asks Valerie to name the various stories her mind tells. Valerie identifies quite a few, including "I could do something with my life if I didn't have back pain," "I'm not going to keep this job," "Everything was better before I was depressed," and "All of my friends have real lives." As she names each story, the social worker writes it on a piece of paper and tapes it to the office wall. The office eventually has a ring of "stories" encircling it. The social worker asks Valerie to take them all in.

Social Worker: (*After a few moments.*) What's it like to look at these stories from this perspective?

Valerie: I wasn't even aware of some of them.

Social Worker: Is there one you get especially stuck on when you look at it?

Valerie: "I could do something with my life if I didn't have back pain." It just jumps right out at me.

Social Worker: When that one shows up, how do you respond?

Valerie: I sort of freeze. Everything else becomes less important.

Social Worker: How so?

Valerie: I spend all my time focusing on it.

Social Worker: And do you neglect anything in your life?

Valerie: If I'm with Pia, I'm not really there mentally. If I'm at work, I slow down and things don't get done.

Social Worker: Is there anything different about looking at it like this instead of being in the middle of it?

Valerie: It's like it's just a thing, not the way my life really is.

Social Worker: Maybe we can get out of the business of deciding whether or not it's the way your life really is. Maybe we could get into the business of something else, like putting your energy into what you care about—your job and your family.

As homework, the social worker gives Valerie a worksheet which helps her observe how fusion dominates her actions (figure 1.2).

Noticing Thoughts That Get You Stuck

Date and situation	What thoughts got you stuck?	How did these thoughts influence your actions?	Did this cost anything in terms of what's important to you?	If you had not been stuck, what would you have done differently?
Saturday, sitting on the couch watching TV.	"My life is going nowhere."	I sat there for the next few hours feeling guilty.	I could've taken a walk to help my back, and I could've played with Pia. I want to be a better parent.	I would've taken Pia to the park to feed the ducks.

Figure 1.2   A sample client worksheet.

Throughout the rest of their work, Valerie and the social worker continue to observe which thoughts become especially "sticky" for her and how her behavior changes as a result.

Contact with the Present Moment

Contact with the present moment means deliberately bringing one's attention to lived experience as it occurs. This can be contrasted with the kind of "experiencing" that is filtered through the mind. For example, a person with a history of panic, despite surviving many panic attacks with no enduring physiological consequences, can perceive his racing heart and tingling extremities as evidence of an oncoming heart attack. Alternatively, without a layer of meaning superimposed over them, he can notice these phenomena simply as bodily sensations. Contacting the present moment involves flexibly attending to experience as it occurs, outside of thinking and meaning making, the way one might momentarily take in a backyard garden—now seeing the colors of the flowers, now feeling the breeze against one's skin, now smelling the freshly cut grass, now hearing the children playing next door, now noticing the pleasant feeling in one's body. It is different from the inflexible attention one might bring to worrying about an upcoming job interview or playing a video game for hours on end (Wilson & Dufrene, 2008). Becoming present to experience can be facilitated through any kind of mindfulness exercise, from counting breaths for a few minutes to begin a session to observing the feelings in one's body during an intense moment in the therapeutic conversation to engaging in more formal and lengthy exercises such as Kabat-Zinn's body scan (see chapter 3).

In the third session following intake, after reviewing the "Noticing Thoughts That Get You Stuck" worksheet, the social worker introduces Valerie to the concept of "being present" and teaches her a brief mindfulness exercise in which she observes various components of her immediate experience: the sensations of her breath in her body; the feeling of her body in the chair; the feeling of her feet inside her shoes, the sensation of her skin exposed to the air; the ambient sounds in the room; and the shapes, colors, and textures in her visual field. She encourages Valerie to practice this exercise once a day for 5–10 minutes as homework. When they meet two weeks later, Valerie reports she often became distracted during the exercise but now notices she is beginning to pay a little more attention to the world around her, even when she is in pain or feeling depressed.

Self as Context

Self as context involves making a distinction between one's self and the thoughts and feelings one experiences. The ACT practitioner helps the client adopt the perspective that he or she is the context or "container" of all he or she experiences. The self as context, often referred to in ACT as the "observing self," is not a true or essential self, but merely a safe and stable vantage point from which to notice private experiences. Whereas the observing self is stable and continuous—it is the same perspective the client has looked out from throughout his or her life—thoughts and feelings are always changing from moment to moment. Taking this perspective helps the client to experience private experiences, especially the ones that usually invite struggle, as transient and therefore less dominant.

The observing self is cultivated through metaphors and experiential exercises. The social worker might offer the "Chessboard Metaphor" (Hayes, Strosahl, & Wilson, 2012) in which "good" and "bad" thoughts are rooks, pawns, and other chess pieces in an ongoing, unwinnable game and the observing self is the board that experiences their movements with no investment in the outcome. The social worker could also facilitate an extended mindfulness exercise called the "Observer" (Hayes, Strosahl, & Wilson, 2012) in which the client is asked to look back over his or her life at various points, noticing the endless stream of thoughts and feelings that have come and gone while the self has remained the same. Or the social worker might have the client embody a troublesome private experience in an object and carry it around as a welcome guest for a week to make literal the distinction between the observing self and what it experiences ("Practicing Willingness with an Avatar"; Boone & Canicci, 2013).

In the fourth session, after leading Valerie through the "Observer," the social worker gives Valerie the assignment to carry an object in addition to practicing daily mindfulness. Because Valerie struggles so much with physical pain, the social worker suggests she embody that pain as part of the exercise. To add an element of acceptance, she suggests Valerie pick an object with which she feels she can cultivate a warm and caring relationship. Valerie identifies one of her daughter's stuffed animals, a small bunny that Pia never took to but Valerie has always been fond of. The social worker suggests Valerie carry it around with her as much as possible between sessions, even if she needs to keep it hidden in her purse if she is in public. Valerie finds the exercise a bit silly, but says she's willing to try it. In the fifth session, they discuss how it went.

Valerie: I forgot about it at first, but then I saw the bunny in Pia's room and I started carrying it with me all over the house. Pia thought it was really funny. I didn't tell her what it was about. When I was cooking dinner, it sat on the counter next to the stove. When I went to work, it sat in my purse. I secretly petted it while I was sitting on the bus and on my breaks. It seemed kind of dumb at first, but after a while the bunny became kind of like my little buddy. A couple of times when I felt back pain, I remembered the bunny and thought, "It's okay, pain, you can be here."

The exercise, though primarily about helping Valerie make a distinction between herself and her pain, also encourages her to be more accepting of the pain, bringing it with her (and even petting it) rather than pushing it away. Notice that what the exercise helps to change is not the pain itself, but rather Valerie's relationship to it.

Values and Committed Action

Values are chosen life directions that guide behavior. *Committed action* is any behavior, large or small, that serves these values. ACT encourages clients to identify what matters most in their lives and move in that direction. Values can be any personally chosen statement about how to live one's life, but they are best described using verbs, adjectives, and adverbs to better capture qualities of acting in the world. When asked to identify how he or she wants to act in relationships, the client might identify "lovingly" and "patiently." At work, the client may want to be "engaged" and "hardworking." In the realm of fun and leisure, the client may want to "have fun" and "build friendships." Though many words that describe feelings can be chosen to describe values, values are very different from feelings. For example, a person choosing "loving" as a value may not experience that feeling at any given moment. But he or she can act in a loving way, no matter what the circumstances. Furthermore, living according to one's values is not chosen once and for all. Just as in mindfulness practice, where the mind will inevitably drift off again and again, living according to values means frequently finding oneself moving *away* from values. In these moments, ACT encourages clients to gently redirect themselves, just as they would gently redirect their attention during mindfulness practice.

Values and committed action can be facilitated formally or informally. The social worker could simply ask, "If you were not devoting so much energy to struggling with this anxiety, what would you be doing with your energy?" Or the social worker could use any one of the many values worksheets and exercises available in ACT literature, such as the Valued Living Questionnaire-2 (Wilson & Dufrene, 2008). With the help of the four mindfulness processes—acceptance, defusion, contact with the present moment, and self as context—the social worker helps the client build ever-increasing patterns of valued action in the service of creating a meaningful life.

In session six, the social worker asks what life would look like were Valerie living according to what's most meaningful to her. She gives Valerie a homework assignment to imagine she is at the end of her life and writing a thank-you note to her younger self, the person she is at this moment in time. She is to imagine expressing gratitude for all the values-directed living she has done from this moment on, identifying specific actions she took. In the next session, Valerie explores the exercise.

Valerie:	I was kind of sad when I was writing it. I realized just how much I'm not doing in my life. But I also felt kind of motivated—I'm beginning to feel like these things are not out of reach. I thanked myself for spending more time with Pia, for being a good mother to her. And I wrote a lot about taking care of my health—like not drinking so much anymore, and taking walks for my back like the doctor said. I also thanked myself for going to physical therapy and sticking it out *(laughs)*. I hate physical therapy! It hurts, and it's hard to keep up with when I'm working. But maybe things would be better if I was going.
Social Worker:	Anything else?
Valerie:	One of the things that I wrote about was relationships, like a boyfriend or a girlfriend. I think I want someone special in my life again. I've been so focused on myself, so worried about parenting and pain, that I haven't really put any energy toward meeting someone. And if I'm honest with myself, I think that's something I really want…. *(With tears in her eyes.)* I thanked myself for building a family.

The social worker spends the rest of the session helping Valerie identify small, specific actions she can take in these directions, like going for at least one walk over the week, spending quality time with Pia every day, and being more engaged with people she meets. Over the next two months, Valerie continues practicing mindfulness for homework, incorporating other exercises like walking meditation. The social worker continues to help her notice when she is struggling with feelings and getting wrapped up in thoughts. Homework assignments include taking more small actions in the service of her values, writing out goals and the steps to achieve them, and practicing exposure to her pain and anxiety by visualizing breathing in and out of them, which Valerie finds especially helpful. After fourteen sessions, Valerie says she is ready to wrap up the work.

Social Worker: You seem really different these days.

Valerie: I *am* different. I'm walking a lot now, and I'm spending more quality time with Pia. I mean, I've always spent time with her, but I was usually far away in my mind. Now I feel like I can really be with her more of the time. My back still hurts a bit every day. And I still get anxious and sad. But my feelings don't stick the way they used to. I'm drinking less, too. And guess what: I'm starting physical therapy next week! (*Laughs.*)

Social Worker: (*Smiles.*) You hate physical therapy.

Valerie: I know, but that's one of the reasons I think we should stop meeting for now. I need to devote some time to my health in other ways. I feel like I have the tools to keep going. And I'm still carrying that bunny around!

Conclusion

Valerie has learned to relate differently to her physical pain and her emotional reactions. Whereas before she would respond with the same inflexible pattern of inertia, avoidance, and rumination no matter what the situation, she can now respond effectively to her pain without unnecessary struggle and live in a way that is more consonant with her values. In short, she has become more psychologically flexible.

Though the social worker's interventions focused primarily on helping Valerie live differently in the world, other social work interventions that target the world in which Valerie lives could be seamlessly incorporated into the work. There is nothing in ACT that suggests all interventions must remain in the office. ACT is based on a contemporary version of behaviorism called *functional contextualism* (see chapters 4, 10, and 11), and behavioral theory focuses on changing the context of a behavior in order to change the behavior itself. So if the behavior that needs changing is ruminating on thoughts about hopelessness, then the social worker could address a very localized context, such as Valerie's relationship to ruminating (e.g., treating thoughts as equivalent to what they represent versus simply noticing thoughts and acting in the service of values), or a broader context, like the client's access to needed resources and engagement with other services. Either one might have an effect on the behavior of ruminating, and it would be up to the social worker to decide which intervention—if not both—was clinically appropriate.

References

Boone, M. S., & Cannici, J. (2013). Acceptance and commitment therapy (ACT) in groups. In Pistorello, J. (Ed.), *Mindfulness and acceptance for counseling college students: Theory and practical applications for intervention, prevention, and outreach.* Oakland, CA: New Harbinger.

Bricker, J., Wyszynski, C., Comstock, B., & Heffner, J. L. (in press). Pilot randomized controlled trial of web-based Acceptance and Commitment Therapy for smoking cessation. *Nicotine and Tobacco Research.*

Eifert, G. H., & Forsyth, J. P. (2005). *Acceptance and commitment therapy for anxiety disorders: A practitioner's treatment guide to using mindfulness, acceptance, and values-based behavior change strategies.* Oakland, CA: New Harbinger.

Flaxman, P. E., & Bond, F. W. (2010). Acceptance and commitment training: Promoting psychological flexibility in the workplace. In R. A. Baer (Ed.), *Assessing mindfulness and acceptance processes in clients: Illuminating the theory and practice of change.* Oakland, CA: New Harbinger.

Fledderus, M., Bohlmeijer, E. T., Fox, J. P., Schreurs, K. M. G., & Spinhoven, P. (2013). The role of psychological flexibility in a self-help acceptance and commitment therapy intervention for psychological distress in a randomized controlled trial. *Behaviour Research and Therapy, 51,* 142-151.

Harris, R. (2010). *ACT made simple.* Oakland, CA: New Harbinger.

Hayes, S. C., Strosahl, K. D., Bunting, K., Twohig, M., & Wilson, K. G. (2004). What is acceptance and commitment therapy? In S. C. Hayes and K. D. Strosahl (Eds.), *A practical guide to acceptance and commitment therapy* (pp. 1-29). New York: Springer.

Hayes, S. C., Strosahl, K., & Wilson, K. G. (1999). *Acceptance and commitment therapy: an experiential approach to behavior change*. New York: Guilford Press.

Hayes, S. C., Strosahl, K., & Wilson, K. G. (2012). *Acceptance and commitment therapy: The process and practice of mindful change* (2nd ed.). New York: Guilford Press.

Lillis, J., & Hayes, S. C. (2007). Applying acceptance, mindfulness, and values to the reduction of prejudice: A pilot study. *Behavior Modification, 31*, 389-411.

Luoma, J., Hayes, S. C., & Walser, R. (2007). *Learning ACT*. Oakland, CA: New Harbinger.

Masuda, A., Hayes, S. C., Fletcher, L. B., Seignourel, P. J., Bunting, K., Herbst, et al. (2007). The impact of acceptance and commitment therapy versus education on stigma toward people with psychological disorders. *Behavior Research and Therapy, 45*, 2764-2772.

Montgomery, K. L., Kim, J. S., & Franklin, C. (2011). Acceptance and commitment therapy for psychological and physiological illnesses: A systematic review for social workers. *Health & Social Work, 36*, 169-181.

National Association of Social Workers (NASW). (2008). *Code of Ethics*. Retrieved from https://www.socialworkers.org/pubs/code/code.asp

Ruiz, F. J. (2010). A review of acceptance and commitment therapy (ACT) empirical evidence: Correlational, experimental psychopathology, component and outcome studies. *International Journal of Psychology and Psychological Therapy, 10*, 125-162.

Wicksell, R. K., Melin, L., Lekander, M., & Olsson, G. L. (2009). Evaluating the effectiveness of exposure and acceptance strategies to improve functioning and quality of life in longstanding pediatric pain—A randomized controlled trial. *Pain, 141*, 248-257.

Wilson, K. G., & DuFrene, T. (2008). *Mindfulness for two: An acceptance and commitment therapy approach to mindfulness in psychotherapy*. Oakland, CA: New Harbinger.

CHAPTER 2

Social Work and Dialectical Behavior Therapy

Felicia Marohn, LMSW

Private Practice, Santa Fe DBT

Cedar Koons, MSW, LISW

Private Practice, Santa Fe DBT

Behavioral Tech, Seattle, WA

Social workers are committed to the dignity and worth of each client, the importance of human relationships, the social worker's personal integrity, and professional competence (National Association of Social Workers, 2008). Social workers also commit to working with underserved and stigmatized populations, including those with severe personality disorders. Dialectical behavior therapy (DBT) is a principle-driven, intensive, and evidence-based treatment that values these social work principles. DBT's overarching goal is to help clients, many of whom struggle with suicidal thoughts, build a "life worth living." Linehan (1993a, 1993b) created DBT to treat clients with a diagnosis of borderline personality disorder (BPD) and other severe, multiproblem, and difficult-to-treat disorders that arise from pervasive emotion dysregulation. Until Linehan and her colleagues (1991) presented data from the first randomized DBT trial, there had been no psychotherapy treatment shown to be effective for clients who suffered from BPD.

DBT is based on the hypothesis that the problematic behaviors of BPD are the result of emotional vulnerability interacting with skills deficits. Therefore, much of DBT consists of the teaching, strengthening, and generalization of skills so that clients learn to become more mindful, regulate emotions, tolerate distress, and improve their interpersonal effectiveness. In creating DBT, Linehan drew from her personal studies in mindfulness, meditation, and spirituality, especially Zen Buddhism—so much so that mindfulness skills became the core skills taught throughout the yearlong treatment program.

Many DBT clients grow up in environments that invalidate their rights for safety, worth, and dignity. This invalidation ranges from, for instance, traumatic verbal, physical, or sexual abuse to discrimination based on gender, race, or socioeconomic status. As social workers who practice DBT, we frequently hear some version of the following self-invalidating client statement: "I am a bad person.... I think I was born that way. I am a bad seed—bad to the core... Otherwise all those things would not have happened to me." Many of our clients question their personal worth and dignity, moving frequently between shame, guilt, and self-loathing. As clinical social workers, we see it as our ethical obligation to help our clients arrive at a place where they are able to experience their inner wisdom as well as their inner worth and dignity. Furthermore, since DBT is an evidence-based treatment, making an effort to deliver it with fidelity is a responsible choice grounded in social work's value of professional competence. Considering the severity of our clients' suffering and the need for reducing this suffering to a bearable amount as rapidly as possible, it is essential to provide *effective compassion*, which means offering an evidence-based treatment for fast and long-lasting behavioral changes.

Furthermore, social workers value human relationships. In DBT, the therapeutic alliance, as one form of a human relationship, is of crucial importance. To work from a relational perspective means to recognize and acknowledge that our interpersonal relationships contribute to long-term happiness or unhappiness. Through the therapeutic alliance and through the examination of other relationships, our clients may achieve interpersonal healing. As DBT therapists, we embody and model ways to arrive at a place of self-love, self-empathy, and self-confidence, helping our clients shift from self-loathing to self-acceptance. Herein, the social worker's personal integrity is of essence. In DBT, as in most cognitive-behavioral treatments, the therapeutic relationship is acknowledged as a real—rather than a transferential—relationship between equals, even though the therapist is a professional who must honor all professional and ethical standards. Linehan (1993a) highlights that, at times, the therapeutic DBT relationship *is* what keeps our clients alive.

In the following chapter, we will present the evidence base, theory, and practice applications of DBT. Client excerpts will be woven throughout the chapter to provide the reader with an experience of what DBT in action may look like. Further, we will highlight the complementarities between social work values and a social worker's DBT practice.

Evidence Base

DBT is recognized as an evidence-based treatment with high rates of success (Feigenbaum, 2007; Kliem, Kröger, & Kosfelder, 2010; Lynch, Trost, Salsman, & Linehan, 2007; Scheele, 2000). DBT has been shown to reduce the frequency and severity of (a) self-injurious behavior, (b) days of psychiatric hospitalization, and (c) symptoms of depression, binge eating, and substance abuse. Further, DBT has been shown to increase social functioning and global adjustment (Robins, Schmidt III, & Linehan, 2004). Moreover, DBT has been widely disseminated in North America and in Europe and is being utilized in a variety of treatment settings serving different populations, including outpatient, intensive outpatient, inpatient, residential, forensic, juvenile justice, and vocational rehabilitation settings. DBT has been adapted for treating a number of comorbidities of

BPD, including post-traumatic stress disorder (Steil, Dyer, Priebe, Kleindienst, & Bohus, 2011), eating disorders (Chen, Matthews, Allen, Kuo, & Linehan, 2008; Robinson & Safer, 2012), and addiction (Linehan et al., 1999). It has also been shown to be effective in treating victims of domestic violence (Iverson, Shenk, & Fruzzetti, 2009). Throughout this book chapter, the phrase "standard DBT" refers to outpatient DBT delivered with fidelity to the evidence-based treatment model. As practiced by the authors, standard DBT stands in contrast to "DBT-informed" programs. DBT-informed programs are partial and have been modified to the needs of a particular agency or practitioner yet do not adhere to all characteristics of Linehan's (1993a, 1993b) development of the DBT treatment model.

Theoretical Foundation

DBT is based on the integration of three diverse philosophical orientations, each of which contributed equally to the development of the treatment. The three orientations are behaviorism, dialectics, and mindfulness practices. Before we describe the structure of the treatment, it is important to explain a little of how these orientations are present in its foundation.

Behaviorism

Behaviorism, a theory backed by a great deal of scientific research, explains human behavior in terms of learning, especially learning acquired through modeling and conditioning. DBT's behavioral change strategies include skills training, contingency management, cognitive restructuring, and exposure, all of which are standard interventions in cognitive behavioral therapy (CBT).

In DBT, behavior is defined not only as observable behaviors but also as thoughts, emotions, and bodily sensations. DBT posits that most of the problematic behaviors seen in emotionally dysregulated clients are the result of skills deficits, primarily deficits in managing emotions. The skills to manage emotions, tolerate distress, and function interpersonally are usually learned in childhood, but adequate modeling and teaching of skills is not present in every home and every community. Furthermore, problematic behaviors that are shaped in the absence of skills are conditioned by unhelpful reinforcing contingencies, while adaptive behaviors are punished in many contexts. For example, in some environments, children are not attended to until their demands become impossible to ignore, thereby punishing adaptive communication efforts while reinforcing extreme communication styles. Social work and behaviorism share the recognition that we need to understand the person within his or her environment in order to enter a change process.

Dialectics

Dialectics can be defined as an inquiring into and holding of opposing truths. From a DBT perspective, dialectics focuses on the "whole as well as the complexity of the whole" (Linehan, 1993a, p. 32). There is no ultimate truth, final answer, or absolute experience. Rather each truth, perspective, viewpoint, or answer (i.e., thesis) also includes an opposing truth (i.e., antithesis). The primary dialectic upon which DBT rests is that clients need both to change their self-defeating behaviors and to simultaneously accept themselves for who they are in this very moment. DBT acceptance strategies are rooted in validation and mindfulness; DBT change strategies are derived from behaviorism. The goal in DBT is to engage in a *dialectical dialogue* and create a cycle of knowledge generation, learning, and growth throughout the length of the treatment contract.

DBT and dialectics are based on a systems perspective, which aligns with basic social work principles. In DBT, we acknowledge the interdependent and transactional forces that transpire in families and in life, as well as in the therapeutic relationship. Sometimes, the transactional forces are not readily apparent, and we need to inquire into the pieces of the puzzle we are not seeing. For example, Marie, a new client in a private practice setting who has not yet begun skills group, asks to be seen three times a week for individual therapy. She has the means to pay for this amount of treatment. The social worker knows she is struggling because she recently separated from her husband of ten years. Marie reports being "emotionally dependent" on her husband. She says she is "in a hurry to feel better." Marie is not employed and has few structured activities on most days. The social worker, Carla, in consultation with the DBT team, considers the dialectical dilemmas presented by Marie's request. On the one hand, Marie is suffering from feelings of abandonment and is seeking support for the painful loss she is experiencing. On the other hand, Carla feels that Marie is at risk for becoming dependent on therapy at a time when she really needs structures in her life that will build self-efficacy and independence. The consultation team helps Carla arrive at a synthesis. Marie needs more support to be able to establish structure in her life and, until she is able to start group, she needs a "jump start" on distress tolerance and mindfulness skills to help her tolerate her pain. Carla offers Marie a second session each week until she will be able to start skills group—a session that will be focused on skills acquisition and activity scheduling. This synthesis then becomes the thesis of the next problem. Even though Marie has the second session (i.e., thesis), she will likely find it difficult to reengage in the world as a newly separated woman who has to overcome her isolation (i.e., antithesis). Moreover, the idea of using skills on her own (i.e., thesis) contrasts with seeking soothing and support from her therapist (i.e., antithesis). The hope is that the next synthesis will be for Marie to learn and master skills to become more independent. Marie's story is an illustration of how DBT treatment proceeds in a dialectical manner.

Mindfulness

The third piece of DBT's foundational triangle is mindfulness. Mindfulness skills are at the core of the DBT skills curriculum and are taught at the beginning of each of the skills modules. Furthermore, a mindfulness practice is required of DBT therapists so that they may be able to teach the skills and deliver the treatment effectively.

Linehan derived the DBT mindfulness skills in consultation with her Zen teacher, Willigis Jäger, Roshi, and DBT was the first psychotherapy to employ mindfulness as part of the treatment. No dismantling studies of DBT have yet been completed, making it difficult to gauge the exact role mindfulness actually plays in improving outcomes, but the mindfulness skills as well as the distress tolerance skills are designed to balance the relentless pressure clients feel to confront painful realities and change their behaviors. These acceptance strategies and the empathic validation from the therapist address the profound misery of clients and assist them with learning to stay present and improve the quality of their lives.

Biosocial Theory

In her biosocial theory, Linehan (1993a) hypothesizes that BPD might arise in a client's life as a result of specific transactions that may have occurred between a child and his or her developmental environment. DBT emphasizes the importance of working with clients from a dialectical systems perspective that considers the client within his or her environment. Causes and conditions neither arise from a vacuum nor exist within a vacuum. In this way, the biosocial theory of the etiology of BPD mirrors social work's person-in-environment conceptualization.

The biosocial theory is taught to clients in skills classes. Halfway through the psychoeducational lecture, we usually hear someone comment, "That is exactly what happened in my family while growing up. Now everything makes so much more sense, and I understand that none of this is my fault." DBT's biosocial theory as a person-in-environment perspective appears to have a healing effect upon many of our clients by mitigating some of their pervasive shame and self-blame.

BIOLOGICAL UNDERPINNINGS

Linehan (1993a) proposes that people who later develop pervasive emotion dysregulation may have been born with a higher emotional sensitivity or vulnerability than the average person. What does it mean to be more emotionally vulnerable than the average human being? A person may have been born highly sensitive to external cues or stimuli—much more sensitive than other people in similar situations. For example, it may not take much to arouse a highly sensitive baby; this baby may be more easily startled, afraid, or even excited than other babies. Furthermore, a more sensitive child may have a higher level of emotional intensity, throwing a tantrum in response to stimuli that might not affect other children so intensely. Lastly, people who experience high emotional vulnerability may have a slower return to their baseline, meaning that their reactions last longer. For example, while one client's brother would usually calm down within five minutes of becoming upset, it took this client an hour to stop crying when faced with a similar situation. Our clients often describe themselves as emotional burn victims or emotional sponges, without sufficient skin, boundaries, or a stable sense of self.

Linehan (1993a) also suggests that biological causes for a higher emotional sensitivity may be genetic, intrauterine, or based on unfavorable early childhood events that may have effected brain development, such as sexual abuse (p. 49).

THE INVALIDATING ENVIRONMENT

Linehan (1993a) proposes that an "invalidating environment" is the social component that may contribute to the development of pervasive emotion dysregulation and an inadequate sense of self. Among other things, invalidating environments can include stereotypical gender role expectations, sexism, racism, or ongoing sexual abuse.

In an invalidating environment, a child's private experiences are quashed or even punished over an extended period of time. When a child feels emotionally distressed, she may be told that she is overreacting, she is oversensitive, there is nothing to worry about, and she should pull herself up by the bootstraps and go on with life. By definition, invalidating environments are intermittently nonresponsive to a person's needs and emotional expressions. Thus, clients need to become very creative in devising survival strategies. As one client stated, "If I wanted to get a response from my parents, I needed to scream at the top of my lungs." A teenage client reported: "Unless I engage in self-harm behaviors and cut, I am invisible to my parents."

THE TRANSACTION BETWEEN BIOLOGY AND AN INVALIDATING ENVIRONMENT

Not every child who is emotionally sensitive experiences pervasive emotion dysregulation later in life. Nor does every person who grew up in an invalidating environment later present with BPD. The essential component for developing an emotion regulation disorder appears to be the transaction between emotional sensitivity and an invalidating environment. Linehan (1993a) suggests a reciprocal influence between invalidation from the environment and the emotionally sensitive individual. This reciprocal influence may lead to *pervasive* invalidation and *increased* vulnerability for the individual (e.g., child) *and* the environment (e.g., family and school). Subsequently, the ongoing transaction between pervasive invalidation and increased emotional vulnerability leads to pervasive emotion dysregulation in the child (p. 58). Linehan suggests that an inadequate sense of self and feelings of chronic emptiness may also result from persistent invalidation.

Structure of Treatment

DBT divides treatment into four stages, with clear priorities as to what is treated in each stage. In stage one, the goals are to establish a therapeutic working alliance, support basic client safety, and teach basic skills. Stage one clients are often in complete behavioral chaos, possibly engaging in life-threatening behaviors, as well as behaviors inconsistent with a reasonable quality of life. Thus, the goal of stage one is to develop the skills to move from behavioral dyscontrol to basic behavioral control.

In stage two, clients have learned various skills and gained control over severe behaviors. Clients are now ready to focus on increasing their emotional experiencing and processing pain or trauma in their pasts. During this stage, social worker and client increase the client's skill and comfort with experiencing strong or painful emotions while also treating and resolving any traumatic stress that may be present. In addition to informal emotional exposure, DBT uses evidence-based trauma treatments such as prolonged exposure.

During the third treatment stage, clients work on increasing self-respect, solving ordinary problems of living, and achieving individual goals. Clients now learn to validate their own opinions, emotions, and actions and develop self-respect independent of the therapist. During stage three, clients learn how to generalize their behaviors and effectively ask for help from other people. At the same time, when help is not available, clients now need to practice self-soothing and tolerating the distress that comes with having to solve problems on their own.

Stage four is conceptualized as a time when the client is able to focus on introducing more joy and more personal freedom into his or her life. Individuals who have suffered a great deal and struggled to attain stability and a decent quality of life often want to continue to grow in their capacity to fully embrace and enjoy living. In a social work context, DBT may be considered a holistic treatment that honors higher-order needs such as belonging and self-actualization. Thus, DBT social workers recognize the human need for more than just symptom reduction. In stage four, we help our clients express a connection to self and community, spirituality, and acceptance of the world as it is, while also contributing to positive change. From personal experience, we can say that many of our clients leave DBT and become involved in formal mindfulness practices or engage in community in other enriching ways.

Treatment Target Hierarchy

Each stage of treatment has its own treatment target hierarchy that prioritizes specific behaviors—behaviors that need to change before another stage begins. For example, the therapist does not begin stage two trauma work until clients have acquired basic mindfulness, emotion regulation, and distress tolerance skills. In this introduction to DBT, we will focus only on the primary targets of stage one.

The four primary targets in stage one are decreasing life-threatening behaviors, decreasing therapy-interfering behaviors, decreasing quality of life–interfering behaviors, and acquiring, strengthening, and generalizing behavioral skills. If we want to decrease maladaptive behaviors, we must replace them with something else. That is why DBT explicitly focuses on skills acquisition (Linehan, 1993a, p. 177). Furthermore, all the skills that have been learned must be generalized by being applied with increasing frequency in the client's life.

Decreasing Life-Threatening Behaviors

The highest priority target in DBT is to decrease suicidal behaviors, including nonsuicidal self-injury (NSSI) such as cutting. NSSI has been shown to increase the risk of suicide (Andover & Gibb, 2010). Reducing suicidal and NSSI behaviors is the highest priority target because, as DBT therapists often say in their characteristically irreverent style, we can only treat clients who are alive. Therefore, whenever suicidal or NSSI behaviors occur, the therapist conducts a thorough behavior chain analysis (BCA), a detailed investigation of the behavior, its antecedents, its reinforcing consequences, and its function. This is followed by a solution analysis in which the social worker and client generate alternative behaviors. DBT therapists also ask clients to track behaviors, urges, and skills on a weekly diary card, which they then bring to their weekly individual therapy sessions for assessment and discussion. These strategies are illustrated in the following vignette.

Jenna, fourteen years old, was recently discharged from the hospital after a suicide attempt. Jenna had been in DBT for about a month and was attending the multifamily skills group with her parents. Jenna had been cutting for over a year, sometimes superficially, and sometimes, as before her hospitalization, quite severely. Since starting DBT, the cutting had diminished.

Her therapist, Ann, had started Jenna on a diary card to track behaviors such as taking her medication, doing homework, and exercising, as well as problem behaviors such as fighting with her parents, suicidal ideation, self-harm urges, and self-harm behaviors. The diary card was used to structure the session.

"Do you have your diary card?" Ann asks at the beginning of an individual session.

"You are going to be mad at me."

"How come?"

"I cut."

"Hmm. No, I'm not mad but I want to understand why. Let's do a behavior chain analysis. When did you cut?" (The social worker undertakes a formal BCA in a matter-of-fact tone so as to neither punish nor reinforce the problematic behavior. The goal is to understand the controlling variables of Jenna's behavior as well as raise Jenna's awareness of the causes and conditions of cutting.)

"Monday."

"What happened on Monday?"

"My mother found out I'd been ditching school."

"You didn't tell me you'd been ditching school. You have to tell me these things. We need to put that on your diary card. But anyway, your mother found out when?"

"The assistant principal called her at work on Monday."

"Did you two have a fight?"

"Yes, a big one."

"Then what happened?"

"She grounded me from everything, took away my phone, turned off the Internet. I called my dad but he didn't answer…"

"You could have called me for coaching…" (The social worker attempts to help Jenna with skills acquisition and learning to reach out for help.)

"I couldn't stand it. I went in my room and cut with a ball point pen, because, of course, you made me get rid of my razors."

"What couldn't you stand?" (The social worker attempts to understand the discriminative stimulus, or the "straw that broke the camel's back.")

"How I felt. The anger."

"Okay, we need to work on skills to handle anger. So, how did you feel after you cut with the pen?"

"It didn't really work. I just kind of jabbed myself a lot. But I calmed down eventually."

"So the pen wasn't as effective as the razor at bringing relief?"

"Not really. I know you told me that relief isn't a good thing, because it makes it more likely I'll do it again."

"That is right, it's reinforcement. The bad feelings go away. But it sounds like it worked anyway."

"Yeah, just not as good as the razor."

"That's progress. Did you show your mother what you'd done?" (The social worker comments on the reduction in reinforcement and assesses whether the behavior was a means of communication.)

"No, of course not! She would just punish me more."

"How do you feel about telling me about it?"

"Pretty bad. I had urges to cut again before our session."

"I'm glad you didn't. Bravo! (The social worker validates skillful behavior.) So we have to work on you calling for coaching before you cut, and we have to work on skills to manage your anger at your mother. Right?" (The social worker targets solutions.)

"Right," Jenna smiles and looks relieved.

Decreasing Therapy-Interfering Behaviors

Therapy-interfering behaviors are behaviors in which either the client or the social worker acts in a way that interferes with effective treatment. For example, the client may come late for sessions, fail to report a problematic behavior or lie about it, or refuse to complete homework or a diary card because she "does not feel like it." A social worker who is inattentive, begins sessions late, or does not take a dialectical stance would also be considered to be engaging in therapy-interfering behaviors. Addressing therapy-interfering behaviors of both the client and social worker underscores the importance of one's professional social work integrity in respecting the therapeutic relationship and diffusing the power differential inherent in the therapeutic relationship. DBT honors the social work values of integrity and competence by orienting clients toward what behaviors are likely to be therapy-interfering while also encouraging clients to hold the individual therapist accountable for his or her therapy-interfering behaviors.

Decreasing Quality of Life–Interfering Behaviors

Quality of life–interfering behaviors can be manifold and should be prioritized. At times, it may be advised to solve the problems that are most detrimental to a client's quality of life. For example, if a client has extreme financial and housing problems, these must be addressed first in order to help the client maintain a certain standard of living conducive to engaging in weekly psychotherapeutic treatment. If alcohol or drug abuse prevents a client from either maintaining financial stability or being able to do the therapeutic work, then the addiction may need to be addressed first. Other quality of life–interfering behaviors may include social isolation; avoidance behaviors such as not attending work or school; spending; gambling; noncompliance with medications; eating disorder behaviors such as bingeing, restricting, and purging; or other impulse-control problems. Instead of addressing the most pressing issues first, one may also choose to begin with solving those problems that seem the most easily solvable. This sets the client up for success and reinforces active problem solving.

The fourth target in the DBT treatment target hierarchy is the acquisition, strengthening, and generalization of behavioral skills, which is achieved via group skills training, individual therapy, and intersession phone coaching.

Modes of Treatment

Standard DBT has four modes of treatment: individual psychotherapy, group skills training, intersession telephone contact for coaching, and team consultation for the therapists. Weekly individual therapy is the central mode of treatment. In individual therapy sessions, client and social worker individualize the treatment plan and focus on the client's target behaviors in a hierarchy of severity. Intersession contact for coaching is provided by the individual therapist to reduce suicidal behaviors and suicide crises and to further the generalization of DBT skills. DBT skills groups are conducted in a psychoeducational format that includes lectures and discussion in order to help clients acquire and strengthen behavioral skills. The DBT team consultation is a weekly meeting for all the therapists treating a cohort of clients. These meetings emphasize case consultation to maintain fidelity to the evidence base and increase therapists' capabilities and effectiveness through education and mutual support.

Mindfulness is at the core of every mode of treatment. It is theorized that core mindfulness skills increase clients' abilities to experience rather than avoid their emotions (Linehan, 1993a, p. 62). In DBT, mental and physical pain and discomfort are considered to be an unavoidable part of life; trying to avoid pain just adds unnecessary suffering. Moreover, core mindfulness skills are also the skills that support therapists in holding the central dialectic of acceptance and change (Robins, Schmidt III, & Linehan, 2004, p. 37). Therefore, all skills groups and consultation team meetings start with a mindfulness exercise for three to five minutes.

Individual Therapy

In weekly individual therapy sessions, social worker and client prioritize and individualize treatment goals, identify problematic behaviors, and prioritize time in the session according to the severity of behaviors present and the stage of treatment. At times, client problems appear so complex and pervasive that both social worker and client may feel overwhelmed and confused about which problem needs to be addressed first. In order to mediate this challenge, DBT therapists rely on the treatment stage and treatment target hierarchies.

Further, the individual therapist is the client's primary therapist and his or her biggest cheerleader, giving encouragement and support for the strenuous task of accepting life as it is, while trying harder to solve the problems that can be solved. Within this context, the social worker models dialectical thinking and dialectical behaviors.

Moreover, DBT utilizes several case management strategies to determine when to intervene in the client's environment and when to teach and coach the client regarding ways to help herself. DBT's primary case management strategy is providing "consultation-to-the-client." In consultation-to-the client, the social worker helps the client learn how to advocate for her needs in the most skillful way rather than having the therapist solve the client's problems. From a social work perspective, consultation-to-the-client may be considered a self-empowerment practice. Linehan (1993a) states: "Patients may not have caused all their problems, but they need to solve them anyway" (p. 107). It behooves the clinical social worker to do the utmost to teach clients how to solve the problems they can solve and accept those that cannot be solved at this time. However, there might be instances in which a client is unable to be effective on his own. For example, the client may lack power or skill—yet the outcome may be essential. In those cases, the therapist may use more traditional environmental strategies, such as calling up the staff of a psychiatric hospital to intervene on the client's behalf rather than asking the client to advocate on his own behalf.

Group Skills Training

In group skills training, the skills trainer focuses on teaching clients new behavioral skills as well as on strengthening and generalizing those skills (Linehan, 1993a, p. 186). During the twelve-month standard DBT program, clients learn skills from four modules: (a) core mindfulness, (b) interpersonal effectiveness, (c) emotion regulation, and (d) distress tolerance.

Core Mindfulness

Mindfulness can be understood as a universal human potential that can be cultivated through training. Mindfulness is both a process and an outcome—a fundamental way of being that penetrates one's moment-by-moment experience. DBT core mindfulness skills are divided into two categories—three core mindfulness *"what" skills* and three core mindfulness *"how" skills*. The three "what" skills (i.e., what to do in order to become more mindful) are observing, describing, and participating. The three "how" skills (i.e., the attitude to take in practicing mindfulness) are nonjudgmentally, one-mindfully, and effectively (Linehan, 1993a, 1993b).

"What" skills. The three "what" skills help clients lead a lifestyle characterized by awareness rather than impulsive and mood-dependent behaviors (Linehan, 1993a, p. 144). For example, when practicing *observing*, the client is asked to watch the coming and going of thoughts, sensations, or environmental occurrences without reacting. The skill of *describing* refers to verbally labeling one's experiences—that is, naming thoughts, sensations, or environmental occurrences without judgment. *Participating* is the ability to fully and spontaneously engage in one's present-moment experience without self-consciousness (Linehan, 1993b, pp. 63-64).

"How" skills. The purpose of the three "how" skills is to specify the manner in which one practices the "what" skills. One of the most important attitudes in DBT is embracing a nonjudgmental stance, and *nonjudgmentally* is the first "how" skill. Linehan (1993a) explains: "Taking a nonjudgmental stance means just that—judging something as neither good nor bad" (p. 146). DBT therapists encourage clients to focus on consequences of behaviors and events as opposed to regarding behaviors or events as good and bad, worthy or worthless. The second core "how" skill is *one-mindfully*, which means doing one thing at a time with full and undivided attention. The third "how" skill is to do things effectively. Linehan (1993a, 1993b) recommends using an attitude derived from Zen Buddhism called *upaya*, which translates as using "skillful means," in order to achieve one's intrapersonal and interpersonal goals. Accordingly, a common question asked by DBT skills trainers is, "Do you want to be right, or do you want to be effective?"

Wise mind. Wise mind is another central mindfulness concept in DBT. DBT operates on the premise that individuals experience three states of mind—reasonable mind, emotion mind, and wise mind (Linehan, 1993a, 1993b). *Reasonable mind* is the state of mind in which people are able to access logic and rational thinking, utilizing the left brain, thinking linearly, and feeling cool, calm, and focused. However, an overemphasis on reasonable mind may make us feel detached and distant, leaving out values and morals. *Emotion mind* is the state of mind that is driven by feelings, desires, and aversions. Emotion mind feels hot; we may feel overwhelmed and out of control. However, emotion mind connects us to our right brain and is the seat of love, passion, intuition, and creativity. *Wise mind* is conceptualized as the synthesis of reasonable mind and emotion mind—a synthesis between intuitive knowing/emotional experiencing and logical analysis (Linehan, 1993b, p. 63).

Linehan suggests that therapists and clients need mindfulness skills in order to access and realize wise mind. Linehan (1993b) elaborates that the goal of core mindfulness skills is learning how to be in control of one's attention instead of letting a wandering mind run the show. In order to master and control one's attention, clients need to practice mindfulness with dedication and perseverance (p. 65). We would like to suggest that controlling one's attention, impulses, thoughts, and emotions might be equally important for clinical social workers. DBT core mindfulness skills seem to relate directly to the social work value of respect for the worth and dignity of each client. When being mindful, we are more likely to engage with our clients in a manner that is attentive, transparent, and nonjudgmental.

Interpersonal Effectiveness

Clients with a diagnosis of BPD and clients who suffer from pervasive emotion dysregulation often report long histories of intense and unstable interpersonal relationships. Linehan (1993a) points out that, although clients who suffer from pervasive emotion dysregulation often have the needed social skills, the application of their social skills is often inhibited by uncontrollable affective responses and rigid beliefs. Therefore, in the interpersonal effectiveness module, skills trainers emphasize how to apply social and communication skills more effectively. As clinical social workers, we support clients in prioritizing their interpersonal goals. In this context, interpersonal effectiveness addresses the primary objectives of (a) obtaining what the client wants, (b) keeping the relationship, or (c) keeping one's self-respect.

Emotion Regulation

For clients who suffer from pervasive emotion dysregulation, emotions are experienced as too intense, painful, and ultimately intolerable. Moreover, these clients have often been socialized in an environment that has taught them that it is unacceptable to feel the way they do. To counteract the clients' prior learning history, emotional sensitivity, and persistent invalidation from the environment, emotion regulation skills teach clients that emotions have important functions and cannot be avoided. The emotion regulation module explicitly addresses how to increase one's mindfulness to current emotions, identify and label emotions correctly, and reduce one's vulnerability to emotion mind.

Distress Tolerance

In DBT, distress tolerance is regarded as a natural consequence of mindfulness. The purpose of distress tolerance is to teach the client how to tolerate and survive crises without doing things that make matters worse. When tolerating distress, the client is asked to take a nonjudgmental stance toward the situation at hand—without resisting his or her current experience. The distress tolerance module shows clients how to "bear the pain more skillfully," since mental pain and anguish are part of living and cannot be avoided.

One key ingredient for practicing distress tolerance is *radical acceptance*. Radical acceptance means accepting without adding or taking away anything from the experience of this very moment. In order to tolerate distress by radically accepting whatever life presents, one needs to cultivate an attitude of *willingness*—an attitude of being willing to turn one's mind away from maladaptive behavior toward skills with curiosity and openness. However, it is crucial to note that radical acceptance and willingness do not mean approval. The DBT premise is that a willingness to radically accept one's current reality—such as, for instance, being obese—is the only effective means for change. DBT poses that we cannot change anything unless we fully recognize and embrace the situation, its facts, and its consequences.

Intersession Contact for Coaching

Intersession contact for coaching, usually by phone, but also by e-mail and text, is an important part of DBT treatment. The aim of the five-to-fifteen-minute coaching interaction is to (a) reduce and eliminate suicide crises by teaching clients how to ask for help before harming themselves, (b) support clients in learning how to apply DBT skills in a specific situation, and (c) provide an opportunity for the repair of a relational rupture that might have occurred during the previous therapy session. In this way, intersession coaching honors the human relationship between social worker and client.

Clients with pervasive emotion dysregulation and an unstable sense of self often struggle with asking for help and often experience therapy sessions as strenuous; as a result, they may leave the office in an emotionally vulnerable state. Being able and encouraged to call the therapist for coaching helps the emotionally sensitive client resolve issues when they arise instead of having to wait for another week to see the therapist again. However, intersession contact for coaching is not therapy conducted on the phone. Calls are typically brief and focused on how to use skills to get through a difficult episode until the next session when problem solving can take place. While conducting this protocol, it is important for the social worker to fully orient the client regarding what to expect from intersession coaching. Moreover, it is essential that the social worker observe his or her own personal limits, as the following case vignette illustrates.

Keith, a DBT therapist with a caseload of depressed elderly adults who are also diagnosed with personality disorders, received a call from his client Vernon on the weekend. Keith noticed on the caller ID that the call was from Vernon and let it go to voice mail because he was grocery shopping for his family. Once Keith had finished shopping, he checked his voice mail and heard that this was not an emergency call. Vernon was upset about something Keith had said during their last session. After he had come home and put away the groceries, Keith called Vernon back from the privacy of his study.

"Hey Vernon, this is Keith. I got your message. What's up?"

"Keith, listen, I'm sorry to call you on your day off. I don't want to inconvenience you, but...something you said has been bothering me..."

"Vernon, you know it is okay to call for coaching or if something is bothering you about our last session. (The social worker validates Vernon's behavior for keeping their agreement.) What is it?"

"Well, I've been dealing with this depression..."

"Vernon, you said I said something that bothered you. What was it?" (The social worker reinforces boundaries and clarifies purpose of phone coaching.)

"You said that I had something to do with my own depression? Like I caused it or something?"

"If you thought I was saying that, no wonder you are upset. That would not only be wrong, it would be hurtful. (The social worker validates Vernon's feelings in light of a misunderstanding.) But that wasn't what I said. (The social worker clarifies facts.) What I said was, 'Staying in bed makes your depression worse and so does drinking alcohol and not having any social interactions.' Do you remember me saying that?"

"Yes. But, see, it is so hard to get out of bed when I feel this bad. And I'm not drinking that much, and…"

"Vernon, do you feel better now that you know what I was really saying?" (Social worker redirects to help Vernon stay on target and resolve the therapeutic rupture that had occurred.)

"Well, yes."

"Are you out of bed?" (The social worker now focuses on change strategies, problem solving, and skills acquisition and generalization.)

"Yes."

"Are you going to bingo at church tonight?"

"Wasn't planning on it."

"You were planning on it when we met on Wednesday, remember? You committed to going. I need to hear that you are indeed going."

"Okay, Keith, I'll go."

"Terrific. I can't wait to hear about it! (The social worker cheerleads Vernon.) Be sure and speak with John and Betty. Remember you wanted to thank them for having you over." (The social worker continues with emphasizing problem solving and solution focus.)

"I will."

"Good. That is how you build relationships. Take care and I'll see you in group on Monday."

"Okay, Keith, thanks."

Consultation Team

In DBT, a community of therapists treats a community of clients (Linehan, 1993a). Linehan acknowledges that treating clients with BPD and pervasive emotion dysregulation can be "enormously stressful" for the clinician (p. 104). Therefore, during the required weekly two-hour consultation team meetings, individual therapists and skills trainers receive mutual emotional, psychological, and structural support to sustain their own well-being while also improving the delivery of DBT to their individual clients.

The weekly team consultation in standard DBT addresses the social work values of personal integrity, professional competence, and the importance of human relationships. In our experience, the weekly meetings provide a rejuvenating form of self-care for the therapists, preventing the burnout that may occur when working with a high-risk client population. Moreover, these weekly check-ins help each clinician adhere to dialectical thinking and dialectical behaviors in the therapeutic work. For example, a client's ongoing, unbearable suffering may be so overwhelming that a therapist engages disproportionately in soothing the client while change strategies remain unexplored. In such an instance, an overemphasis on validation would disregard DBT's dialectical stance and prevent helping the client to learn new skills to reduce his or her suffering. Just as frequently, therapists will find themselves insisting clients change problematic behaviors without attending adequately to the need for validating the difficulties involved in making such changes, or recognizing that the client may lack the necessary skills needed to make such changes. In these situations, having a community of therapists to assist each social worker is believed to improve client outcomes by balancing treatment.

Conclusion

Clients with BPD, NSSI behaviors, and pervasive emotion dysregulation often lead unbearably painful lives. As social workers, it is our ethical obligation to help our clients ameliorate their suffering effectively and in a timely manner. As an evidence-based treatment grounded in core mindfulness skills, DBT appears to be an excellent choice for social workers who wish to help clients improve the quality of their lives in ways that are effective, holistic, and long lasting. In its theory and practice, DBT incorporates many social work values such as honoring the social worker's personal integrity and professional competence, human relationships, and the worth and dignity of each client.

Over the past decade, researchers have urged clinical social workers to develop a more scientifically rigorous approach and deliver more evidence-based treatments. Nonetheless, the majority of clinical social workers continue to be trained in nonspecific general practice rather than in targeted evidence-based treatments (Howard, Allen-Meares, & Ruffolo, 2007; Mullen, Bellamy, Bledsoe, & Francois, 2007; Weisman et al., 2006). We believe that, in addition to honoring several values of the social work profession, DBT offers social work a means by which it can increase its delivery of evidence-based treatments to those who need it most. Occupational stress and burnout remain a high risk in the mental health profession, particularly for social workers, who often work in high-stress situations and with the most vulnerable populations (Newell & McNeil, 2010). Empirical research provides data confirming that mindfulness training seems to decrease stress and increase psychological, emotional, and physical well-being for clients as well as clinicians (Baer, 2003; Davis & Hayes, 2011). Moreover, research also suggests that therapist mindfulness may enhance treatment outcomes (Grepmair et al., 2007). Therefore, DBT may be especially useful for social workers because it encourages practitioners to practice core mindfulness skills themselves, which may support and enhance personal well-being as well as professional excellence.

References

Andover, M. S., & Gibb, B. E. (2010). Non-suicidal self-injury, attempted suicide, and suicidal intent among psychiatric inpatients. *Psychiatric Research 178*, 101-105.

Baer, R. A. (2003). Mindfulness training as a clinical intervention: A conceptual and empirical review. *Clinical Psychology: Science & Practice, 10*, 125-143.

Chen, E. Y., Matthews, L., Allen, C., Kuo, J. R., & Linehan, M. (2008). Dialectical behavior therapy for clients with binge-eating disorder or bulimia nervosa and borderline personality disorder. *International Journal of Eating Disorders, 41*, 505-512.

Davis, D. M., & Hayes, J. A. (2011). What are the benefits of mindfulness? A practice review of psychotherapy-related research. *Psychotherapy, 48*, 198-208.

Feigenbaum, J. (2007). Dialectical behavior therapy: An increasing evidence base. *Journal of Mental Health, 16*, 51-68.

Grepmair, L., Mitterlehner, F., Loew, T., Bachler, E., Rather, W., & Nickel, M. (2007). Promoting mindfulness in psychotherapists in training influences the treatment results of their patients: A randomized, double-blind, controlled study. *Psychotherapy and Psychosomatics, 76*, 332-338.

Howard, M., Allen-Meares, P., & Ruffolo, M. C. (2007). Teaching evidence-based practice: Strategic and pedagogical recommendations for schools of social work. *Research on Social Work Practice, 17*, 561-568.

Iverson, K. M., Shenk, C., & Fruzzetti, A. E. (2009). Dialectical behavior therapy for women victims of domestic abuse: A pilot study. *Professional Psychology: Research And Practice, 40*, 242-248.

Kliem, S., Kröger, C., & Kosfelder, J. (2010). Dialectical behavior therapy for borderline personality disorder: A meta-analysis using mixed-effects modeling. *Journal of Consulting and Clinical Psychology, 78*, 936-951.

Linehan, M. M. (1993a). *Cognitive-behavioral treatment of borderline personality disorder.* New York: Guilford Press.

Linehan, M. M. (1993b). *Skills training manual for treating borderline personality disorder.* New York: Guilford Press.

Linehan, M. M., Armstrong, H. E., Suarez, A., Allmon, D., & Heard, H. L. (1991). Cognitive-behavioral treatment of chronically parasuicidal borderline patients. *Archives of General Psychiatry. 48*, 1060-1064.

Linehan, M. M., Schmidt, H., Dimeff, L. A., Craft, J., Kanter, J., & Comtois, K. A. (1999). Dialectical behavior therapy for patients with borderline personality disorder and drug-dependence. *American Journal on Addictions, 8*, 279-292.

Lynch, T. R., Trost, W. T., Salsman, N., & Linehan, M. M. (2007). Dialectical behavior therapy for borderline personality disorder. *Annual Review of Clinical Psychology, 3*, 181–205.

Mullen, E. J., Bellamy, J. L., Bledsoe, S. E., & Francois, J. (2007). Teaching evidence-based practice. *Research on Social Work Practice, 17*, 574-582.

National Association of Social Workers (NASW). (2008). *Code of Ethics of the National Association of Social Workers.* Washington, DC: NASW.

Newell, J. M., & McNeil, G. A. (2010). Professional burnout, vicarious trauma, secondary traumatic stress, and compassion fatigue: A review of theoretical terms, risk factors, and preventive methods for clinicians and researchers. *Best Practice in Mental Health, 6*, 57-68.

Robins, C. J., Schmidt III, H., & Linehan, M. M. (2004). Dialectical behavior therapy: Synthesizing radical acceptance with skillful means. In S. C. Hayes, V. M. Folette, & M. M. Linehan (Eds.), *Mindfulness and acceptance: Expanding the cognitive-behavioral tradition* (pp. 30-44). New York: Guilford Press.

Robinson, A. H., & Safer, D. L. (2012). Moderators of dialectical behavior therapy for binge eating disorder: Results from a randomized controlled trial. *International Journal of Eating Disorders, 45,* 597-602.

Scheele, K. R. (2000). The empirical basis of dialectical behavior therapy: Summary, critique, and implications. *Clinical Psychology: Science and Practice, 7,* 68-86.

Steil, R., Dyer, A., Priebe, K., Kleindienst, N., & Bohus, M. (2011). Dialectical behavior therapy for posttraumatic stress disorder related to childhood sexual abuse: A pilot study of an intensive residential treatment program. *Journal of Traumatic Stress, 24,* 102-106.

Weisman, M. M., Verdeli, H., Gameroff, M. J., Bledsoe, S. E., Betts, K., Mufson, L., et al. (2006). A national survey of psychotherapy training programs in psychiatry, psychology, and social work. *Archives of General Psychiatry, 63,* 925-934.

CHAPTER 3

Mindfulness-Based Stress Reduction and Social Work

Elana Rosenbaum, LICSW

Center for Mindfulness in Medicine, Health Care, and Society
Worcester, Massachusetts

What is life?
It is the flash of a firefly in the night.
It is the breath of a buffalo in the wintertime.
It is the little shadow which runs across the grass and loses itself
in the sunset.

—last words of Crowfoot
Blackfoot warrior and orator, 1890
(In Miner & Rawson, 2006, p. 381)

"Why are you here? Why are you really here?"

This question begins the mindfulness-based stress reduction (MBSR) class at the University of Massachusetts Medical School. The question is repeated as the teacher invites the participants to investigate their true underlying motivations.

"Imagine that this question is like a pebble dropped into a deep well, and as it falls deeper and deeper into the well, ask yourself again, 'Why am I really here? What do I hope to gain?'"

Initially the answer revolves around "the problem."

"I suffer anxiety attacks."

"My wife made me come."

"I'm in a lot of pain."

"I have cancer."

"My loved one just died."

"I had a car accident and now I can't _____."

"I had a heart attack and I can't stop worrying it will happen again."

"I have GI problems."

"My doctor suggested I come."

"I have multiple sclerosis."

As the participants are encouraged to go beneath the surface of their initial responses, their original reason for coming begins to lose its centrality and their perspective broadens. As the mind quiets and people connect to their inner desires, the goal almost universally is to be at peace, be happier, and live with greater ease.

The Stress Reduction Program

The Stress Reduction Program was founded by Jon Kabat-Zinn in 1979 at the University of Massachusetts Medical School in Worcester, Massachusetts (Kabat-Zinn, 1990). Since that time, over 20,000 people have completed the program, and it has spread to over forty-two states in the United States and more than fifty-three countries worldwide. The program is now embedded in the Center for Mindfulness in Medicine, Healthcare, and Society at the university and has been renamed Mindfulness-Based Stress Reduction. It is described on the center's website as "an intensive training that asks participants to draw on their inner resources and natural capacity to actively engage in caring for themselves and finding greater balance, ease, and peace of mind" (Center for Mindfulness, n.d.).

MBSR requires a major commitment of time and energy. It consists of eight consecutive weeks of classes ranging from two-and-a-half to three hours in length. The program is experiential and highly interactive. Each class includes mindfulness practices, didactic material, and a class discussion, and there is a daylong session that is primarily silent. Participants are expected to do forty-five minutes of daily homework, which consists of mindfulness and awareness practices. Classes are heterogenous, with men and women seeking help for a variety of mental and physical problems, including stress-related symptoms, chronic pain and illness, anxiety, depression, and life-threatening illnesses. No prior experience in meditation is required, but participants are expected to practice diligently and are screened for their ability to engage fully in the program.

The MBSR Curriculum

Kabat-Zinn defines mindfulness as "paying attention in a particular way: on purpose, in the present moment, and nonjudgmentally" (1994, p. 4). This practice, based on awareness, forms the core of MBSR. Mindfulness is first introduced through sensory experience in the exploration of a raisin. Class members are each given two or three raisins and asked to observe one of them "as if you've never seen it before." Thus, the ability to have a fresh perspective on the familiar and to take the time to pay attention and use all one's senses as free of expectation as possible lays the foundation for the meditations that follow.

One of the first formal mindfulness exercises is the body scan, a guided meditation that takes a person slowly through his or her body from the feet up through the crown of the head. This practice enhances awareness of the body and cultivates the ability to sustain attention on sensation, thoughts, and feelings with greater neutrality and acceptance. Other exercises include mindful breathing, gentle yoga (which can be adapted for persons with disabilities), walking meditation, and mindful movement. As the class progresses and participants become adept at focusing not just on the breath but also on sounds, sensations, thoughts, and feelings, they are encouraged to practice "choiceless awareness," in which they attend to whatever arises from moment to moment. These exercise, most of which are assigned as homework, also serve as vehicles to examine one's relationship to what arises. The willingness to make a continued effort to acknowledge what arises without judgment and gently but firmly return attention to one's direct experience is reinforced throughout the eight weeks.

Each mindfulness practice is conducted in class first and is accompanied by discussion to clarify its meaning and its relevance to enhanced wellness. Sharing by group members also serves as support and normalizes their experiences. Furthermore, it serves as a motivator for making a commitment to continue practicing outside of class and encourages participants to persist with an attitude of curiosity rather than self-criticism. Acceptance is emphasized, as is the noticing of thoughts, feelings, and sensations, regardless of how they are being appraised. The appraisal of what arises becomes itself an object of attention, and participants are encouraged to simply allow feelings, thoughts, and sensations to go by returning attention to the body or breath.

Group discussion continues throughout the eight weeks, as does informal practice to bring mindfulness into daily life. Homework assignments include being mindful when brushing teeth, eating, and checking e-mail, and noting stressors and one's reactions to them. There is also a section on mindful communication during classes six and seven. Furthermore, as people settle into meditation and become more able to recognize conditioned patterns of thoughts and feelings, they are asked to keep a journal of events they appraise as pleasant or unpleasant. This is the springboard for didactic material on stress and the power of the mind to create happiness and ease versus stress and dis-ease.

The all-day session, which is conducted in silence except for the last hour, occurs after the sixth class and is attended by all members of current classes and "graduates" from prior ones. Being in a large group for a full day strengthens the ability to sustain attention and be mindful with greater acceptance. Participants feel empowered by the realization that they made it through the day and that all mind states changed, even anxiety. This boosts the ability to make practice really practical. Class members report that they are more able to catch themselves being reactive, reanchor attention on their breath or another neutral object, and calm down. An acronym for this is process S.T.O.P. It means *stop, take a breath, open and observe*, and then *proceed*. This fosters self-regulation and affect management.

MBSR and Its Impact

MBSR is an evidence-based program with a burgeoning literature supporting its effectiveness in addressing a range of illnesses. It has been applied to depression, anxiety, substance abuse, eating disorders, binge eating, insomnia, chronic pain, psoriasis, type 2 diabetes, fibromyalgia, rheumatoid arthritis, ADHD, cancer, and heart disease. A recent meta-analysis (de Vibe, Bjorndal, Tipton, Hammerstrom, & Kowalski, 2012) of twenty-six randomized controlled trials of MBSR found "a moderate and consistent effect on a number of measures of mental health for a wide range of target groups" (p. 8). The authors of the study also conclude that MBSR "appears to improve measures of personal development such as empathy and coping,...enhance both mindfulness [and] quality-of-life[,] and improve some aspects of somatic health" (p. 8). Hoffman and colleagues (Hofmann, Sawyer, Witt, and Oh, 2010), reviewing thirty-nine studies with 1140 participants, found that mindfulness-based therapies—that is, MBSR and treatments derived from it—were moderately effective for improving anxiety and mood symptoms and even more effective for people with actual anxiety and mood disorders.

MBSR has been adapted as mindfulness-based cognitive therapy (MBCT; Segal, Williams, & Teasdale, 2013) to treat chronically recurring depression and mindfulness-based relapse prevention (MBRP; Bowen, Chawla, & Marlatt, 2011) to prevent relapse in addictions. These programs combine the basics of MBSR (mindfulness meditation, the body scan, etc.) with interventions that are specific to depression and substance abuse treatment. There are also adaptations of

MBSR for cancer patients (Rosenbaum, 2012; Carlson & Speca, 2011), eating disorders and obesity (MB-EAT; Kristeller & Wolever, 2011), and childbirth and parenting (MBCP; Bardacke, 2012), as well as "Cool Minds," a program for teenagers developed by Florence Meyer at the Center for Mindfulness. There is an Association for Mindfulness in Education (http://www.mindfuleducation.org), and new programs are continuing to emerge. Like MBSR, all these programs require a mindfulness practice and a belief that change is possible if there is a willingness to make a commitment of time, energy, and consistency.

Social Work and MBSR

Both social work and MBSR are committed to improving people's lives. Both began in response to conditions within the context of a system and a culture that either created suffering or perpetuated it. Both value and respect the rights of an individual and believe in their worth. Social work began by focusing on the ills of society and addressed external conditions such as sweatshops, child labor, low wages, and poor housing. MBSR focuses on internal processes, attitudes, beliefs, and patterns of behavior. Mindfulness cultivates awareness by directly observing thoughts, feelings, and sensation as they arise. By consciously attending to what is here, people cultivate the ability to evaluate for themselves what helps and what hinders health. Though MBSR is imbedded in a medical school, it is a departure from the medical model. Rather than focusing on what is wrong, it focuses on what is right. Like social work, it builds on strengths and empowers people to trust their inner wisdom. Rather than having a doctor fix the problem, it provides tools for people to recognize their own resources for healing. This can include a physician, but the locus of responsibility is placed on the self. To paraphrase a quote often attributed to Thomas Merton, "We have what we seek and if we give it time it will become known to us."

What is common to social workers and MBSR teachers is the intention to do what benefits the self and others and a commitment to do so throughout each day. All can agree that it is impossible to live life fully without encountering difficulties, but some conditions support well-being and others create pain. No one can escape the natural processes of aging, illness, death, and loss. Change, which is a stressor, is part of the human condition. MBSR addresses the manageability of change by focusing on attitude and attention. As the mind quiets, there is an acknowledgment of reality—what cannot change and what is possible. With awareness there is choice and an inner sense of control. What we do and where we place our attention is relevant. Living fully requires a willingness to face what is true and maintain the equanimity to foster what helps rather than hurts well-being.

Buddhism and the Origins of MBSR

Buddhism, which forms the frame for mindfulness-based interventions such as MBSR, is derived from the teachings of one man: Siddhartha Gautama, the Buddha. He was most likely born sometime in the fifth century BCE. According to the Theravada tradition, shortly after Siddhartha's birth, his father, a chieftain or king, was visited by an astrologer who prophesied that his son would either be a great king or a great holy man. The king wanted Siddhartha to follow in his footsteps and did all he could to give his son a perfect life and shield him from suffering. This, of course, was impossible, and Siddhartha took secret trips outside his father's province where he discovered the suffering of others. Vowing to find a way to alleviate suffering, he left his family and the protective shell of his home to seek enlightenment. He sought all the great teachers of the day and practiced severe asceticism, becoming very weak and coming close to dying. Only through the kindness of a milkmaid who saw he needed to eat and fed him did he discover "the middle way"—neither too harsh nor too indulgent. Following the beliefs of others had nearly killed him. From this, he learned to focus on direct experience. Accepting what was real and true, be it good or bad, brought peace.

This is the work of mindfulness and a challenge not only for the participants in a mindfulness-based program, but for the teacher as well. Teaching mindfulness requires awareness of self and other and the ability to discriminate wisely between wholesome and unwholesome. Awareness goes back and forth between the inner and outer world and facilitates the recognition of personal limitations and "hooks" that trap the mind in repetitive thoughts, as well as cultivating the discipline to catch them as they arise without harsh criticism so new, healthier patterns can emerge.

Mindfulness is a practice and a way of life, not a technique. It requires determination and effort, impelled by suffering and the desire to be free from suffering. MBSR is a secular program and is not Buddhist, but it is based on the principals of self-discovery and direct experience originated by the Buddha. It is adapted to fit Western culture and address the stresses of today's world.

Jon Kabat-Zinn, who founded and developed MBSR in the late 70s, writes, "From the beginning of MBSR, I bent over backward to structure it and find ways to speak about it that avoided as much as possible the risk of it being seen as Buddhist, 'New Age,' 'Eastern Mysticism,' or just plain 'flaky.' To my mind this was a constant and serious risk that would have undermined our attempts to present it as commonsensical, evidence-based, and ordinary, and ultimately a legitimate element of mainstream medical care. This was something of an ongoing challenge, given that the entire curriculum is based on relatively (for novices) intensive training and practice of meditation and yoga, and meditation and yoga pretty much defined one element of the 'New Age'" (2011, p. 282).

Wakefulness, Compassion, and Wisdom

Karen, a physician training in MBSR, was concerned about how she could bring MBSR to her patients. She was not Buddhist and worried that she might have to be Buddhist to teach the program. When questioned what "Buddhist" meant to her, it became apparent that she believed that she had to take it on as a religion and identify herself in that tradition. She thought she had to be something she was not.

Karen had recently had a powerful experience being with her mother as she died. In tears, she described what this was like for her. She quietly sat with her mother and even got in bed next to her. Karen described the deep connection she felt as she shared the heat of her body and her love. She stayed with her mom until her last breath, calmly breathing with her, easing her passage with her quiet heart and caring presence, connecting to her with attention and love. This is the heart of MBSR. There is no Buddhism, only mindfulness—moment-by-moment awareness and loving care.

Kabat-Zinn (2011) writes, "'Buddha' means one who has awakened, and mindfulness, often spoken of as 'the heart of Buddhist meditation,' has little or nothing to do with Buddhism per se, and everything to do with wakefulness, compassion, and wisdom" (p. 283).

What the Work Requires

There are many paths to accepting life as it is and alleviating suffering. One of these is social work, which identifies problems in society. It arose to address the concerns of the underserved and the disenfranchised, people who were poor and needed assistance. It aimed to do more than provide support and treat emotional and physical concerns; it also sought to investigate the ills of society and the conditions that perpetuate injustice and change them. Social work includes work with groups and individuals; the focus is on human rights, social justice, mental and physical health, and systemic change. It also encompasses community organization, case management and assistance in interpersonal relationships, child welfare, and education and training, as well as the creation and location of resources for people in need. Focusing attention on a particular area or problem is inherent in this work. It requires mindfulness to discern what requires change, and it requires determined effort, patience, and compassion to make change happen. There is a recognition of our common humanity and our interdependence. What one person does affects us all, and everyone is subject to disappointment and change as well as love.

A classic story in Buddhism is the parable of the mustard seed. In it, a woman is bereft as her son, an only child whom she had given birth to after many years of failing to conceive, is gravely ill and soon to die. Complicating the situation is the fact that this is not only an emotional loss, but it dramatically lowers the woman's status in her husband's family. Refusing to accept her child's illness, she hears that there is a very wise man in her village who has the power to bring a person back from the dead. She goes to this person, the Buddha, which means "awakened one," and asks him to save her son. He says he will do so if she can bring him a mustard seed from a family who has never experienced death. Happily, the woman sets off with the child in her arms and goes from household to household. She asks all the people she meets whether they have ever experienced a death in their family. Sadly, as she travels near and far, she cannot discover any person who has not been touched by death. When she returns to the Buddha, still holding her now dead son, she realizes the universality of death and knows she is not alone. Comforted with this knowledge, she is able to put down her baby and accept his passing.

Some of the power of MBSR is due to the connectivity and community of the group. From the very first session, people realize that they are not alone. All of the people in the room have committed themselves to doing the intensive work of mindfulness with the hope of improving the quality of their life and developing skills to help them feel better. One person's problem affects them all.

Choice

Stress is inherent in living a full life. There are, however, choices in how a person relates to life events, and these choices are contextual. Mindfulness-based interventions in the West address contemporary problems. They are adapted to fit this culture, conveyed in the vernacular, and designed to be compatible with all belief systems. Some people report that mindfulness connects them more deeply to their own spiritual practice, but this arises spontaneously within an individual rather than in the classroom. Mindfulness exercises hold up a mirror to ourselves. For example, everyone has preferences, and most of us are drawn to getting what we want and like. This is not a problem unless we fall into despair, bitterness, or anger when this does not happen and we cannot move on. Craving for anything, be it money, health, change, or simply what used to be, is counterproductive. However, rather than lecture or have people read a scholarly article or Buddhist treatise on the hazards of holding on, MBSR asks participants to do an exercise that demonstrates this. They are asked to list what comes to mind as they say to themselves, "If only...then": "If only I had more money, if only I wasn't sick, if only I hadn't _____ or had _____, then I'd be happy, fulfilled,..." Without judging or being self-critical, participants are encouraged to note when a thought of this type arises and observe the effect it has in the body as well as the reaction it provokes. This applies not only to "if only" statements, but also to anything that is held on to so tightly that it is blinding and creates tension. If they can identify what preceded the thought and learn more about the conditions that created it, this too is helpful. Mindfulness has to be practical and make sense. It is a process of self-discovery and is based on each person's unique experience. All individuals need to discover for themselves what works and what does not.

• *Case Example: Rachael*

Rachael's husband brought her to class every week. She came wearing a baseball cap and dark sunglasses and sat in a corner in the room as far away from the light as possible. Rachael was very determined to get her life back after a major car accident. Light hurt her eyes, as did loud noise. It was challenging for her to be in a group because the voices of more than one person speaking would jam her mind. She reported that the accident caused brain damage that "changed everything big and little in my life." She was filled with self-criticism and holding on to her past. Prior to the accident, she could teach, write poetry, work with emotionally challenged children, manage her house, and care for two teenagers and a husband. Now she was isolated, easily fatigued, and unable to fully care for herself. Her husband had to retire early to care for her, which made her feel guilty and created financial difficulty. She worried what would happen to her if he got sick.

Rachael enjoyed the company of others in class but had to strain to listen. She had difficulty tracking conversations and trouble with word retrieval and memory. This increased her sense of isolation. In addition, she had tinnitus (ringing in her ears) and sometimes felt dizzy and nauseous. Her goal was to accept the changes in her life and to "be happy." She sometimes had to sequester herself in a corner of the room to tune out the din when the class was broken into small groups for a discussion, but she was very diligent with the homework, and the class accommodated her needs. The lights of the classroom were dimmed, and people were careful to speak one at a time when they were in a small group. The intensity of her desire to listen and use what she was learning was inspirational. Around week five, after a discussion on stress, she read a poem she wrote about her struggle to refocus attention and be more accepting of her condition.

Movement, motion, swaying, gliding, rolling, waving, dizziness, nausea. How can movement be so painful?

Why can't I accept this?

Why can't I be instead of do?

Why can't I be happy being, living a life of ease, accepting myself for who I am today? Why can't I accept that life is a journey, bodies wear out and accidents happen. This is life. You can't change it.

Acceptance of the way things are here on earth, right here and now. Today.

Bring relief from suffering...

Can I let go and experience the beauty in the ordinary.

Comfort in soft shades.

Joy in soft sounds.

And

Find

The peace
That surpasses all understanding
Ready and waiting
inside of me.
Listen…
Be still and know that I am Here
Be still and know that I am here.

There was silence after she read this poem. It was courageous to acknowledge out loud how hard it is to accept what we don't like: pain, change, disabilities, and sorrow of the heart, the head, and the body.

The Process of Investigation

Rachael was held by the silent empathy of the class, all of whom also struggled with acceptance. It calmed her and validated her feelings.

"How is this for you now?" the teacher asked her.

"It feels good to read out loud how I feel. I have an easier time writing than talking. I don't feel so afraid."

"What are you observing in the body?"

"I still have ringing in my ears and the light hurts my eyes, but it's okay. I can manage it…. I feel happy that I could share this. I feel grateful that I am here. I often feel isolated and I don't now."

Rachael's breathing had slowed, and her tone of voice pitched lower. Her honesty opened space for others in the class to talk about their difficulty in accepting their own conditions and their reactivity to them. She had normalized difficulty and named some of the obstacles.

The teacher was aware that Rachael's description of her own struggle touched others in the class. She moved from her investigations of Rachael's response to those of the whole group. She wanted to know how they were affected by what had just transpired. Her questions were designed to humanize and make universal this resistance and aversion to change.

"Does anyone else have trouble accepting change?" (Most raised their hands.)

The teacher went on to ask more questions that illuminated the dynamics of their resistance to change.

"What are some of the changes you're experiencing? How are you adapting to them? What allows you to return to a state of balance? How is balance (or equanimity, calm, or steadiness) experienced in the body? Are there thoughts that accompany it? What are they? Can you recognize them? Are there thoughts or sensations that signal distress? What are they? When do they occur?"

These questions then became the object of attention and investigation in class and at home.

The group serves as a container to explore what might be too difficult to examine alone. Sharing experience in an atmosphere of honesty and confidentiality is a source of support and comfort for the group members. Self-disclosure is voluntary, but honesty becomes the norm and people learn from each other. Whether a person speaks in class or reflects quietly to him- or herself, there is an exchange of compassion and an encouragement to jettison self-criticism and examine one's pattern of thought and action. There is no "fixing," but instead an agreement to investigate and be as nonjudgmental and forgiving of entrenched habits as possible. The recognition that it is human to make mistakes and resist change and discomfort cushions this process, and helps a person accept that this too will pass, whatever "this" happens to be.

Qualities of the Teacher

A mindfulness teacher and a social worker share qualities in common. In *The Art and Science of Mindfulness: Integrating Mindfulness into Psychology and the Helping Professions* (2009), Shauna Shapiro and Linda E. Carlson list qualities of mindfulness teachers. These are acceptance, patience, trust, curiosity, letting go, gentleness, nonreactivity, and loving-kindness. The US Department of Labor says social workers should be emotionally mature, objective, and sensitive to people and their problems (Bureau of Labor Statistics, 2013). The National Association of Social Workers has a standard of ethical conduct (NASW, 2008) that includes service, integrity, and respect of the dignity and worth of the individual with whom a social worker is working. The ability to create a haven of safety and be the holder of this space so that pain can be explored with compassion and respect encompasses all of these qualities. This is conveyed through the presence of the mindfulness instructor and is often nonverbal and felt. It is embodied. An effective teacher must not only know the curriculum but speak from her own experience so it emerges fresh and relevant to the population served. Her authenticity inspires change. Knowing when to inquire deeply, when to move away, when to be silent, and when to encourage further investigation is also important. Even as one works with an individual, there is always an awareness of the group. If mindfulness is not being done in a group context, there is the larger context of culture, values, and beliefs to be considered. This requires flexibility, openness, and skill.

Leading Meditation

To be able to translate meditation instructions and make mindfulness meaningful for daily life is a skill. One can intellectually know that being fully alive means residing in the present moment, but experiencing this presence requires intentionality and commitment. We resist awareness when we don't like what it brings. Accepting this moment, be it pleasant or unpleasant, with equanimity requires practice. Different meditations are used in MBSR including a body scan, walking meditation, yoga, and a sitting meditation.

Sitting Meditation

A sitting meditation might begin with instructions about grounding the body—sitting with an upright spine in a dignified position, legs uncrossed and feet on the ground (if in a chair), and finding a natural posture rather than an overly stiff one. If sitting on a cushion, the legs should be supported and the body stable, with arms resting comfortably on the lap. Participants are invited to close their eyes or gaze softly at a spot on the floor a little in front of them. Instructions might continue as follows:

> Being aware of your intention: nothing to do, nothing to reach for, an inner attitude of openness, fresh, awake, curious, and welcoming. Meeting the present moment to really experience what is here. Being aware of breathing where the breath is experienced most vividly. When thoughts appear, acknowledging thinking but letting them be like clouds moving through the sky. It is common to experience restlessness, boredom, impatience, anger, even sleepiness, but there is no need to change something. Practicing being aware and bringing your attention back to your breath or even a sound and allowing the experience to be the experience.

"Languaging"

Instructions are phrased in gerund form rather than as a command. For instance, in the example above, the facilitator says "being aware of breathing" rather than "be aware of breathing." This helps facilitate the experience of impermanence. People are invited to do a meditation or an exercise rather than instructed to do it. Vocabulary from everyday life is used. Responsibility is placed on each person, but a person can choose to opt out of an exercise or be self-disclosing. There is always choice. The work is to bring what is unconscious and below the level of awareness into consciousness. It is human to want to resist what we don't like, and the courage to stay with it is recognized and acknowledged.

Working with Resistance and Aversion

As people engage in practice for a longer time, awareness grows of negative habits of mind, or even aches and pains that might have previously been ignored or defended against. Observing these automatic responses can be very useful.

Participant: I don't like the body scan. It is too slow. I get impatient and angry.

Teacher: Are there other times when this happens? Is this a pattern?

Often the answer is "yes" and this is investigated further.

"Could you notice a particular thought or sensation right before you felt anger?"

Or, "What does anger feel like? Can you locate it in the body?"

A willingness to observe and make connections between cause (which is usually a thought or feeling) and action enhances control and interrupts the automatic response. After doing this for some time a person might report:

"I notice when I'm getting angry sooner, and I have more patience with my kids now. When I'm getting upset with them I pause and take a breath and it helps."

"When I do the sitting meditation I notice pain in parts of my body I didn't before. Then I ask myself, 'What have I been doing?'"

"I'm checking out my position when I use the computer. Maybe I should raise it or hold my hand differently… I think I need to get up more often."

Each person is met individually, but the conversation between teacher and participant is usually relevant to the group as a whole. The teacher investigates process. Some typical questions or instructions might be:

"Anyone discovering something they hadn't noticed before?"

"When does this occur? What is it telling you?"

"Is this a familiar pattern? How often does it occur? How long does it last?"

"Are you willing to refocus attention and anchor it with your breath or perhaps a sound?"

"What are you noticing? When? What preceded it? What happened next?"

"Can you locate it [meaning a strong emotion] in the body?"

"How can you nurture yourself?"

Falling asleep during the body scan is often a topic of discussion. This is investigated.

"Do you notice when you are feeling sleepy? What do you do then?"

"When do you do the meditation?"

"Where are you when you wake up? Are you here and awake?"

"How can you make this work for you?"

"Were you tired and did you need some sleep?"

"What is possible?"

The Stress Reaction

Richard Lazarus and Susan Folkman (1984) defined stress as a demand that is appraised as overwhelming our resources and ability to cope. The mind, hardwired for survival, automatically reacts by fleeing, freezing, or fighting. They believed that people make automatic, often unconscious, assessments of what is happening and what it may mean for them or those they care about, and these assessments may or may not be true. Mindfulness helps us catch this automatic response and appraise it without bias. In mindfulness-based cognitive therapy, the adaptation of MBSR for depression, people are taught to remember that thoughts are not facts and ask themselves, "What is the evidence of this?" In MBSR it is enough to simply note the automatic response, feel the rush of adrenaline that accompanies the stress reaction, and allow it to pass. Participants practice noting this conditioned automatic response and catching any self-critical judgment. The instruction is to stop when this is observed and refocus attention on a more neutral object, usually their breath.

Attitude

Simply noticing automatic reactions and being present with pain is counterintuitive. Intention is powerful. One sees the constellation of thoughts, feelings, and sensations that one usually identifies as one's "self." This sense of self is disrupted. Anything that disrupts our sense of self and forces us to reexamine our belief system is change, and change can be frightening.

"You are not your thoughts," the teacher may say again and again.

"What is the evidence for that thought?"

"You don't have to like it, but it's here. Can you acknowledge it?"

Creating a mind flexible and resilient enough to come to a new balance takes time, effort, and compassion. We like to think we have control over events, but do we really? What is our attitude toward hardship and disappointment? Viktor Frankl, a survivor of a concentration camp in World War II, wrote in *Man's Search for Meaning* (2006), "Everything can be taken from a man but one thing: the last of the human freedoms—to choose one's attitude in any given set of circumstances, to choose one's own way" (pp. 65-66). One class member said he pasted slogans such as "You can't stop the bluebird of sorrow from flying over your head but you can stop it from nesting in your hair" in strategic spots in his house.

This ability to choose one's attitude in any given set of circumstances applies to all mindfulness-based interventions. Our desire to maintain the status quo, to hold on to the pleasant and avoid or push away what is unpleasant, can delude us and blind our perception of events. Everything is always changing, so how can a person find the stillness within in the midst of difficulty? What allows a person to again and again accept the "monkey mind" that jumps all over the place and return again and again to this moment and the way things are? A teacher cannot answer these questions, but she can pose them and trust participants to find the answer for themselves. Entering into a mindfulness-based program is a big first step and provides structure and support, but taking responsibility for one's actions and practice is up to the participant. For example, when the stress reduction program ended, Rachael decided that she was still suffering from post-traumatic stress and needed some one-on-one therapy specific to this incident, and she found a therapist to help her. Later she came to a graduate class that focused on kindness and worked with her excessive self-demands.

Compassion and Acceptance: A Personal Story

Compassion can be defined as a quivering of the heart, a tenderness and caring that is filled with love. Compassion is essential in accepting what we don't like, be it a mental state or a physical one. To be able to cradle ourselves as we might a crying infant and learn to self-soothe is also the work of mindfulness. Noticing what is here now, in this moment, means opening to the pleasant and the unpleasant, the good and the bad. It is like a dance. We are always coordinating our steps to the rhythm of life, trying to keep the beat and stay in step with the changing tempo. When we are loving, constrictions dissolve and there is flow and harmony—even when sadness emerges.

I have taught at the Center for Mindfulness since 1984 when it was called the Stress Reduction Clinic. In 1995 I was diagnosed with non-Hodgkin's lymphoma, which tested the principles of the program. Could I move through the treatment for cancer and its aftermath and truly not suffer? In *Here for Now: Living Well with Cancer Through Mindfulness* (2007), I wrote:

> Staying present and paying attention without judgment was vital if I didn't want to get lost and swallowed up by self-pity or despair. It became imperative that I focus on what I did have control over—my attitude—in order to maintain a sense of well-being. There's more right with you than wrong, I'd tell my classes, even in the face of a life-threatening illness. But acting on this belief and staying happy requires effort. My diagnosis forced me to confront habits that kept me from being well. It forced me to pay attention and really notice what helped me stay well and what I needed to let go or change. Caring for myself properly meant I really had to listen to my body and nurture myself, mind and body. I needed to remind myself to come back to this moment again and again. I needed to maintain an open, steady heart and forgive myself if I strayed. I also needed to be able to accept support... As I

kept on doing my best to keep my spirits up through a series of blood transfusions, anemia, and isolation following a bone marrow transplant, I was forced to confront physical limitations. It became clear that the more I could let go and accept these limitations, the better I felt and the freer I became. The more I lived in the present moment as it was, rather than what I wished it would be, the happier I felt. (p. 19)

Research

Before I was confronted with a cancer diagnosis, I was a clinical social worker with a practice in psychotherapy for many years, as well as an MBSR instructor and meditator. The question arose whether MBSR helped in my recovery and my ability to cope with the uncertainties and difficulties of being a cancer patient. After I recovered from my illness, a feasibility study that introduced an adaptation of MBSR for people undergoing stem cell transplant was funded. The criteria to enter this study included having no prior experience with mindfulness or MBSR. MBSR was adapted to conform to the conditions of an intensive care inpatient unit in a hospital for people undergoing a stem cell transplant, a high-risk procedure. The intervention was done on a one-on-one basis, and mindfulness was introduced for the first time during a period of high anxiety prior to transplant in the phoresis unit of the hospital. This is an environment that is often crowded and noisy and in which there is little privacy. Mindfulness was introduced by an instructor using a seventeen-minute CD. The CD led the patient in grounding attention to the present moment with greater acceptance and riding the waves of thoughts, feelings, and sensations. The patient was instructed to continue daily use of the meditation at home prior to transplant, as well as during hospitalization. The patient also met with a mindfulness instructor. Statistically significant decreases in heart and respiratory rates and improvements in symptoms immediately before and after each session were found, and 87 percent of patients felt more mindful and positive three months after hospitalization (Bauer-Wu et al., 2008). Upon being interviewed, patients commented:

"Sometimes I'd listen to the breath of the air and the wind blowing and the calmness of the whole thing just put you in a different mindset and I found that very relaxing."

"It surprises me that I am still doing it. When I signed up I didn't think I would be doing it when I got home and look, I am."

"I don't knowingly practice now, but it's just my approach to things is a lot better, and I think that is a result of being more mindful overall."

"It has changed the whole quality of my life and has become a daily ritual… Was one of the most important parts of my recovery… Lowered my anxiety and increased my sense of control… Now I'm focused on the pleasure of the moment, and the days are not agonizing—even if I'm feeling really ill."

"In a way I kind of let go of that frantic clinging of life and I'm willing to go with the flow."

"I do find that mindfulness thing helpful because it helps you to not reach for repression right away. It acknowledges that something is going on."

"I think it gave me a heightened awareness of the level of care I was getting. The other day I was standing at the radiator, and I was just ready to pick something up to read, and I thought, "Ahh, I am at the radiator. It is warm. I am in my home. Isn't this lovely?"

As a result of this study, a larger NIH grant was funded for a multi-site randomized controlled trial to evaluate the longitudinal and short-term effects of mindfulness meditation training. Two hundred and forty patients were divided into three groups (Bauer-Wu et al., 2011). One group received a mindfulness instructor; a second group, a nurse educator; and a third group, usual care. The mindfulness intervention included individual sessions with an instructor and between-session "homework" practice with a meditation CD. Sometimes the patients were too sick to listen to the CD or meet with the mindfulness instructor, and some patients were reluctant to admit a mindfulness instructor if they were acutely nauseous. No longitudinal group differences were identified, but significant group differences were identified in short-term effects: the mindfulness group demonstrated greater decreases in tension, unhappiness, pain, and respiratory rate compared to control groups. A secondary analysis revealed that the amount of time the patients were able to listen to the guided mindfulness meditation on the CD and the number of sessions they had with the mindfulness instructor made a difference.

This was the first large-scale randomized controlled study of a mindfulness intervention for seriously ill, hospitalized persons, and much was learned. The mindfulness instructors met with the principal investigator, Susan Bauer-Wu, and this author weekly for support and uniformity in the intervention. It was discovered that the biggest difficulty for the instructors was their empathy for the patients and their wish to "fix" what was wrong. At times, maintaining a calm presence and "letting be" was a challenge for them as well as the patients.

Summation

MBSR provides a taste of mindfulness, but it is only the beginning of a lifetime of work and practice. Paying attention and observing the stream of consciousness with acceptance sounds simple, and it is, but it takes intention to do so. To observe, free of judgment, and accept all that is here in mind and body requires not only persistence but courage. Doing so, however, opens possibilities of new ways of thinking and being that enhance life and its challenges with greater equanimity and joy.

References

Bardacke, N. (2012). *Mindful birthing: Training the mind, body, and heart for childbirth and beyond*. New York: HarperOne.

Bauer-Wu, S., Sullivan, A. M., Rosenbaum, E., Ott, M. J., Powell, M., McLoughlin, M., et al. (2008). Facing the challenges of hematopoietic stem cell transplantation with mindfulness meditation: A pilot study. *Integrative Cancer Therapies 7*, 62-9.

Bauer-Wu, S., Carmody, J., Cooley, M., Reed, G., Whitworth, R., Rosenbaum, E., et al. (2011). A randomized controlled trial of mindfulness training for cancer patients undergoing stem cell transplant [Abstract]. *Annals of Behavioral Medicine 41* (2, suppl. 1), 1-278.

Bowen, S., Chawla, N., & Marlatt, G. A. (2011). *Mindfulness-based relapse prevention for addictive behaviors: A clinician's guide*. New York: Guilford Press.

Bureau of Labor Statistics, U.S. Department of Labor (2013). *Occupational Outlook Handbook, 2012-13 Edition*. Retrieved from http://www.bls.gov/ooh/community-and-social-service/social-workers.htm

Carlson, L. E., & Speca, M. (2011). *Mindfulness-based cancer recovery: A step-by-step MBSR approach to help you cope with treatment and reclaim your life*. Oakland, CA: New Harbinger.

Center for Mindfulness in Medicine, Health Care, and Society (n.d.). *Center for Mindfulness in Medicine, Health Care, and Society at the University of Massachusetts Medical School Home Page*. Retrieved July 20, 2013, from http://www.umassmed.edu/cfm/index.aspx

de Vibe, M., Bjorndal, A., Tipton, E., Hammerstrom, K., & Kowalski, K. (2012). *Mindfulness-based stress reduction (MBSR) for improving health, quality of life and social functioning in adults*. Oslo, Norway: Campbell Systematic Reviews. Retrieved from http://campbellcollaboration.org/lib/project/117/

Frankl, V. (2006). *Man's Search for Meaning*. Beacon Press. [Kindle for PC edition]. Retrieved from Amazon.com.

Hofmann, S. G., Sawyer, A. T., Witt, A. A., & Oh, D. (2010). The effect of mindfulness-based therapy on anxiety and depression: A meta-analytic review. *Journal of Consulting and Clinical Psychology, 78*, 168-183.

Kabat-Zinn, J. (1990). *Full catastrophe living: Using the wisdom of your body and mind to face stress, pain, and illness*. New York: Delacorte.

Kabat-Zinn, J. (1994). *Wherever you go, there you are: Mindfulness meditation in everyday life*. New York: Hyperion.

Kabat-Zinn, J. (2011). Some reflections on the origins of MBSR, skillful means, and the trouble with maps. *Contemporary Buddhism, 12*, 281-306.

Kristeller, J., & Wolever, R. Q. (2011). Mindfulness-based eating awareness training for treating binge eating disorder: The conceptual foundation. *Eating Disorders, 19*, 4-61.

Lazarus, R. S., & Folkman, S. (1984). *Stress, appraisal and coping*. New York: Springer.

Miner, M., & Rawson, H. (Eds.). (2006). *The Oxford Dictionary of American Quotations*. New York: Oxford University Press.

National Association of Social Workers (NASW). (2008). *Code of Ethics*. Retrieved from https://www.socialworkers.org/pubs/code/code.asp

Rosenbaum, E. (2007). *Here for now: Living well with cancer through mindfulness* (2nd ed.). Hardwick, MA: Satya House Publications.

Rosenbaum, E. (2012). *Being well (even when you're sick): Mindfulness practices for people with cancer and other serious illnesses.* Boston: Shambhala Publications.

Segal, Z. V., Williams, J. M. G., & Teasdale, J. D. (2013). *Mindfulness-based cognitive therapy for depression* (2nd ed.). New York: Guilford Press.

Shapiro, S. L., & Carlson, L. E. (2009). *The art and science of mindfulness: Integrating mindfulness into psychology and the helping professions.* Washington, DC: American Psychological Association.

CHAPTER 4

Social Work and Behavioral Activation

Jonathan W. Kanter, PhD
Ajeng Puspitassari, MA
Maria Santos, MA
Gabriela Nagy, BA

University of Wisconsin—Milwaukee

Social work is grounded in the values of service, social justice, integrity, and competence, and is committed to promoting the dignity and worth of individuals and human relationships (National Association of Social Workers, 1999; Reamer, 2006). Given these founding principles, the profession's primary mission is to enhance individual and family well-being by helping clients take action to meet their basic needs, with a focus on assisting those who are vulnerable and oppressed. In practice, social workers emphasize the role of environmental and cultural factors that cause or contribute to individuals' problems, and promote clients' meaningful participation in the decision-making process.

Consistent with social work practice, behavioral activation (BA) is designed to help clients effect change in their lives to meet their needs and improve well-being. BA's basic idea is to help clients overcome depression by identifying and activating behaviors in line with their goals and values. Throughout therapy, the social worker and the client collaborate to specify behavioral assignments for the client to complete in between sessions. These activities are discussed in detail during each session to ensure that the activity targets the client's problems as the client defines them, is compatible with the client's values, and can be feasibly implemented given the client's capabilities and resources. A primary obstacle that is addressed in BA is avoidance. Challenges such as fatigue, anxiety, and hopelessness oftentimes overwhelm clients and make it difficult to engage in life. Clients are taught to problem solve to overcome avoidance, and mindfulness and acceptance techniques are taught to enable activation in the face of difficult environmental and personal circumstances.

BA's underlying theory and therapeutic concepts are harmonious with the social work profession. Specifically, BA theory is consistent with the notion of the person-in-environment, which emphasizes the importance of considering the individual in context, a conceptual thread that cuts across major social work frameworks (Greene, 1999). Moreover, BA's basic treatment ideas are compatible with the profession's values and mission. BA techniques are designed precisely to help clients effect change in their environments and, by extension, in society at large. This action-oriented treatment is intended to be executed collaboratively. Of particular relevance to social workers' target populations, it accommodates flexibility and creativity in tailoring the treatment to the needs of the individual. Society's most vulnerable and impoverished are facing tangible obstacles that may contribute to their experiences of depression. Mindfulness in particular holds promise as an empowering technique that can allow a client to activate and remain engaged in life despite societal barriers such as discrimination and disenfranchisement, among others. Given the congruence between BA techniques and social work's mission, we suspect many professionals already engage in "behavioral activation."

What, then, does BA contribute to social work knowledge and practice? BA provides a coherent, easy-to-use framework that organizes and consolidates activation techniques that practicing social workers likely use and that can serve to guide the implementation of the techniques. Accordingly, this chapter's function is to outline the BA framework to help the social worker recognize aspects of his or her approach that should be emphasized and elaborated more fully, and to provide guidelines for doing so. We aim to present an introduction to BA ideas and techniques that can be integrated seamlessly into the ongoing work of the social worker, amplifying his or her effectiveness with depressed and other clients.

Our belief in BA for depression as an effective, efficient, easily trainable, and acceptable treatment approach for social workers and clients across diverse settings and cultures is based on three factors. First, BA is an empirically supported approach to depression with a solid scientific basis. Second, we have directly observed BA working for many of our clients, including impoverished clients, minority clients, and clients with whom other forms of treatment have failed. Finally, BA techniques have worked at the personal level. Each one of us, the authors, use BA in our own lives to stay active in the presence of difficult obstacles and to structure and organize our days to maximize meaning and productivity. This chapter represents our collective scientific, clinical, and personal wisdom.

BA and Social Work Theory

BA's underlying theory of functional contextualism parallels social work's person-in-environment perspective in which the individual can only be understood in the context of his or her environment (Andreae, 2011) and an intervention's major objective is to adjust the person-in-environment configuration (Bartlett, 1970; Greene, 1999). Although interested social workers may choose to increase their knowledge of functional contextualism as a general framework (see, for example, Hayes, Barnes-Holmes, & Wilson, 2012 and chapters 10 and 11 in this volume), training in BA theory may be unnecessary due to the strong congruence between functional contextualism and social work's systems theory and ecological perspective. The consistencies between the BA and social work frameworks may allow the typical social worker to practice BA while operating completely within his or her theoretical approach. Here, we briefly outline a few of the major tenets of functional contextualism as applied in BA.

First, functional contextualism suggests that when conducting BA, it is important for the social worker to understand the various interrelated contextual systems that influence the individual (consistent with Bronfenbrenner, 1989). For example, consider the different systems affecting two Latino clients. Take Lucia, a twenty-eight-year-old lesbian, US-born Latina woman of Puerto Rican descent, who is finishing her undergraduate degree and working part time as a nursing assistant. Now, consider Manny, a fifty-eight-year-old male immigrant originally from a small Guatemalan village and of limited education, who has lived in a large city's Latino enclave where he has not needed to understand or use English. A BA worker's goal is to understand the various individual, familial, social, cultural, and political influences on these two individuals, and how these may present obstacles to each when they aim to engage in activities that lead to a productive, meaningful, values-based life. The presenting obstacles for these two clients will likely differ given their different life contexts.

Although the traditional BA model (e.g., Lewinsohn, 1974) emphasized specific negative life experiences as triggers for depression, such as loss of a job or divorce, modern BA takes a much more flexible approach to understanding context that creates space to consider chronic stressors, such as structural barriers, discrimination, oppression, neglect, daily hassles, and family dynamics and conflict, to provide a few examples. An individual's entire life context, encompassing the current and historical, is the cause of depression.

Second, rather than focusing on simple cause-and-effect relationships in which the individual is mindlessly responding to stimuli (Andreae, 2011; Skinner, 1974), the focus is on the person and situation as a complementary, interdependent whole. Likewise, although "inner" causes of depression, such as genetic, biological, personality, and other psychological factors (e.g., cognitive) are acknowledged as important to a full understanding of the individual, the social worker focuses on "outer" causes in practice. Specifically, the social worker identifies problems in living and in the environment as the targeted causes of depression through an evaluation of the interaction between an individual and his or her environment.

Third, significant parallels exist between BA and an empowerment approach, which involves helping individuals act for themselves (Lee & Hudson, 2011). The important practice elements here include reducing self-blame, helping the client take personal responsibility for effective change, and strengthening self-efficacy to do so. BA's person-in-environment approach within the context of empowerment prevents social workers from blaming the client and from failing to recognize that problems can be addressed through environmental change.

The process of helping the client recognize how his behaviors may contribute to the cycle of depression may also help the client recognize alternate behaviors that may result in change and for which he can take responsibility. For instance, the BA practitioner working with a client who is avoiding talking to her boss about harassment she is experiencing at the hands of coworkers helps the client recognize the behavioral pattern of avoidance (e.g., changing the topic when the boss attempts to inquire about the issue in public) and identify and activate alternative behaviors (e.g., find a time and place in which the client is comfortable raising the problem with her boss), so that she can carry out change. Once the client understands her behavioral pattern and is able to recognize alternate behaviors that may be more effective, she is given responsibility to change her circumstances. Then the social worker helps the client with all the details involved in executing the new behavior to maximize the chance of success. Overall, the social worker and client work to change the environmental and structural arrangements that are oppressive (to the extent that the client identifies this as a treatment goal).

Fourth, in BA, "behavior" is broadly defined as everything that a person does. BA assignments target not only explicit behaviors, such as exercising and job searching, but also subtle behaviors, such as expressing one's needs assertively or engaging in intimate self-disclosure, and private behaviors, such as grieving and ruminating. For example, the BA social worker may attend to times when the client is ruminating, treating rumination as something a person *does*.

Treatment may focus on helping the client notice when he is ruminating and engage in more productive behavior instead, such as active problem solving in the form of making to-do lists or lists of pros and cons. Thus, BA does not restrict the social worker to only target superficial behaviors that may not address the client's core issues. BA guides the worker to find ways to view the core issues behaviorally and help the client get more active with respect to them.

Finally, functional contextualism encourages thinking functionally about behavior. In addition to asking, "What is the depressed person doing?" social workers are encouraged to ask, "What is the function of engaging in these behaviors?" A primary function to recognize is avoidance. For example, consider a client who proposes scheduling a gardening activity assignment. On the surface and without considering the behavior's function, gardening seems like a healthy behavior and good activation target. Although gardening may function to reengage a client in her life and result in increased satisfaction and self-efficacy related to successfully nurturing a garden, for another client, gardening could function as an escape from a difficult family life. At home, the client may have children who need help with homework or a partner who feels neglected and ignored. Gardening helps the client experience relief from the problem in the short term but does not help the client effectively address the problem. In this case, other behaviors more directly related to the core issues should be discussed and assigned. In BA, every client behavior should be analyzed in terms of its function.

Research Evidence for BA

BA is an empirically supported treatment for depression (National Institute for Health and Clinical Excellence, 2009; Sturmey, 2009) comparable to other empirically supported treatments (e.g., antidepressants and cognitive therapy [CT]). Moreover, its efficacy and effectiveness have been well-documented in several meta-analyses (Cuijpers, van Straten, & Warmerdam, 2007; Ekers, Richards, & Gilbody, 2008; Mazzucchelli, Kane, & Rees, 2010). BA is an especially promising treatment for severely depressed clients, as it was found to reduce depression equally as well as an antidepressant medication (Paroxetine) and better than CT in the severely depressed subsample of a landmark randomized controlled trial (Dimidjian et al., 2006).

A number of research studies have been conducted to evaluate BA for different diagnoses and populations, including patients with substance use disorders, comorbid health or physical conditions, obesity, and a variety of age groups from adolescents to the elderly (reviewed by Dimidjian, Barrera, Martell, Munoz, & Lewinsohn, 2011). Our own research team has modified BA for Latinos in the United States and found favorable results when a treatment team, made of primarily of social workers, were trained in this approach and delivered it in Spanish at a community clinic (Kanter, Santiago-Rivera, et al., 2010).

Behavioral Activation, Mindfulness, and Acceptance

The primary goal of BA is to help clients increase engagement in a diverse array of important, personally meaningful activities. BA treatment is action-oriented, and these actions often occur in the context of the client's thoughts and feelings, and the tangible barriers that work against action. BA acknowledges that activation may trigger different types of negative, unpleasant emotions and thoughts, particularly when clients try to engage in activities that are important but relatively challenging. For some clients, experiencing these negative emotions may lead to avoidance of targeted activities (e.g., exercising often results in physical and emotional discomfort, so a client chooses to watch TV instead). In this case, negative emotions and thoughts become barriers to engaging in targeted activities, and BA provides specific strategies to deal with this particular issue that are in line and consistent with the concepts of mindfulness and acceptance (Martell & Kanter, 2011).

In BA, negative emotions and thoughts that increase avoidance of targeted activities are considered seriously. The goal in BA, however, is not to directly focus on or change the content of thoughts and emotions. Instead, BA strategies highlight the importance of helping clients to take actions consistently and strategically even when experiencing negative emotions in the process. This does not mean that clients are encouraged to just ignore their emotions and thoughts. In fact, clients are taught to intentionally notice their internal reactions, observe how these reactions often trigger avoidance, and accept these experiences in the service of moving toward their goals.

Mindfulness and acceptance are not directly taught in BA. The assumption is that by mainly focusing on engaging in targeted activities and nonjudgmentally noticing (but not changing) negative emotional and cognitive reactions, clients are implicitly asked to be mindful and accept these internal reactions.

Summary of BA Techniques

BA has a long history, with variants of BA developed continuously since the early 1970s (Kanter, Manos, et al., 2010). The summary of techniques described herein is consistent with current variants but also includes other techniques that have been incorporated in BA variants over the years (Kanter, Manos, et al., 2010; Kanter, Busch, and Rusch, 2009). Specifically, we attempt to identify the primary BA techniques common in BA treatment packages and present them in an integrated, clear, simple, and easy-to-train fashion. The treatment strategies reviewed include providing the rationale, assessment, activity scheduling, and additional strategies when initial activation is not successful. The following techniques will be presented in the context of the case below to demonstrate how each strategy is often delivered to clients.

> Mr. Lee Thao was a fifty-three-year-old Hmong refugee who came to the United States thirty-three years ago. He was recently laid off from his job as a factory worker and was

unemployed at the time of referral. He lived with his wife and three children. Mr. Thao presented with symptoms of depression due to unemployment and a history of experiencing microaggressions at his previous job, such as comments about his accent, denial of training opportunities for unclear reasons, and overhearing jokes about the food that he brought for lunch. He reported that he had difficulty finding motivation to apply for a new job.

Providing the BA Rationale

A rationale for BA should be given early in treatment to ascertain the client's enthusiasm for the approach and willingness to move in this direction. There are five main skills in providing a BA rationale, which are integrated into a typical assessment of the client's presenting problems and related experiences. The first skill is identifying the depressing life context, which simply consists of asking the client what has happened in his or her life that has caused him or her to seek treatment. The second skill is to identify and discuss emotional and behavioral responses to these negative life experiences. How has the client been feeling in response to these experiences? Are there activities that the client now does less of? Third, the social worker should validate and express genuine understanding of these reactions. When people are depressed, their reactions can be counterproductive (e.g., staying in bed instead of engaging with family); these reactions are understandable but can perpetuate problems. Therefore, the fourth skill is to explain the impact of the natural emotional and behavioral responses in perpetuating a depressive cycle. The fifth skill involves explaining the goal of BA, which is to help clients engage in more productive behaviors to solve problems, contact more rewards in their lives, and behave according to their life plans and values.

It is important for the social worker to avoid jargon and use language that clients can understand. The social worker should also provide opportunities for clients to ask questions or provide feedback to increase collaboration and build good rapport. Delivery of the BA rationale is consistent with person-in-environment social work frameworks that emphasize consideration of the client's life context in identifying problem areas. It is also consistent with the social work value of working collaboratively with clients because social workers are encouraged to evoke questions and client feedback about the rationale that help the client establish whether he or she buys into the treatment. In the following example, a social worker presents the rationale to Mr. Thao.

Social Worker: Mr. Thao, I understand that you have been feeling down and depressed for a while now. You started to feel depressed while you were still working with people who mistreated you, but your depression got even worse after you lost your job. Some of the reactions that you have reported to me include feeling very sad, guilty, angry, and afraid. You have stopped looking for a job and talking to your friends and now spend most of your time sleeping or listening to songs in your room. These reactions make sense to me. You experienced real unfair treatment in your life, so of course you are going to feel down and react in certain ways. To me, this does not mean that you are weak or that there is anything wrong with you. I believe that any person in your situation would react similarly. You came here, however, noticing that you need to do something different because what you have been doing is not helping you to make improvements in your life. Instead, you feel stuck and even more depressed, and there are new problems that occur as a result, such as social isolation and more financial problems. So my suggestion for our work together is to work as a team to help you get unstuck and start engaging in life again. We can discuss specific activities you used to do but stopped doing, problems you need to solve, and other activities that will increase a sense of meaning and purpose in your life. Some activities may focus on solving your problems related to unemployment, and these activities may be challenging but consistent with your values as a father, a husband, and a productive citizen, such as starting to look for a new job.

When delivering the treatment rationale in BA, it is important for the social worker to ask for feedback about the model and discuss the congruence between the model and the client's feelings about the appropriate tasks and goals of therapy. Consistent with social work values, the work should always be collaborative. If the client expresses resistance to the model, it should be discussed fully, and the work should be adjusted to take into consideration the client's preferences and beliefs about how treatment should proceed.

Assessment

Assessment in BA functions primarily to collect information so the social worker will be able to collaboratively identify personally meaningful and relevant activities for the client to engage in over the course of treatment. Carefully choosing activities that will actually address the client's core issues and values is important in BA. The social worker and client should not pick arbitrary activities without examining the function of the behaviors. To do this, at the least, when assessing the client's behavior, the social worker can identify the relationship between specific behaviors and any resulting changes in the client's mood, sense of pleasure, mastery, or productivity. These observations will be helpful in designing activation assignments that are functionally healthy and improve mood.

The client's values are an important source of guidance in generating meaningful and relevant activities to schedule. In understanding a client's values, it is important to be attuned to what clients say about their personal, local, social, and cultural worlds, and tailor activation assignments accordingly (Lakes, López, & Garro, 2006). What is at stake for this individual? What deeply matters? What are the cultural subgroups in which the client lives? For example, Mr. Thao's value as a parent was to be a strong role model and responsible father. He also valued being a productive and contributing member of his Hmong community. A specific goal that was in line with these values was to be more involved in cultural and political activities in his community, such as participating as a board member in preparing a cultural festivity.

As the social worker learns about the client's life, he or she identifies possible activities to schedule. This is essentially case conceptualization in BA. There are several aspects of the client's life to assess. First, the social worker should assess important activities that the client used to do but has stopped doing since he or she became depressed, including pleasant activities, problem-solving activities, and other meaningful activities. Second, the social worker should assess possible new and important activities that the client would like to start doing. When assessing these activities, the social worker should always be noticing and highlighting their function (e.g., avoidance), not just their form (i.e., what they look like on the surface). Third, social workers should assess the existing patterns and daily routines in their clients' lives. Any routine disruptions should be noticed (e.g., inconsistent sleep and eating schedules, no exercise, poor daily hygiene). Clients with depression often find that their days are not structured well, and it is important to help them build better routines. Fourth, the social worker should explore activities that the client has increased since becoming depressed, which generally consist of behaviors that function to help the client avoid important but more aversive or difficult activities.

Activity Scheduling

The heart of BA is concrete activity scheduling based on the client's goals and values. Each session is devoted primarily to scheduling activities and reviewing the client's success with activities scheduled from the previous session. Activity scheduling should be based on what was learned during assessment, and this is an iterative, evolving process. Our general tip is to start by scheduling two or three specific activities per session, although for some clients, more may be scheduled. Social workers and clients should collaborate to generate the type, amount, and intensity of activities based on what the client needs and is able to manage.

It is often helpful to schedule the important activities in concrete detail, with the social worker and client clearly identifying the type of activity and when, where, and with whom the activity will be completed. This should be a collaborative process, although with some very depressed clients, the social worker may be quite directive, suggesting activities and seeking feedback on the suggestions. The intensity of the activity should also be considered; it may be helpful to choose an activity that is not too hard but also not too easy for the client. When the activity consists of many steps (e.g., applying for a job), each step should be considered and scheduled properly. Possible obstacles that may get in the way of successful activation, and potential solutions to these obstacles, should be identified.

In the beginning of the following session, the social worker should check in with the client about activation in the previous week. Any progress the client made should be reinforced in session. Social workers should also ask if conducting the scheduled activities had any effect on the clients' mood. When clients fail to do the scheduled activities, social workers should assess barriers to activation and use additional strategies to address the issues that occurred.

Mr. Thao and his social worker agreed that looking for a new job was an important activation assignment that would be beneficial for him. The social worker helped Mr. Thao to break the seemingly overwhelming task—"finding a new job"—into smaller tasks. This took several minutes of discussion. The first task assigned was to look over at least one newspaper for possible job openings a day. Mr. Thao initially suggested that he would look over several newspapers, but upon curious, open questioning from the social worker, he decided that that was too ambitious and likely to fail. They identified avoidance as the most common barrier, and Mr. Thao imagined in session looking at the newspaper to evoke how he might feel during the actual task, and he and the social worker practiced being mindful of that feeling while taking action based on the agreed upon plan instead of responding to his feeling through avoidance. The social worker also discussed how making small progress in looking for a job affected Mr. Thao's feelings in the beginning of each session.

Additional Strategies

Several additional strategies are used in BA to maximize the likelihood of the client completing activation assignments. These strategies generally have been lifted from traditional behavior therapy techniques, and many social workers may already be familiar with them. Here, we review four primary strategies: stimulus control, skills training, contingency management, and dealing with avoidance.

Stimulus control. Often clients simply forget to complete activities, and when this occurs, the social worker should take a nonblaming, problem-solving approach. Primarily, the goal is to help the client remember about the assignment with well-designed reminders. Social workers and clients can work together to choose a method that is most effective.

Skills training. When activities are not completed, it is always possible that the client does not possess the necessary skills to successfully complete them. Additional skills training can be the solution to this barrier. For instance, if the client is planning to post his resume online but is not familiar with the process, a visit to an employment agency may be the first step of activation. Some clients may need to learn how to talk to social workers at social service agencies, or how to ask their primary care doctors about medication side effects. In these cases, clients and social workers may be able to role play in session how to communicate more effectively. Other clients may choose to take classes to learn English or a new skill. In these cases, signing up for and attending the classes regularly can become activation assignments on their own. Some clients may need help making difficult financial decisions, and the social worker may choose to teach the client more effective problem-solving skills such as breaking the problem into steps and making pros and cons lists.

Contingency management. Some activities are not very fun or rewarding, but are still important for clients to complete. For example, exercising may not immediately result in lower blood pressure or increased energy. In this case, an arbitrary reward (e.g., going to a movie after thirty minutes of walking) can be arranged as a short-term strategy to help with activity completion. The key here is for clients to discipline themselves such that they withhold the reward until after completing the activity. For some clients, this will be possible; for others who may struggle with this strategy, it should not be relied upon.

Strategies targeting avoidance. The most common obstacle to activation is avoidance. We all know the experience of not doing something because we were too tired, too anxious, too overwhelmed, too angry to think straight, or too filled with hopelessness that the situation will change. Here, BA offers strategies that are in line with mindfulness and acceptance strategies. In BA, engagement in nondepressed activities is guided by strategic planning and the client's values instead of the client's mood. Put simply, the goal is to help clients learn to act according to plans rather than moods. While we all know how it feels to avoid, we can also think of instances in which we were able to act even though we did not feel like it. This is often the case with exercise, taking a risk to make an assertive request or trying something new, or simply getting out of bed in the morning when we are feeling tired. These small lessons in acting according to plans rather than moods can serve as the basis for action in the face of avoidance tendencies in BA. Clients are asked to follow the activation plan even in the presence of negative thoughts and feelings.

Another way to conceptualize this is that BA takes an "outside-in" approach to behavior change. Specifically, the typical view is that our feelings (on the "inside") determine our behavior (on the "outside"). For example, a client may say, "I don't think I can get active until I feel better first." This is the "inside-out" approach. The "outside-in" approach reverses this sequence. All of the examples above, in which we acted first, even though we did not feel like it, are consistent with "outside-in." We act first, then, as a result of the action, our feelings change. We start to exercise, and then we feel more energetic. We make the assertive request, and then the next time the opportunity to be assertive arises, it feels easier. However, the goal of activation should not be to immediately change mood, but rather to create an overall pattern of active engagement in life based on values.

To target avoidance, several specific strategies may be employed. The first strategy is to guide clients to notice thoughts and feelings when they engage in the scheduled activity. Social workers can simply ask, "What do you feel or what do you think about when you start [the scheduled activity]?" It is then important for social workers to validate these reactions in a nonblaming, nonjudgmental way. Consider Mr. Thao again, who responded to this question by saying that he initially felt stupid and silly for having so much difficulty getting active, and then he felt anxious and overwhelmed.

Social Worker: These feelings and thoughts that occur every time you start looking for a job make sense to me. These are natural reactions you are having. In the past, it was easy for you to do this sort of thing, and now that you are depressed, it is really hard. So it makes sense that you would feel stupid and silly, and then not want to even start. Most people in your situation would have similar reactions.

After clients become more mindful of their own natural reactions, social workers should reiterate that the goal in BA is not to change or control these negative feelings and thoughts directly, because these reactions are seen as normal and, therefore, not problematic. Instead, clients are encouraged to be open to these natural reactions and view them nonjudgmentally, which is in line with the concept of acceptance. Clients are then guided to examine their typical behavioral reactions toward negative feelings and thoughts. Most clients are usually aware that experiencing negative feelings and thoughts tends to lead to avoidance of the scheduled activities. It is then important for social workers to remind the clients that having negative thoughts and feelings in reaction to activation is not the problem, but letting these reactions control their behaviors is. Then, the social worker and the client can revisit the specific activation assignment and redesign the assignment to make it less challenging and more likely to be successful in the face of strong and understandable tendencies to avoid.

Social Worker: Now that you notice feeling anxious and overwhelmed whenever you try to look for job openings, I want to help you to follow our activation plan by maybe just holding the newspaper in your hands, even with the anxiety. This will be the first step for you. How does this first step sound to you? The second step is to flip the newspaper to the job opening section, even with the anxiety. And the third step is to read at least one or two possible job openings, even with the anxiety. We can even try it now in session. I brought this newspaper. Are you willing to practice it with me now? Later we will check how this practice affects your feelings.

Conclusion

Our belief is that BA is appropriate for and relevant to the field of social work, and we hope this chapter provides an introduction to the practice that successfully makes this case. Social work theories that emphasize the client's environment fit well with BA's functional contextualist perspective, and BA's pragmatic, action-oriented focus is compatible with how many social workers approach the clinical interaction. We believe that a great potential strength of BA is that the model can be easily adapted for clients who are not from the mainstream culture, and this adaptability is important given that social workers work regularly with clients from diverse backgrounds (e.g., racial and ethnic minority groups), lower socioeconomic status, and histories of disenfranchisement (e.g., undocumented immigrants). For some of these clients, a successful course of BA will not only reduce depression but increase efficacy and yield a sense of empowerment to join the fight for structural and systemic social and racial justice improvements.

For some clients, issues of racism and discrimination become primary core treatment issues. For example, consider how Mr. Thao, who does not speak English well, was paid less than other workers, and worked under harsh conditions because he could not successfully assert himself to improve his work conditions. Or consider a teenage client who endures bullying at school for being "different," or an African-American male client who perceives that he was followed in a store because the owner thought he was shoplifting. In BA, these experiences of racism and discrimination are taken seriously, validated, and seen as negative life experiences that may contribute causally to depression. Activation with respect to experiences of racism and discrimination is determined on a case-by-case basis, in collaboration with the client and in the context of the client's goals and values. In line with accepting the things one cannot change and working to change what can be changed, BA adheres to the slogan, "Think globally, act locally." In other words, some acknowledgement that racism exists and will continue to exist is required, and the focus is on what the individual can change in his or her life.

Some clients may choose to activate to fight against local experiences of racism, while others will not. It is important that the choice to take action in this regard is the client's, not the social worker's, and that the pros and cons of taking action are explored objectively, in line with the client's goals and values. For those who do choose to activate in this way, activation assignments may include engaging in political advocacy, working with community organizations, or taking specific workplace actions to redress perceived racial biases and actions. For the teenager who was bullied for being different, an activation goal might be to volunteer at an elementary school and talk to children about the importance of not bullying others. For another individual, the activation may be related to maintaining good study habits to gain acceptance to college, or to learn English. For the individual who contacts explicit instances of racism (e.g., a racist boss), activation may include problem-solving to explore if there is possible action in which to engage. The social worker might work with the client to discuss the pros and cons of assertively confronting the racist individual directly. Small actions would be scheduled each week until the client is behaving in ways consistent with his or her goals and values on a local basis. The BA worker can equip the client with mindfulness techniques to help the client stay active while enduring the distress that accompanies engaging in acting against racism and other forms of discrimination.

Many depressed clients fit the BA model well. They start treatment significantly shut down, passive, and hopeless, with many core valued activities they have stopped doing in life. Some depressed clients, however, do not seem to fit the model well, and using the BA model with them may be more challenging. We end this chapter with a discussion of how to work with some of these more challenging issues. For example, some depressed clients are depressed but still quite active. They have not shut down. This is particularly the case for individuals in poverty or financial distress. For example, consider a depressed father who is the primary breadwinner for his family and works over seventy hours weekly to provide for them, as his wife is disabled and cannot work. Additionally, consider a depressed single mother with three children who provides for them financially, takes them to school and extracurricular activities, cooks meals for them, bathes them, cleans the home, and so forth. Both of these clients are very active, but their activity is dominated by the daily hassles and stress of poverty.

Does BA fit for such individuals? What is the nature of activation for already active but still depressed clients? There are several issues to consider here. First, the BA model keeps us humble and empathic. By focusing on contextual causes of depression, in some instances the model may suggest that there is in fact not much we can do to improve the client's situation. When a client is already very proactive in trying to solve life's problems and acting according to her values, but remains depressed, we look to the environment—not to what's inside the client—for the source of the problem. Thus, we celebrate the client's strengths in staying active in the face of adversity and predict that the depression would be considerably worse if she shut down and gave up. We support the client in maintaining action in the face of ongoing adversity and maintain optimism that with continued action, the environment will change. One thing we know for sure: If the client quits and gives up, then the client's life will never improve. These clients, however, often already know this fundamental BA axiom.

At the same time, we do not give up or become passive in our attempts to intervene with sensitive activation efforts. We continually question and explore the balance of activities in these clients' lives, seeking to find opportunities for new activities that bring pleasure, enjoyment, or simply respite, and new creative ways to solve problems. We help clients schedule and manage their lives successfully. We help clients understand that when their lives are dominated by efforts to simply make ends meet and to stay afloat, it takes effort to carve out time to take care of oneself and build in routines that offer some modicum of pleasure and relief, and that these routines are important. A therapy goal for some clients like this might be to integrate meaningful time and conversations with loved ones into the ongoing routine.

Acceptance and mindfulness are important strategies here, not in accepting one's environmental situation but rather in accepting and becoming mindful of the frustration and despair that accompany the continued effort to change. Paradoxically, in BA, clients are taught to activate and stay active in the presence of frustration and despair, and this, in turn, may decrease these experiences over time. In contrast, efforts to avoid the frustration and despair of life may lead to unhealthy avoidance moves such as drug use or lashing out at others. In fact, acceptance of pain and hardship is consistent with how many minority groups respond to life's hardships, as evidenced by well-known Latino *dichos* (sayings) such as "Todo pasa por una razón" ("Everything happens for a reason"), "Cuando una puerta se cierra otra se abre" ("When one door closes, another opens"), and "Al mal tiempo buena cara" ("During hard times, put on a good face and continue on"). The serenity prayer also has its place here: "God, grant me the serenity to accept the things I cannot change, courage to change the things I can, and wisdom to know the difference." In this way, BA can be seamlessly integrated with cultural idioms that emphasize acceptance and mindfulness to help clients activate in a way that is consistent with their goals and values.

References

Andrae, D. (2011). General systems theory: Contributions to social work theory and practice. In F. J. Turner (Ed.), *Social work treatment, Interlocking theoretical approaches* (5th ed., pp. 242-254). New York: Oxford University Press.

Bartlett, H. M. (1970). *The common base of social work practice.* New York: Putnam.

Bronfenbrenner, U. (1989). Ecological systems theory. *Annals of Child Development, 6,* 187-249.

Cuijpers, P., van Straten, A., & Warmerdam, L. (2007). Behavioral activation treatments of depression: A meta-analysis. *Clinical Psychology Review, 27,* 318-326.

Dimidjian, S., Barrera, M. R., Martell, C., Muñoz, R. F., & Lewinsohn, P. M. (2011). The origins and current status of behavioral activation treatments for depression. *Annual Review of Clinical Psychology, 7,* 1-38.

Dimidjian, S., Hollon, S. D., Dobson, K. S., Schmaling, K. B., Kohlenberg, R. J., Addis, M. E., et al. (2006). Randomized trial of behavioral activation, cognitive therapy, and antidepressant medication in the acute treatment of adults with major depression. *Journal of Consulting and Clinical Psychology, 74,* 658-670.

Ekers, D. D., Richards, D. D., & Gilbody, S. S. (2008). A meta-analysis of randomized trials of behavioural treatment of depression. *Psychological Medicine, 38,* 611-623.

Greene, R. R. (1999). Human behavior theory, person-in-environment, and social work method. In R. R. Greene (Ed.), *Human behavior theory and social work practice* (2nd ed., pp. 1-30). Hawthorne, NY: Aldine de Gruyter.

Hayes, S. C., Barnes-Holmes, D., & Wilson, K. G. (2012). Contextual behavioral science: Creating a science more adequate to the challenge of the human condition. *Journal of Contextual Behavioral Science, 1,* 1-16.

Kanter, J. W., Busch, A. M., & Rusch, L. C. (2009). *Behavioral activation: Distinctive features.* New York: Routledge/Taylor & Francis Group.

Kanter, J. W., Manos, R. C., Bowe, W. M., Baruch, D. E., Busch, A. M., & Rusch, L. C. (2010). What is behavioral activation?: A review of the empirical literature. *Clinical Psychology Review, 30,* 608-620.

Kanter, J. W., Santiago-Rivera, A. L., Rusch, L. C., Busch, A. M., & West, P. (2010). Initial outcomes of a culturally adapted behavioral activation for Latinas diagnosed with depression at a community clinic. *Behavior Modification, 34,* 120-144.

Lakes, K., López, S.R., & Garro, L. (2006). Cultural competence and psychotherapy: Applying anthropologically informed conceptions of culture. *Psychotherapy: Theory, Research, Practice, Training, 43,* 380-396.

Lee, J. A. B., & Hudson, R. E. (2011). Empowerment approach to social work practice. In F. J. Turner (Ed.), *Social work treatment, Interlocking theoretical approaches* (5th ed., pp. 242-254). New York: Oxford University Press.

Lewinsohn, P. (1974). A behavioral approach to depression. In R. J. Friedman, & M. M. Katz (Eds.), *Psychology of depression: Contemporary theory and research* (pp. 157-185). Oxford, England: John Wiley & Sons.

Martell, C. R., & Kanter, J. W. (2011). Behavioral activation in the context of "third wave" therapies. In J. D. Herbert & E. Forman (Eds.), *Acceptance and mindfulness in cognitive behavior therapy* (pp. 193-209). Hoboken, NJ: John Wiley & Sons.

Mazzucchelli, T. G., Kane, R. T., & Rees, C. S. (2010). Behavioral activation interventions for well-being: A meta-analysis. *The Journal of Positive Psychology, 5,* 105-121.

National Association of Social Workers (NASW). (1999). *Code of Ethics.* Washington, DC: Professional Standards Committee of the Clinical Social Work Federation. Retrieved from http://www.socialworkers.org/pubs/code/code.asp

National Institute for Health and Clinical Excellence. (2009). *Depression: The treatment and management of depression in adults.* London: National Institute for Health and Clinical Excellence.

Reamer, F. G. (2006). *Social work values and ethics,* 3rd edition. New York: Columbia University Press.

Skinner, B. F. (1974). *About behaviorism.* New York: Vintage Books Edition.

Sturmey, P. (2009). Behavioral activation is an evidence-based treatment for depression. *Behavior Modification, 33,* 818-829.

PART II

New Directions: Emerging Applications of Mindfulness and Acceptance in Social Work

CHAPTER 5

Radical Acceptance: Mindfulness and Critical Reflection in Social Work Education

Yuk-Lin Renita Wong, PhD

York University

"We cannot let go of anything we do not accept."

—Ondrea Levine (2012)

The pursuit of social justice is central to the mission and values of the social work profession (CASW, 2012; IASSW, ICSW & IFSW, 2012; NASW, 2012). As social workers, we witness the daily realities of personal, social, and community challenges. We

Portions of this chapter were previously published in Wong, Y. R. (2013). Returning to silence, connecting to wholeness: Contemplative pedagogy for critical social work education. *Journal of Religion & Spirituality in Social Work: Social Thought, 32,* 265-285. They are reprinted here with permission from Taylor & Francis.

are committed to helping people in need, especially those who are vulnerable and oppressed; addressing social problems; and challenging the systems that have a negative impact on people's lives. We work to facilitate personal and social change.

In order to fulfill this mission of the profession, social work educators are called upon to guide future practitioners into becoming agents of change and assist them in developing their critical reflective ability for social work practice. *Critical reflection* involves identifying the deep-seated assumptions we have about the social world and our connection with it, recognizing how political and social contexts shape our values and theories, and challenging the embedded beliefs about what is normal or acceptable in social work practice. The purpose of teaching critical reflection is to enable social work students to become critical thinkers and practitioners who can reflect on society, the role of social work, and social work practices (Bay & Macfarlane, 2011). Critical reflection "aims to uncover power relations and how structures of domination are created and maintained, through a process that involves questioning dominant structures and relations, laying the ground for change" (p. 746). It incorporates "an understanding of personal experiences within social, cultural, and structural contexts" (Fook & Askeland, 2007, p. 522).

In this chapter, I propose that radical acceptance is the grounds for critical reflection and change. In the following discussion, I will introduce a mindfulness-based pedagogy, one that I adopt in my teaching of critical reflection and critical social work. Critical social work is an approach that examines the social construction and structural conditions (e.g., social policies, economic forces, racism, sexism, homophobia) of social problems and human experiences. Critical social work also brings practitioners' awareness to our power relations with clients along identities of race, gender, class, sexual orientation, religion, age, and dis/ability; and how we may be implicated in reproducing existing social power structure. I will show how an attitude of radical acceptance, which is integral to mindfulness, increases students' awareness of what is going on inside and outside. It also enhances their capacity to stay with their internal mental and emotional experiences nonjudgmentally, to see clearly what those experiences are, and to move beyond the limiting dualistic thinking of right and wrong. As students stop their habitual reactions of judgment and preference, they have more internal space to reflect on the structural context of their experiences, to hold multiple views, and to act appropriately to bring about change.

Mindfulness and Radical Acceptance

In his seminal work, *Full Catastrophe Living*, Jon Kabat-Zinn (1990) identifies acceptance as one of seven attitudinal foundations of the practice of mindfulness. (The others are nonjudging, patience, beginner's mind, trust, nonstriving, and letting go.) According to Kabat-Zinn, acceptance means "seeing things as they actually are in the present" (p. 38). Tara Brach (2003) describes acceptance as "an inner process of accepting our actual, present-moment experience" (pp. 25-26). If we feel pain, we accept that pain is present. If we have a negative thought about someone or something, we recognize it and do not judge the thought or judge ourselves for having the thought. We are simply aware of what is happening and whatever we are feeling or thinking, without trying to control or judge or pull away.

Nonjudging is thus integral to acceptance. When we pay attention to our mental activities, it is common to notice that the mind constantly labels, categorizes, and judges our experience and our thoughts: good/bad, right/wrong, pleasant/unpleasant, liking/disliking. We react to everything we experience through these attitudes of the mind and see it through the lens of judgment. We cannot see what is actually happening clearly, just as it is. We waste a lot of energy grasping what we like or resisting what we do not like. These judgments prevent us from growth, as we are too busy with our conditioned reactivity.

"Clearly recognizing what is happening inside us, and regarding what we see with an open, kind and loving heart" is what Tara Brach calls "radical acceptance" (2003, p. 26). Clear seeing is intrinsic to radical acceptance and sets the stage for acting appropriately to bring about change. "We can't honestly accept an experience unless we see clearly what we are accepting" (p. 28). To see clearly, we need to let go of those judging thoughts and the impulses of the mind to grasp what is pleasant or push away from what is unpleasant. In the practice of mindfulness, we recognize these thoughts and impulses but do not pursue them.

According to Tara Brach, alongside clear seeing, compassion—our capacity to relate to our grasping or judging with gentleness and care—is also essential to radical acceptance. It allows us to stay close to what is alive inside us in this moment. It makes our acceptance wholehearted. Together, clear seeing and compassion "help us remain in the experience of the moment, just as it is. When we do this, something begins to happen—we feel freer, options open before us, we see with more clarity how we want to proceed" (p. 29). Radical acceptance thus does not mean we give up on our desire to change and grow, or that we tolerate injustice or do not get involved in changing the world. As we see clearly what is happening, rather than being clouded by the mind's judgments and reactivity, we become more aware of the conditions that produce the thoughts, feelings, bodily experiences, and their intertwined effects; the intentions that motivate our behavior; and the consequences of our actions on both ourselves and others. This larger view in an accepting awareness is described as "clear comprehending" or "clear understanding" in the classic Buddhist text on mindfulness, *Satipatthana Sutta (Sutra on the Four Establishments of Mindfulness)* (Nhat Hanh, 2006a). Likewise, in her reflection on the use of mindfulness in anti-oppressive pedagogies, Orr (2002) writes that out of the process of this nonjudgmental awareness comes the possibility of change.

Critical Reflection and Radical Acceptance

From their experience with teaching critical reflection, Fook and Askeland (2007) identify the need to set up an alternative cultural environment for the purpose of critical reflection. It is a culture of "critical acceptance" in which one's position, interpretation, and practice are deconstructed nonjudgmentally, so that students can find out the "why" of their thoughts and actions, rather than approving or disapproving of them (Fook, 2003). I suggest that the practice of mindfulness, with its foundational attitude of radical acceptance, can help cultivate this alternative environment.

As critical reflection involves unearthing our deep-seated assumptions and unquestioned cultural norms, it provokes resistance and anxiety among learners. Many social work educators identify a broad range of strong reactions among students when their fundamental beliefs about themselves and society, which they have not yet been aware of, become highlighted through critical reflection: emotions such as distress, shame, guilt, and anger; responses such as defensiveness and claims to innocence; and feelings of loss and grief (Chapman, 2011; Garcia & van Soest, 2000; Mishna & Bogo, 2007; Sullivan & Johns, 2002; Wong, 2004). They propose various principles and strategies for instructors to adopt in the classroom, including setting ground rules to prepare students for the possibility of conflict, anticipating their emotions, fostering "a sense of contextual community connectedness and resonance" through the narrative practice of outsider-witnessing (Chapman, 2011, p. 728), and so forth. All recognize the need to prepare students for the emotional experiences they will have during critical reflection.

Fook and Askeland (2007) contend that the emotional experience is a necessary condition for developing the more connected knowing that is crucial for change in critical reflection. They critique the dominant rational and intellectual approach to teaching and learning in the traditional classroom, and argue for the need to create an alternative learning environment that incorporates emotions into the process of critical reflection. Like many, however, they stop short of discussing the pedagogical process (i.e., the "how") to support students to stay with their difficult emotional experiences during critical reflection without pushing them away.

In 2000, in a course titled "Identity and Diversity," I began to develop a mindfulness-based pedagogy to enable students to befriend their emotional discomfort as they engaged in critical reflection on their power and privilege (Wong, 2004). Over the years, as I deepened my own mindfulness practice and studied the original source of Gautama's instruction on mindfulness in the *Satipatthana Sutta* (Nhat Hanh, 2006a), as well as his teachings on the mind in the *Abhidhamma* literature (Davids, 1976; Nhat Hanh, 2006b), I have gained further insight into the interdependent links between the body, feelings, and mental states in Buddhist psychology, which has received increasing interest from those studying the body-mind sciences during the last decade (Goleman, 2004; Pagis, 2009; Siegel, 2010). Subsequently, I have made further systematic attempts to introduce mindfulness into other critical social work courses. In this chapter, I will discuss the students' experiences with the pedagogical process of mindfulness in a more recent course.

The Course: "Spirituality and Critical Social Work"

In May and June 2010, I taught a six-week graduate elective summer course, "Spirituality and Critical Social Work," which integrated bodily, emotive, cognitive, and spiritual knowing into critical reflection in social justice and social work. Integrating spirituality into social justice, this course provided a contemplative space where students reflected on what it means to take spiritually-grounded action for individual and community healing from all forms of oppression and colonization. The course adopted the deep ecology framework of the "interbeing" of the person and the environment (Nhat Hanh, 1991; 2012) that goes beyond the person-in-environment perspective in social work. In this framework, the environment is not outside of people. Rather people and the environment are ultimately one. We embody the environment and we are the environment, both physical and social.

While Fook and Askeland (2007) urge educators to create an alternative learning environment to incorporate emotions in critical reflection, my mindfulness practice of observing the busy judging and reactive mind helps me see the importance of a space for contemplative silence as the foundation for the nonjudgmental presence to one's emotions that is necessary for critical reflection. For many spiritually-based activists, including Gandhi, Thomas Merton, and Thich Nhat Hanh, contemplative silence is the ground for meaningful personal and social change and action that goes beyond dualistic us-versus-them thinking. Unlike most critical social work courses that encourage talking and discussion among students in order for them to process their thinking, I cultivated a space for contemplative silence in this course through both in-class exercises and outside-class assignments.

Class Format and Learning Activities

Classes normally began with a ten-minute mindful breathing meditation and/or another fifteen to twenty minutes of mindfulness exercises such as mindful eating and mindful walking, based on the instructions given by Jon Kabat-Zinn (1990) and Thich Nhat Hanh (2000), and loving-kindness meditation. In one session, students were introduced to a thirty-minute "listening to trees" exercise. All contemplative exercises were followed by a thirty-to-forty-minute "circle sharing" exercise in which students sat in a circle and took turns sharing their experiences. They could pass on the sharing if they wished.

The fifth session was a six-hour silent retreat on a Saturday. The retreat format and its preparatory assignment were adapted from a similar learning activity developed by Teresa Macias, who had taught the course two years before. Prior to the retreat, students submitted a two-page plan to identify one area of their spiritual journey that they wanted to reflect on. For instance, they might have identified one aspect of their spirituality that posed challenges for them in their personal and/or professional life; a set of beliefs they wanted to reflect more deeply on; or an area of spiritual development they would like to explore. Or they might want to reflect on their experience of connecting with the silence within or staying present with their inner experience, moment to moment, and the implications of this for their personal and professional lives. In the retreat plan, they also specified the contemplative practices, texts, or scriptures they would use to guide and carry out their reflection. If reading and writing were chosen, these activities were not to take up more than half of the retreat time. Three readings were recommended to help students plan their retreat (hooks, 1996; Kabat-Zinn, 2005; Nouwen, 1975). On the day of the retreat, students first met in class for a fifteen-minute meditation, after which I encouraged them to allow the flow of the day to guide them and not to be bound by their retreat plan. They were then free to find a spot on campus to conduct their contemplative practice in solitude. Students came back for an outdoor silent meal together. Before closing, they shared briefly their experience of the day.

Every week students also wrote a two- or three-page ungraded reflective journal comprised of two components. First, to honor students' diverse spiritual practices, they were asked to engage in a ten-to-twenty-minute daily "centering practice" of their choice, which might be a mindfulness exercise introduced in class or any contemplative practice that helped them stay centered and grounded. Many students chose mindful breathing, walking, and eating, along with other contemplative practices such as prayer, poetry, calligraphy, painting, gardening, yoga, mountain biking, and music. Students reflected on what they noticed during the practice and how it helped them relate differently to themselves, others, and the world. Second, students engaged reflectively in the weekly assigned readings, which covered topics such as ecology and social justice, indigenous knowledges and decolonization, spirituality and social activism, and so on. They reflected on a sentence or quote from each reading that opened their heart or awakened their spirit, raised a question of significance for contemplation, or invited them to practice critical social work differently.

Course Evaluation and Interviews

An anonymous course evaluation at the end of the course showed overwhelmingly positive feedback—"very good" or "excellent" on a five-point scale—from all of the twenty-one students who took the course. There were ten questions about the course or the instructor, including the students' overall rating of the course, the relevance and value of the course to the overall program, the level of intellectual challenge, and the instructor's knowledge and ability to stimulate critical thinking. Additional anonymous written comments included: "The course addresses a very important part of a social work education: internal processes and state of being." "It created a space for difference." "It helped stimulate critical thinking in a way that purely academic courses miss." "It helped refocus and re-ground my critical social work practice." And "Thanks for restoring my faith in critical social work and the freedom of exploring ideas from different places within myself." Many students also commented on the helpfulness of the mindfulness exercises or the silent retreat.

In February 2011, all of the twenty-one students were invited to participate in a semi-structured in-depth interview of approximately an hour to talk about their experience with the contemplative pedagogy of the course and its impact on their personal lives and critical social work practice. Some of these students had graduated in fall 2010, while some expected to graduate in June 2011. I was not teaching any of the students at the time. Two students could not be reached as their e-mail contacts were no longer valid after graduation. Ten out of the remaining nineteen students contacted responded and participated in the interviews between March and July 2011, a period when graduating students were preoccupied and overwhelmed with the completion of practicum, course work, major practice research papers, and job searches.

Students' Experiences

"Silence," "awareness," and "wholeness" stood out in all the interviews as the students each recalled their experience in the course. Contemplative silence was a new and "surprisingly powerful" experience for the students during their learning of critical reflection. Most commented on how much they appreciated the space for silence and reflection, which they had never had in other courses. It helped them pause, slow down, and take a step back from their habitual fast pace and mental and conceptual criticality. It enabled them to turn inward, recenter, and watch their mental activities with less reactivity. It allowed them to reconnect to all parts of themselves, especially those parts—their bodies, hearts, and spirits—that had been shunted aside in the academic and professional world. Their awareness of what was going on inside and outside was deepened through all the senses.

For the purpose, and within the limit, of this chapter on mindfulness and acceptance, I will focus mostly on the experience of one student, Karla, who shared extensively how mindfulness enhanced her radical acceptance of all of herself for critical reflection. Where appropriate, I will also include other students' accounts to further illustrate this process from their different vantage points.

ACCEPTING "IMPERFECTIONS"

Karla shared her experience of mindfulness meditation in relation to critical social work: "Part of doing critical social work is being able to recognize the ways [in which] we were perpetuating oppression and the things that we were carrying with us that we would be embarrassed to share. We would feel like we're bad, or we [would] judge ourselves over [the ways we perpetuate oppression]. I found mindfulness meditation a great way to help me sit with that and look at that, and not have to run away from it, and feel like I'm a bad person if I even look at that or admit that it was there."

Karla recognized that many people would question "how can we just accept what's there" and "sit with" and be complacent about all the injustice in the world. The more she practiced mindfulness, the more she realized that "it's not that everything is okay and we don't challenge things, but it's the way that we challenge things." Before her experience of mindfulness, Karla's response to injustice used to be "very agitated and angry all the time." She would "constantly debate with people and argued." She was "putting out a lot of anger and frustration," rather than "finding a way to do something to change anything." With the mindfulness practice, however, Karla had come to a place where she was experiencing less "automatic reactivity and anger about things" and was more "able to sit with things and see what they are" so as to choose for herself how to respond.

I asked Karla for a specific moment in her critical social work practice to illustrate how her nonjudgmental awareness of things helped her respond differently. Karla recalled an experience of working with a woman who had a difficult time being alone and felt something was wrong with her. It took Karla some time to realize her own unquestioned cultural value of independence when she talked with the client about the "problem." The mindfulness practice helped Karla not to react immediately or judge herself for having biases, and allowed her the spaciousness to see a larger picture and let the conversation unfold in such a way that the dominant discourse that defined the problem was challenged. Karla described the process of her nonjudgmental awareness and response to the situation as follows:

> "I had a situation where I was working with a client. The person was talking about being alone and how difficult it was for her to be alone. When she was alone in her apartment, she felt really uncomfortable. She was talking about this as if this was a problem, something wrong with her, that she didn't like to be alone. So I started exploring that with her a bit, talking to her about her experience of being alone.... As I was talking to her, it occurred to me that she grew up in another country where there are all sorts of family [around her] all the time. And so it suddenly just dawned on me: Is there something wrong with her, or are we just talking about different cultural norms? Is it just the experience that she has versus what North American norms are? So I got into the middle of the session, having gone down that road, and [said]: 'It occurs that to me you're talking about your childhood when you had family with you all the time. Did you spend time alone?' She said: 'No, never. This is the first time I've ever lived alone.' She was in her forties. If I didn't have the practice of mindfulness [which] for me is about not reacting immediately, [but] about exploring [and] creating spaciousness to be thinking about what

she's saying in a larger way...[I would not have been] able to look at myself: 'Oh look at me, I'm actually working from this particular set of norms and pathologizing this person based on these norms. Let me step back for a minute, maybe that's not what I should be doing.' For me to be able to do that and feel comfortable with that, and not feel like a bad person, [and to] actually say: 'Let me step back'.... To me that's critical social work: to be able to talk about what are the dominant discourses [and] to challenge them in the session, [to see that] our whole discussion about what's wrong with her is based on these dominant discourses. If we start looking at other ways of being, and dismantle those discourses, then actually there is not a 'problem' here. So that, for me, is an example of practicing critical social work. It was able to unfold in that way because of the mindfulness meditation practice."

This nonjudgmental awareness of her deep-seated cultural values, and seeing the dominant structure, opened up a different conversation between Karla and the client about her experience of living alone.

Karla further explained how this incident showed that mindfulness practice had enabled her "to accept that [she has] imperfections, and that's okay," and to come to a place of "loving compassion" toward things happening inside her. She further explained: "Not that I can't grow as a person. But I don't need to be embarrassed in wanting to hide parts of myself, or to pretend that I don't have certain parts of myself. I have parts that people might really be excited about. I have parts that people might not be excited about, and that's okay." Mindfulness practice allowed Karla the "spaciousness" of "embracing and turning toward" all the different parts of herself, including what she "hated" and "most wanted to turn away from because it was uncomfortable." "There is room for everything." Karla described her image of this spaciousness as being "like a platter on the top of my head with this slightly raised lip. Any big huge gigantic thing that comes to the platter looks very small, compared to the size of the platter, when it reaches the platter. Okay, there is space for that. There is space for that too. We live in a world of either-or all the time, and we think there is no room for everything."

ACCEPTING "BOTH-AND"

Through the nonjudgmental acceptance of mindfulness practice, Karla arrived at a spacious, nonbinary place which Fook and Askeland (2007) consider crucial for critical reflection in social work education. Fook and Askeland find that the dominant "adversarial ways of knowing" and the "argument culture" in Western societies "conditions us to believe that the 'truth' can be arrived at only through debate or 'fight' between opposing sides." These adversarial ways of knowing create barriers that prevent learners from being able to "value multiple perspectives, appreciate different viewpoints, and the holding of contradictions" in critical reflection (p. 528).

This "fight between opposing sides" is prevalent in social activism seeking structural change. Another student, Sabrina, struggled with this "confrontational" culture in her years of activism, which she found often ended up in "binary thinking" and action. It felt "exhausting" to Sabrina to see that even people who shared the common goal of social justice were in so much conflict trying to impose their "right way" onto others. For a long time, Sabrina felt stuck in this "simplistic dualism" of right and wrong. She appreciated the weekly in-class and outside-class mindfulness practice and the silent retreat for allowing her the contemplative time of silence to reflect on this. The silent retreat gave Sabrina "the incredible opportunity" to reflect on and affirm the value she placed on contemplation as being something necessary in social activism, rather than the common view of contemplation and activism being in opposition to each other. Even though she did not "resolve everything," she felt more able to stay in a place of "both-and," that is, both this and that. She also "definitely came to some new understanding" of the "interconnectedness," rather than binary nature, of all things, and a deeper appreciation of "the humanness and wholeness of our enemies and of ourselves" as the very different foundation of social action promoted in Martin Luther King's "beloved community" and Thich Nhat Hanh's *Love in Action* (1993).

In *The Courage to Teach*, Palmer (1998) identifies the Western thinking in polarities as a legacy of the Enlightenment, where the mind is separated from and elevated above the body, and where rationalism and certainty and control are more valued than emotive, bodily, and spiritual knowing. While recognizing the contribution of binary logic to the development of modern technology, as well as the merits of analytical reasoning, Palmer challenges us to "think the world together": not to abandon binary logic where it serves us well, but to develop a more capacious habit of mind that embraces the paradox of "both-and." Palmer explains: "In certain circumstances, truth is found not by splitting the world into either-ors but by embracing it as *both-and*. In certain circumstances, truth is a paradoxical joining of apparent opposites, and if we want to know the truth, we must learn to embrace those opposites as one" (italics in original, p. 63). Our breathing, for example, is a form of paradox that requires inhaling and exhaling to be whole. This non-dual consciousness is present in ancient wisdom such as tai chi and the *difrasismo* in Aztec ritual speech, which sees complementarities between opposites and results in a "multi-perspectival" yet "unitive" view of the world (Rendón, 2009). In mindfulness, when the mind is not busy labeling, categorizing, or judging, there is space to embrace "both-and," as well as multiple worldviews.

Another student, Rachel, found that "circle sharing" after the mindfulness exercises in the course gave her "more of a space to just be where [she] was in [her] learning process and to share that" without worrying that she had not "figured out" the answer. Nor did she feel the tension she had felt in other courses, where it was like "a debate" or "a combat of ideas," and where everyone was "set up to try to find an answer." While circle sharing is not specifically a mindfulness practice, the pedagogical format of asking students to wait and listen, and to take turns around the circle to share their ideas or experience, helped them not to react immediately or jump into the "argument culture" prevalent in many critical classrooms. Instead, it allowed them to pause and be present to others' experiences, even if they "[did] not feel the same way" about the topic of discussion. As well, the mindfulness exercises that preceded circle sharing might have already cultivated "more openness" within Rachel to "learn by hearing what everyone has to say even though [she] was not responding to them." It also helped her accept where she was in her learning process, her "not-knowing" or not having an answer, while hearing that "others were similarly not quite sure yet." Like mindfulness, circle-sharing allows the openness of a not-knowing mind and a pause of judgment, and enhances students' capacity to appreciate different perspectives.

ACCEPTING AND RECOGNIZING "POWER AND PRIVILEGE"

Karla also commented on how the accepting openness of mindfulness practice created "a space that feels safe" for her and others to explore their "different prejudices or different views." Normally they "feel worried" and "scared" to share these experiences in class because they think "they're going to be judged."

This experience of mindfulness providing a "safe space" was also shared by another student, Tracy, who described how mindfulness practice helped her develop an *embodied awareness through all her senses* of what was going on inside her. Comparing this course with the other courses where students were also taught critical reflection, Tracy noted the difference mindfulness practice made to her recognition of her "power and privilege." Tracy said:

> "[Critical reflection in the other courses] was just [on] paper. There was no real rooted understanding. I can verbalize, sure, in terms of my identity: gender, race, class, and sexual orientation. I can talk about my growing up in social housing and how class [had more of an] impact [on] me than race did, and then acknowledge that I still have privilege as a white woman....[But] that doesn't mean anything without the context of what it means to be in those spaces and what it feels like to be in those spaces....We weren't pushed into those places where we were brought back to: how do you feel, what's

going on, are you being aware? I don't think I was really really aware until I was in the space where I could really feel and experience things in a different way, like in terms of connecting with all your senses: what are you seeing, what are you smelling, what are you feeling, and then what's going on inside of you?…In your course, you pushed us to the space where we had to be aware of what was going on, and of our feelings, and what was coming up. And you created a space that was safe for people to express things that they might have difficulties in understanding…, where people could bring out their biases and experiences and you were able to allow us to challenge each other in a healthy way without feeling persecuted."

Thus this "safe space" is not a place of "feeling good" without challenge. It is a contemplative space of silence where students could quiet their judging minds—both self-judging and judging others—and be aware of all their bodily senses, feelings, and thoughts, and recognize the embedded systemic relations of power. The exercises of mindful breathing, eating, and walking, as well as the silent retreat, enabled Tracy, Karla, and others to cultivate this accepting presence to what was going on inside and outside, which then opened up a nonjudgmental space for them to discuss what they would normally feel ashamed or afraid to talk about, and to really hear and learn from each other.

Conclusion

> "Don't turn away. Keep your gaze on the bandaged place.
> That's where the light enters you."
>
> —Rumi

Acceptance is the ground on which change occurs. This is radical. In Butot's study (2007) of seven people who identified themselves, or were identified by others, as anti-oppressive or critical practitioners who engaged in "loving practice," acceptance together with nonjudgmental and non-dualistic stances emerged as key themes. Butot notes that contrary to much critical theorizing, which suggests challenge is the driving force behind critical practice, her participants focused on attending, supporting, and connecting with what is in others. She goes on to ask, "Can critical social work function with this sense of acceptance, non-judgment and non-interference, without a sense of 'should'? If so, how might that manifest in practice? How might we reconcile the apparent paradox of critical analysis and change with 'as-is' acceptance and non-interference?" (p. 153)

In critical practice, we often focus on what is wrong or unacceptable, and hence needs to be changed. In our best intentions to work toward social justice by exposing power embedded in structural relations, as well as in our internalized assumptions and cultural beliefs, we are easily caught up in a dualistic frame of mind and a world of either-or: either right or wrong, good or bad. And we want to be on the right and good side of the binary.

In mindfulness practice, this categorization of right or wrong, good or bad, acceptable or unacceptable, and our desire to be "right" and "good" are the blinders that obscure a clear view of how things really are or what is really going on inside and outside of us. This mental habit of categorizing and labeling, as well as our desire to be good and right, needs to be included in our field of awareness without judgment. Judgment locks us into a fixed dualistic positionality. It freezes our ability to imagine an appropriate response. Radical acceptance is not about making no changes, but rather about accepting and seeing clearly what is already here, pleasant or unpleasant, without pushing it away. The light of mindfulness helps us recognize our habitual categorical perception and preference of things and delinks our response from this autopilot mental and emotional reactivity. When we can see clearly what is there without the perceptual or emotional entanglement, we feel freer to connect with our internal resourcefulness and to respond skillfully with more options to make changes, inside and outside, for a socially just world. In the class, when the students were more accepting of where they were, as well as all of *who* they were, they were also more accepting of where their peers were and open to their different views. There was more space for "the world together."

In this chapter, I offer no prescription or "right" way to teach critical reflection. Mindfulness is not for everyone or everything. Rather it is an invitation to expand our imagination and pedagogical repertoire by engaging all of ourselves—body, heart, mind, and spirit—through all our senses in our teaching and learning of critical reflection for social justice.

References

Bay, U., & Macfarlane, S. (2011). Teaching critical reflection: A tool for transformative learning in social work? *Social Work Education, 30,* 745-758.

Brach, T. (2003). *Radical acceptance: Embracing your life with the heart of a Buddha.* New York: Bantam Books.

Butot, M. (2007). Reframing spirituality, reconceptualizing change: Possibilities for critical social work. In J. Coates, J. R. Graham, & B. Swartzentruber (Eds.), *Spirituality and social work: Selected Canadian readings* (pp. 143-160). Toronto: Canadian Scholars' Press Inc.

Canadian Association of Social Workers (CASW) (2012). About CASW. Retrieved December 27, 2012, from http://www.casw-acts.ca/en/about-casw

Chapman, C. (2011). Resonance, intersectionality, and reflexivity in critical pedagogy (and research methodology). *Social Work Education, 30,* 723-744.

Davids, C. A. F. R. (1974). *A Buddhist manual of psychological ethics: Being a translation now made for the first time, from the original Pali, of the first book in the Abhidhamma pitaka entitled Dhamma-sangani compendium of states or phenomena* (Davids, Caroline A. F. Rhys, Trans.). (3rd ed.). London: Pali Text Society.

Fook, J. (February 2003). Critical reflection. *Workshop Presented at the Institute of Koorie Education, Deakin University, Geelong, Australia.*

Fook, J., & Askeland, G. A. (2007). Challenges of critical reflection: 'Nothing ventured, nothing gained.' *Social Work Education, 26,* 520-533.

Garcia, B., & Van Soest, D. (2000). Teaching about diversity: Learning from the analysis of critical classroom events. *Journal of Social Work Education, 18,* 149-167.

Goleman, D. (2004). *Destructive emotions: A scientific dialogue with the Dalai Lama.* New York: Bantam.

hooks, b. (1996). Contemplation and transformation. In M. Dresser (Ed.), *Buddhist women on the edge: Contemporary perspectives from the western frontiers* (pp. 287-292). Berkeley: North Atlantic Books.

IASSW, ICSW, & IFSW. (2012). *The global agenda: For social work and social development commitment to action.* Retrieved December 27, 2012, from http://cdn.ifsw.org/assets/globalagenda2012.pdf

Kabat-Zinn, J. (1990). *Full catastrophe living: Using the wisdom of your body and mind to face stress, pain and illness.* New York: A Delta Book.

Kabat-Zinn, J. (2005). Moments of silence. *Coming to our senses: Healing ourselves and the world through mindfulness* (pp. 573-575). New York: Hyperion.

Levine, O. (2012). *The healing I took birth for.* Vista, California: Aperion Books.

Mishna, F., & Bogo, M. (2007). Reflective practice in contemporary social work classrooms. *Journal of Social Work Education, 43,* 529-541.

National Association of Social Workers (NASW) (2012). Helping social workers serve the nation. Retrieved December 27, 2012, from http://www.socialworkers.org/nasw/naswbrochure.pdf

Nhat Hanh, Thich. (1991). Interbeing. *Peace is every step: The path of mindfulness in everyday life* (pp. 95-96). New York: Bantam Books.

Nhat Hanh, Thich. (1993). *Love in action: Writings on nonviolent social change.* Berkeley: Parallax Press.

Nhat Hanh, Thich. (2000). *The path of emancipation.* Berkeley: Parallax Press.

Nhat Hanh, Thich. (2006a). *Transformation and healing: Sutra on the Four Establishments of Mindfulness.* Berkeley: Parallax Press.

Nhat Hanh, Thich. (2006b). *Understanding our mind.* Berkeley: Parallax Press.

Nhat Hanh, Thich. (2012). *Beyond environment: Falling back in love with mother earth.* Retrieved May 12, 2012, from http://www.guardian.co.uk/sustainable-business/zen-thich-naht-hanh-buddhidm-business-values

Nouwen, H. J. M. (1975). Creating space for strangers. *Reaching out: The three movements of the spiritual life* (pp. 101-110). New York: Doubleday.

Orr, D. (2002). The uses of mindfulness in anti-oppressive pedagogies: Philosophy and praxis. *Canadian Journal of Education, 27,* 477-490.

Pagis, M. (2009). Embodied self-reflexivity. *Social Psychology Quarterly, 72,* 265-283.

Palmer, P. J. (1998). *The courage to teach: Exploring the inner landscape of a teacher's life.* San Francisco: Jossey-Bass.

Rendón, L. I. (2009). *Sentipensante (sensing/thinking) pedagogy: Educating for wholeness, social justice and liberation.* Sterling, Virginia: Stylus Publishing, LLC.

Siegel, D. J. (2010). *Mindsight: The new science of personal transformation.* New York: Bantam Books.

Sullivan, E., & Johns, R. (2002). Challenging values and inspiring attitudinal change: Creating an effective learning experience. *Social Work Education, 21,* 217-231.

Wong, Y. R. (2004). Knowing through discomfort: A mindfulness-based critical social work pedagogy. *Critical Social Work, 5.* Available online: http://www1.uwindsor.ca/criticalsocialwork/knowing-through-discomfort-a-mindfulness-based-critical-social-work-pedagogy

CHAPTER 6

Facilitating Mindfulness Using Arts-Based Methods and a Holistic Strengths-Based Perspective

Diana Coholic, PhD

Laurentian University

Social workers have expertise with group work and the use of creative methods to engage clients. We are knowledgeable about the broad field of mental health, often dealing with crises but also helping to shore up clients' defenses and change maladaptive or oppressive systems. We work with vulnerable and marginalized populations, usually from strengths-based perspectives, and we increasingly incorporate holistic approaches into our work. These broad areas of focus have been the foundation of my research and scholarly work over the past several years. My research team and I developed the Holistic Arts-Based Program (HAP) and studied its effectiveness for helping vulnerable children develop their self-esteem and resilience. HAP is a time-limited group that teaches mindfulness using art and other experiential methods and that creates space for existential and spiritual material to emerge when relevant.

Vulnerable Children

Much has been written about *vulnerable children*—children who come to the attention of child welfare services due to abuse, neglect, loss, or trauma. These experiences can have deleterious effects on children's physical, cognitive, affective, social, and behavioral development (Flisher et al., 1997). The consequences of child abuse and neglect include aggression and other externalizing behavior problems, anxiety, fear, developmental delays, and poor relationship-building skills (Mabanglo, 2010). We also know that children involved with child welfare services are at high risk for behavior problems and a myriad of difficulties in later life (Racusin, Maerlender, Sengupta, Isquith, & Straus, 2005; Woodruff & Lee, 2011). They often lack many of the characteristics of more resilient children, such as positive self-concept, hopefulness, emotional management in stressful situations, and interpersonal problem-solving skills (Coholic, 2010; Daniel, 2006). This being said, vulnerable children are a diverse group, and they can become productive contributors to society and live successful and fulfilling lives (Flynn, Dudding, & Barber, 2006). Thus, social workers are encouraged to develop best practices and offer services that are relevant and beneficial to them.

Holistic Arts-Based Group

For the past six years, we have facilitated HAP with children aged eight to fourteen who have been referred by the local child welfare agency or children's mental health service. Many of them have suffered trauma or other serious challenges that have negatively impacted their development. These include being abused or neglected by their biological parents, witnessing violence or substance abuse in their families of origin, being taken into care by the child protection authorities, and suffering with anxiety or low self-worth. In just the past three years, over one hundred children have participated in HAP. Criteria for referrals are not stringent: participants are only required to have a need for self-esteem improvement and an ability to participate in a group with peers.

The objectives of HAP include teaching children to better pay attention, listen, and use their imaginations; explore their feelings, thoughts, and behaviors; practice mindfulness-based exercises; and recognize and develop their strengths. A typical two-hour group begins with a presentation of the plan for the session, followed by a primer (i.e., warm-up) activity and arts-based mindfulness exercises connected to a theme consistent with the group's needs, such as dealing with loss. After a break at the halfway point for nutritional snacks, the children engage in more arts-based mindfulness activities and, finally, a closing activity such as "Thumbs Up, Thumbs Down," in which each child takes a turn sharing one thing that was enjoyable during the group and one thing that was challenging. Initially, the arts-based mindfulness exercises are used to build a foundation of skills, such as listening and paying attention, as well as to build group cohesion and trust before they are enlisted to help facilitate mindfulness (Coholic, 2010).

Our work is part of the emergent body of research that explores the effectiveness of mindfulness practices with children (Burke, 2010; Semple, Lee, Rosa, & Miller, 2010). To date, we have reported both quantitative and qualitative research results. Overall, we have found that HAP helps children to develop self-awareness, feel better about themselves, learn the healthy expression of feelings, and develop more effective coping strategies at school and at home (Coholic, 2011b; Coholic & LeBreton, 2009; Coholic, Lougheed, & Cadell, 2009; Coholic, Lougheed, & LeBreton, 2009). HAP also helps children to improve their emotion regulation skills (Coholic, Eys, & Lougheed, 2012).

HAP's methods are highly relevant for social work practice for three primary reasons. First, vulnerable children require relevant and meaningful services; interventions must be adapted to their constellation of strengths and limitations. Thus, HAP facilitates mindfulness exercises using art and other experiential methods rather than asking the participants to simply sit still for any length of time. Second, HAP is grounded in the strengths-based perspective (Saleebey, 2001), which is the foundation of social work. Though the children in the group often present with multiple problems, facilitators always emphasize their strengths. Finally, HAP is holistic, meaning it focuses on not just the children's minds, but also their bodies and spirits, which fits with social work's systemic nature and humanistic values.

Arts-Based Mindfulness Methods

In HAP, mindfulness is understood and facilitated in a way that reflects Jon Kabat-Zinn's (1990) conceptualization: paying attention on purpose, in the present moment, and nonjudgmentally. However, many vulnerable children lack the skills required to learn mindfulness as it is taught in some approaches (e.g., mindfulness-based stress reduction and mindfulness-based cognitive therapy, see chapter 3). They can become easily frustrated and disengaged, they have poor listening skills, and they often do not want to engage in traditional types of treatment (or lack the familial support to do so) (Coholic, 2011b). More basically, many of the children who participate in HAP simply have trouble sitting still and paying attention. This can lead to an almost comical level of chaos from time to time. For example, in the first session of a boys' HAP group, the facilitator was trying to help the participants create group rules when John, a ten-year-old living in foster care and struggling with poor self-esteem, began talking about a series of seemingly unrelated things: his middle name, apples, and Dracula. Then Pete, a highly distractible nine-year-old with poor listening skills, asked, "What does this look like?" as he held a marker as if it were sticking out from his head. At the same time, Jamie and Alex, two ten-year-olds who were also struggling with poor self-esteem, were talking to each other about something completely unrelated to the activity. The facilitators needed a lot of patience to get everyone back on task. Obviously, these are not children who will easily sit still and count their breaths! Typically, they need to be supported to develop their ability to focus and mindfully listen in alternative ways. We have found that they can make sense of mindfulness with the help of activities that are fun and engaging. Doing so is important because learning to be more mindful can develop abilities to regulate attention, which are the building blocks for all types of learning (Sakai, 2012).

Using Art to Facilitate Mindfulness

The arts-based activities are not complicated, require only basic arts supplies, and are easily adapted for specific clientele and problems. One of the ways we introduce mindfulness is with an activity called the "Thought Jar." In this activity, an empty glass jar is half-filled with water. Participants take beads or baubles of various shapes and colors, which represent thoughts and feelings, and drop them into the jar one by one as they state what each object represents. Each participant can have his or her own jar, or a group jar can be used. If there is one jar, it is passed around the group so the participants can take turns swirling and shaking the jar. (Make sure the lid is screwed on tightly!) A discussion can ensue about how we feel when we have many thoughts and feelings "swirling" around in our minds and, after the objects have settled at the bottom of the jar, how we feel when our minds are calmer and more focused. Mindfulness is then introduced as a practice that can help us keep our minds clear. With a clear mind, we can make better choices and decisions rather than acting out feelings. Many of the children take the jars home, and we often refer to the "Thought Jar" to remind them about the purpose of subsequent mindfulness-based activities. Jennifer, a ten-year-old girl with poor emotion regulation skills living in foster care, told us she brought her mindfulness jar to school. She told her class that the beads were "all of my feelings" and explained how they too could calm down their minds. She explained, "If I don't listen in class, I do listen [now], instead of doing something else."

When we later begin to teach the children how to improve their attention through focusing on their breathing, we use art to make the process more workable for them. For example, we encourage them to sculpt or draw what they imagine in their minds as they listen to a relaxation reading or a guided imagery script. Sculpting while they are listening helps them to pay attention both to the reading and to what they are thinking and feeling in the present moment, which is expressed in the clay creations. Over time, as they develop an ability to maintain focus and be more self-aware, they are encouraged to listen to the guided imagery reading and other meditations with their eyes closed and without using the clay. In addition to using mindfulness-based scripts, we use books like *Relax Kids: The Wishing Star* (Viegas, 2004) because the readings are short, engaging, and tend to hold the children's attention. Many of the children ask us for copies of the readings so that they can review them after school and before they go to sleep.

Another activity that can assist the children to discuss their feelings and thoughts and develop their self-awareness is "Me as a Tree." The participants are encouraged to draw themselves as trees. Everyone can draw a tree and the trees are always diverse; diversity in the group can be discussed as a positive characteristic and strength. Facilitators can leave the instructions vague or actively encourage the participants to think about what the tree might look like and what might be around it. After the trees have been drawn, facilitators can ask exploratory questions about the drawing to help develop a child's self-awareness. Oftentimes, a child will draw a tree from a season that has significance to him or her, such as autumn with the leaves falling off the tree. Some pictures are full, with many objects on the page, while others are bare. Recently, a twelve-year-old girl who had poor self-esteem drew a very simple tree with no roots using only two colors; it appeared to be floating in the middle of the page, and there was nothing else around it. When we reflected on this, she admitted that she did not feel grounded or rooted anywhere in her life (she had just left one parent's home to live with her other parent, who had a new spouse). A similar activity is "Me as a River." Often the rivers are drawn full of obstacles such as rocks and twists and turns that symbolize the challenges the children have experienced. Others have bridges that represent new life paths and directions.

Making It Fun

Arts-based and experiential activities can be a lot of fun. In fact, almost all of the children who have participated in HAP have described the program as "fun," and many of them have asked to keep attending HAP once it ended. We have learned that having fun is inextricably linked to the success of HAP. Using interventions which are fun and creative is sometimes the only way to engage children with high needs. They are oftentimes reluctant participants in the helping process, and these methods can help them experience success without focusing on what is going wrong in their lives (Coholic, Lougheed, & Cadell, 2009). This is crucial given the multiple challenges they face at home and at school. As James (1989, p. 13) explained, "It is fun that keeps the child emotionally receptive so that the intense positive messages can slip through her defenses" (p. 13). For example, the goal of one art exercise, "Painting on a Line," is not to focus on a final product (and on how "good" something looks) but on the process of creating something and having fun while doing so. A line of string is hung, and a piece of paper for each group member is clipped to the string using clothespins; we usually attach the ends of the string to two chairs so the participants have to sit or kneel on the ground to reach the sheets of paper. Then, the children are encouraged to paint something without holding onto the paper with their hands. It is a good idea to place newspapers underneath the hanging papers to catch all of the drops of paint!

On occasion, we encounter parents and guardians who have difficulty understanding how their children are developing skills when "all they are doing is arts and crafts." We also know of parents who have kept their children from attending the group as a punishment for misbehaving. We find it important to explain to parents and guardians how developing self-awareness and learning to talk about feelings can be gained through these methods. As Crenshaw and Hardy (2007) stated, it makes more sense to teach relaxation skills, social skills, and problem-solving skills to some at-risk children than to engage them in interventions that look more like "treatment" at first glance.

Group Work

While the methods used in HAP can easily be adapted for individual work, there are good arguments for working with vulnerable children in groups. Many of the challenges they face, such as poor social skills and difficulty coping, are fully expressed in the interpersonal context of the group. This can provide vital learning opportunities. For example, in a boys' group, Justin, a nine-year-old who was in a class at his school for children with behavior problems, ran away from a group session at break time. Alex, who was prone to hoarding art supplies and the fruit offered at break time, had taken all of the plums from the fruit bowl. Once Justin was found and brought back to the group, it was obvious that he had been crying. When he processed his reactions with the group facilitators, he complained that it was "not fair" that Alex had taken all of the plums. He was shocked that we agreed with him and that we had already spoken with Alex about the need to share the fruit. This event, which could only have occurred in the context of a group interaction, was an opportunity for Justin to learn that it is actually possible to address something that has upset him in an effective way rather than escaping his feelings by running away.

In a group, children can practice interpersonal skills, cooperate toward a shared goal, and alleviate isolation (Whitaker, 1975). As Grief and Ephross (2005) explained, individuals in a group can experience support from their peers and learn that they are not alone. By "tackling the process of exclusion" (Adams, Dominelli, & Payne, 2009, p. 123), group work can contribute to resilience building and lessen social isolation (Finn, 2003). Indeed, many of the children who have participated in HAP have expressed that they were able to be authentic in the group and that meeting other children with similar problems was normalizing. As Sue, a thirteen-year-old girl who felt isolated at school and was living in a group home, stated, HAP group "just made me happier. I just got to be myself. That's not usual; [Usually] I try to be somebody else." Similarly, Beth, a ten-year-old girl who frequently got into trouble at school, found out that another girl in her group had attention deficit hyperactivity disorder like she did.

This made her feel "kind of happy" because, she said, "Now I don't have to hide it." The connections the children build contribute to a sense of cohesion amongst them, which is of vital importance to the development of their resilience (Ungar, Brown, Liebenberg, Cheung, & Levine, 2008). In fact, according to the children, the opportunity to "make friends" is one of the key factors contributing to the success of HAP.

Strengths-Based Practice

Another reason the children enjoy HAP is because of its focus on strengths. Focusing on client strengths, rather than deficits and problems, has become an important guiding principle in Western social work over the past two decades (Saleebey, 2001). The "strengths perspective" suggests that by recognizing and emphasizing the personal resources of clients, social workers can make change more likely as well as more effective. Focusing on strengths involves affirming clients' viewpoints and believing they can change (Saleebey, 2001). This approach is vital for working with children in need because they may receive little genuine praise and respect elsewhere in their lives, and they may have few adults or peers who are truly interested in what they think and feel. Laursen and Oliver (2003) argue that strengths-based groups for children instill hope that their lives can be different and help them identify solutions and behaviors that can help them deal with challenges. I am often struck by how marginalized the children we work with are, and how, for some of them, HAP group is the one place in their lives where they do not have to worry about being criticized, punished, or made to feel bad about their behavior.

Rawana and Brownlee (2009) suggest that focusing on strengths should be woven throughout all clinical interactions. In HAP, strengths are emphasized in a variety of ways. We provide regular reinforcement and encouragement; utilize challenges and problems, as well as group activities, as teaching moments (e.g., by stressing what behavior is desired rather than what is going wrong); provide opportunities for the children to be successful (e.g., by asking a child to teach an activity to the group); adapt exercises so that the children can discuss topics that are of interest to them; explicitly point out the children's strengths; and make a clear distinction between the children and their behavior.

Maintaining a focus on strengths is especially important when the children are disruptive, which they inevitably are from time to time, given their histories. This requires a strong level of patience and compassion coupled with a nonjudgmental attitude. Some common disruptive behaviors include not paying attention, interrupting, not staying on task, and not participating in activities. A child might sing or make noises for no apparent reason, talk out loud about something unrelated to the matter at hand, walk around the room without paying attention, or leave an activity to look at art supplies or write on the whiteboard. However, we do not attend to every problem with a correction; this would be onerous to both the facilitators and the participants and would not promote a strengths-focused environment, especially when the behaviors are not especially disruptive. It is important to have realistic expectations and to respond to significant problems in such a way that the children are encouraged and supported to understand the feelings that may have precipitated their behavior. Such responses are especially important when the behaviors are more serious, such as locking the group room door on a participant, threatening to fight someone, rocking a chair back and forth so that it might tip over, touching or pushing another child, or writing on someone else's creative work.

Applying a Strengths Perspective

An extensive case example will illustrate the strengths perspective in action. Comments in parentheses provide a commentary on the actions of the facilitators. One group of boys was creating a "Coat of Arms," a drawing and collage activity for developing cohesion and promoting understanding among group members. The object was to construct a symbol that represented the group—its members, its characteristics, and its aspirations. During the exercise, Fred, a ten-year-old living in foster care who was often bullied at school, wrote on the group's coat of arms, "I am the dumbest." John, a quiet boy who had a history of witnessing abuse in his family, asked the group why Fred wrote what he had written. Without responding, Fred left the table and went to sit on the floor beneath a nearby countertop. The facilitators pointed out that no one in the group believed Fred was dumb, and, furthermore, they believed all of the boys were creative. They further observed that everyone in the group was there to discuss how they felt about themselves, which was important to do. (The facilitators were supportive of Fred despite his disruptive behavior, reminded everyone of the purpose of the group, and encouraged the discussion of feelings.)

Fred began knocking on the underside of the countertop while the other boys continued the activity. Jamie, another group member, asked in a playful manner where Fred had gone. A facilitator explained that Fred was taking a "time out." She then suggested to Fred that he look inside his "Warm Fuzzy" envelope. "Warm Fuzzies" are short, positive notes stored in decorated envelopes that the group participants write to each other during the group break. (She redirected him toward the positive sentiments of his peers rather than focusing on his disruptive behavior.) After he was done reading, Fred returned to sitting underneath the countertop. The facilitators explained that they would have to cover up what he wrote on the coat of arms with something "cool" because what he wrote was not true, and they wanted the coat of arms to be positive. They encouraged him to come and help them do this. This led to a group discussion about things the group thought were "cool." The facilitators continued to encourage Fred to rejoin the group activity by stating that they would like him to share the "great ideas" that he had. They explained that it was important to have everyone's help and to work together. At this suggestion, Fred moved closer to the group but began writing on the large whiteboard instead. He wrote, "I am a loser. I am an idiot." Both of the facilitators, as well as John, told Fred that he was not a loser, and they asked him if there was something he wanted to talk about. The facilitators discussed the importance of developing awareness of one's feelings and learning how to accept and deal with these feelings by linking this to the concept of mindfulness. They also praised the group's attempts to support Fred. (They used this moment to again encourage the discussion of feelings, reinforce the relevance of mindfulness, and validate the supportive behavior of his peers.)

At this point, Fred decided to leave the group room. One of the facilitators followed him, and when they returned to the group, they explained that they had discussed how it feels good when people tell us they care about us and that often when people say hurtful things they are doing so because they feel insecure. (She made this a teaching opportunity—not just for Fred, but for the whole group.) Fred then explained to the group what had been going on for him: he wrote the negative statements about himself because he had a bad day at school and felt like everyone hated him there. After he shared this, he helped get the group snack prepared and reengaged with his fellow group members.

Throughout the incident, the facilitators spent very little time discussing Fred's disruptive behavior. Instead, they focused on the function of his actions (e.g., dealing with difficult feelings) and more adaptive ways to achieve the same ends (e.g., being mindful of his feelings and sharing them).

A Holistic Approach to Mindfulness

The nature of the social work profession, with its emphasis on social justice and working from a person-in-environment perspective, has influenced my research team to consider mindfulness in a holistic way that incorporates the body, the mind, and the spirit. This is different from how mindfulness is often studied within psychology and medicine—that is, divorced from its spiritual roots, with a focus on creating operational definitions and measuring processes and outcomes. It is certainly not my intent to diminish this body of research, as mindfulness is proving effective for a wide variety of problems and people, including children. However, there is also good reason to consider the ancient history of mindfulness and its complexity as a philosophy and practice. Kabat-Zinn (2003) encouraged researchers to contemplate the complexities involved in splitting mindfulness from its holistic roots and argued that it is important to recognize the unique qualities of mindfulness practice so that it is not "simply seized upon as the next promising cognitive behavioral technique...decontextualized, and plugged into a behaviorist paradigm with the aim of driving desirable change" (p. 145). In one of the first books published on mindfulness and social work, Hick (2009) wondered how we can possibly operationally define mindfulness if it is understood as an experiential and embodied practice.

The practice of mindfulness in a traditional Buddhist context places a strong emphasis on nonattachment to outcome, which is a radical departure from most clinical interventions (Kabat-Zinn, 2003). Furthermore, it offers a lifelong practice that includes an understanding that the fruits of practice will take time to unfold and will often occur in unexpected ways. This differs from treatment applications that incorporate mindfulness as simply a technique within a time-limited intervention and that carry expectations of specific outcomes (e.g., symptom reduction). We believe that a holistic mindfulness approach—that is, one that treats mindfulness as a way to connect to something greater than oneself rather than simply a way to better focus one's attention—can be more creatively attuned to people's specific needs and goals and more likely to generate discourse that is spiritual and existential (Gause & Coholic, 2010).

Holistic Practice

An openness to considering the holistic nature of mindfulness goes hand in hand with a willingness to incorporate spirituality as part of a systemic, person-in-environment approach. Within social work, spirituality is understood as "a universal quality of human beings and their cultures related to the quest for meaning, purpose, morality, transcendence, well-being, and profound relationships with ourselves, others, and ultimate reality" (Canda & Furman, 2010, p. 5). Spirituality is considered one of the biopsychosocial dimensions of human existence and can involve the experience of transcending the ordinary limits of body, ego, and linear space and time. In my prior clinical and research experiences with adults, when room was made for spirituality to enter into the therapeutic space, some people explained how being mindful was a spiritual experience for them or was in fact their spirituality. As clients learned mindfulness, existential discussions often arose, particularly about topics such as life after death, suffering, and making meaning of life events (Coholic, 2005, 2007).

Many children who attend HAP are also interested in discussing spiritual issues if they know there is the space to do so (Coholic, 2011a). As McSherry and Smith (2007) observed, children have a range of ideas about spirituality that are usually linked with their stage of cognitive development and prior experiences. Like adults, children may draw on spiritual beliefs to make sense of life events and to cope with crises. In HAP, we make room for a spiritual dimension to emerge by purposely exploring the topic of spirituality. For example, we encourage the children to draw whatever comes to their minds when they think about spirituality. Common pictures include ghosts, rainbows, and angels. Resulting discussions have included issues such as reincarnation, life after death, death and loss, and the nature of life. Often the children have spontaneously raised these topics. Spiritual discussions have also drawn on the children's cultures. For example, when we have had Aboriginal children (children whose families belonged to First Nations cultures indigenous to Canada) in the groups, they have incorporated symbols and teachings from their cultures, such as the Medicine Wheel, into the creative activities. Medicine Wheels are complex circular structures that can help people understand themselves and develop self-awareness (Hart, 2002; Mawhiney & Nabigon, 2011).

Facilitators use moments when children raise spiritual and existential topics to initiate self-awareness-building conversations. For instance, in a girls' group, one of the children stated that something "touched her soul." The rest of the group was asked what the "soul" meant to them. One girl said, "If we had no soul, then we wouldn't be who we are. It's hard to explain, but if you sell your soul then…it's like you're not living" (Coholic, 2011a). Connections between spirituality and art have been discussed by researchers and practitioners (Bhagwan,

2009; Pearson & Wilson, 2009). As Malchiodi (2007) pointed out, since our earliest recorded history, art has served as a means for transformation and has been used to restore physical, psychological, and spiritual well-being. Thus, one should be prepared for these conversations to emerge when using arts-based mindfulness methods.

Summary

Many vulnerable children are in dire need of services. There is tremendous value in teaching them social skills and problem-solving skills, facilitating their strengths, and helping to shore up their defenses so that they can cope more effectively with daily challenges at home and school. However, vulnerable children are often not interested in traditional counseling or do not have the familial support to engage in counseling. Because it is fun and creative, HAP can engage children who would not otherwise seek out counseling.

The arts-based mindfulness methods discussed in this chapter have the potential to help vulnerable children learn to focus on their feelings and thoughts without judging these experiences. This facilitates a self-awareness that lays the foundation for building new skills and fostering greater self-esteem. Furthermore, arts-based mindfulness methods are flexible and easily adapted so that client needs, cultures, and goals can be addressed. Thus, much like more traditional mindfulness practices, HAP methods can easily be adapted for use with a wide variety of client groups and problems. Furthermore, these methods can bring an element of fun and creativity into our practices, which is not only vitally important for our clients and the communities with which we work, but also for ourselves as we seek to be effective and healthy practitioners over the long term.

Mindfulness can be so much more than a set of techniques. However, the philosophy of mindfulness—letting go of attachment to outcome and being in the present—is so different from the dominant societal messages to which we are all exposed. Helping clients to develop critical analyses of societal messages is something that is an integral part of social work practice. Teaching mindfulness to vulnerable children hopefully plants the seeds for more compassionate, thoughtful, engaged, and aware citizens. For a profession concerned not just with personal development, but also with societal change, these are good goals to have—ones that can be fostered by a holistic, creative approach to mindfulness.

References

Adams, R., Dominelli, L., & Payne, M. (2009). *Critical practice in social work* (2nd ed.). New York: Palgrave Macmillan.

Bhagwan, R. (2009). Creating sacred experiences for children as pathways to healing, growth and transformation. *International Journal of Children's Spirituality, 14*, 225-234.

Burke, C. A. (2010). Mindfulness-based approaches with children and adolescents: A preliminary review of current research in an emergent field. *Journal of Child and Family Studies, 19*, 133-144.

Canda, E. R., & Furman, L. (2010). *Spiritual diversity in social work practice: The heart of helping* (2nd ed.). New York: Oxford University Press.

Coholic, D. (2005). The helpfulness of spirituality influenced group work in developing self-awareness and self-esteem: A preliminary investigation. *The Scientific World Journal, 5*, 789-802.

Coholic, D. (2007). Listening to the soul: Spiritually influenced social work group practice. In F. Gale, N. Bolzan, D. McRae-McMahon & K. Kearns (Eds.), *Spirited practices: Spirituality and the helping professions* (pp. 142-150). Sydney, Australia: Allen and Unwin.

Coholic, D. (2010). *Arts activities for children and young people in need: Helping children to develop mindfulness, spiritual awareness and self-esteem*. London: Jessica Kingsley Publishers.

Coholic, D. (2011a). Exploring how young people living in foster care discuss spiritually sensitive themes in a holistic arts-based group program. *Journal of Religion & Spirituality in Social Work: Social Thought, 30*, 193-211.

Coholic, D. (2011b). Exploring the feasibility and benefits of arts-based mindfulness-based practices with young people in need: Aiming to improve aspects of self-awareness and resilience. *Child and Youth Care Forum, 40*, 303-317.

Coholic, D., Eys, M., & Lougheed, S. (2012). Investigating the effectiveness of an arts-based and mindfulness-based group program for the improvement of resilience in children in need. *Journal of Child and Family Studies, 21*, 833-844.

Coholic, D., & LeBreton, J. (2009). Mindfulness-based practices in group work with children and youths in care. In S. Hick (Ed.), *Mindfulness and social work* (pp. 121-134). Chicago: Lyceum Books Inc.

Coholic, D., Lougheed, S., & Cadell, S. (2009). Exploring the helpfulness of arts-based methods with children living in foster care. *Traumatology, 15*, 64-71.

Coholic, D., Lougheed, S., & LeBreton, J. (2009). The helpfulness of holistic arts-based group work with children living in foster care. *Social Work with Groups, 32*, 29-46.

Crenshaw, D. A., & Hardy, K. V. (2007). The crucial role of empathy in breaking the silence of traumatized children in play therapy. *International Journal of Play Therapy, 16*, 160-175.

Daniel, B. (2006). Operationalizing the concept of resilience in child neglect: Case study research. *Child: Care, Health & Development, 32*, 303-309.

Finn, C. (2003). Helping students cope with loss: Incorporating art into group counseling. *Journal for Specialists in Group Work, 28*, 155-165.

Flisher, A. J., Kramenr, R. A., Hoven, C. W., Greenwald, S., Bird, H. R., Canino, G., et al. (1997). Psychosocial characteristics of physically abused children and adolescents. *Journal of American Academy of Child and Adolescent Psychiatry, 36*, 123-131.

Flynn, R. J., Dudding, P. M., & Barber, J. G. (2006). *Promoting resilience in child welfare*. Ottawa, Ontario: University of Ottawa Press.

Gause, R., & Coholic, D. (2010). Mindfulness-based practices as a holistic philosophy and method. *Currents—New Scholarship in the Human Services, 9*, 1-23.

Grief, G., & Ephross, P. (2005). *Group work with populations at risk* (2nd ed.). New York: Oxford University Press.

Hart, M. (2002). *Seeking mino-pimatisiwin: An aboriginal approach to helping*. Halifax, Nova Scotia: Fernwood Publishing.

Hick, S. (Ed.). (2009). *Mindfulness and social work*. Chicago: Lyceum Books.

James, B. (1989). *Treating traumatized children: New insights and creative interventions*. Massachusetts: Lexington.

Kabat-Zinn, J. (1990). *Full catastrophe living: Using the wisdom of your body and mind to face stress, pain and illness*. New York: Delta.

Kabat-Zinn, J. (2003). Mindfulness-based interventions in context: Past, present, and future. *Clinical Psychology: Science and Practice, 10*, 144-156.

Laursen, E. K., & Oliver, V. (2003). Recasting problems as potentials in group work. *Reclaiming Children and Youth, 12*, 46-48.

Mabanglo, M. (2010). Trauma and the effects of violence exposure and abuse on children: A review of the literature. *Smith College Studies in Social Work, 72*, 231-251.

Malchiodi, C. (2007). *The art therapy sourcebook*. New York: McGraw-Hill.

Mawhiney, A., & Nabigon, H. (2011). Aboriginal theory: A Cree medicine wheel guide for healing first nations. In F. Turner (Ed.), *Social work treatment* (5th ed., pp. 15-29). New York: Oxford University Press.

McSherry, W., & Smith, J. (2007). How do children express their spiritual needs? *Paediatric Nursing, 19*, 17-20.

Pearson, M., & Wilson, H. (2009). *Using expressive arts to work with mind, body and emotions: Theory and practice*. Philadelphia, PA: Jessica Kingsley Publishers.

Racusin, R., Maerlender, A., Sengupta, A., Isquith, P., & Straus, M. (2005). Psychosocial treatment of children in foster care: A review. *Community Mental Health Journal, 41*, 199-221.

Rawana, E., & Brownlee, K. (2009). Making the possible probable: A strength-based assessment and intervention framework for clinical work with parents, children, and adolescents. *Families in Society: The Journal of Contemporary Social Services, 90*, 255-260.

Sakai, J. (2012). Educational games to train middle schoolers' attention, empathy. Retrieved June 10, 2012, from http://www.news.wisc.edu/releases/17368

Saleebey, D. (Ed.). (2001). *The strengths perspective in social work practice* (3rd ed.). Boston: Allyn & Bacon.

Semple, R., Lee, J., Rosa, D., & Miller, L. (2010). A randomized trial of mindfulness-based cognitive therapy for children: Promoting mindful attention to enhance social-emotional resiliency in children. *Journal of Child and Family Studies, 19*, 218-229.

Ungar, M., Brown, M., Liebenberg, L., Cheung, M., & Levine, K. (2008). Distinguishing differences in pathways to resilience among Canadian youth. *Canadian Journal of Community Mental Health, 27*, 1-13.

Viegas, M. (2004). *Relax kids: The wishing Star: 52 magical meditations for children*. New York: Our Street Books.

Whitaker, D. (1975). Some conditions for effective work with groups. *British Journal of Social Work, 5*, 421-439.

Woodruff, K., & Lee, B. (2011). Identifying and predicting problem behavior trajectories among pre-school children investigated for child abuse and neglect. *Child Abuse & Neglect, 35*, 491-503.

CHAPTER 7

Doing ACT Briefly: The Practice of Focused Acceptance and Commitment Therapy

Tom Linde, MSW

Private Practice
Group Health Cooperative Family Medicine Residency,
Seattle, Washington

Kirk Strosahl, PhD

Mountainview Consulting Group
Central Washington Family Medicine, Family Medicine
Residency, Yakima, Washington

In the last two decades, there have been notable shifts in the way clinical services are delivered in the United States. First and foremost has been the impact of the managed care "revolution" on the practice of psychotherapy. Clinicians are now asked to conduct briefer episodes of therapy while simultaneously maintaining the same (or improved) clinical outcomes. In other words, they are asked to see more clients, in less time, at lower cost, and with better results. Indeed, individual patient-consumers, who now manage high deductibles, co-payments, and other increased costs, are echoing the demand for efficiency and demonstrable effectiveness.

Secondly, there have been major reductions in funding for community-based treatment programs. According to one report issued by the Substance Abuse and Mental Health Services Administration (SAMHSA, 2010), behavioral health expenditures in the public sector have fallen to 13.9 percent of total public health care dollars spent, compared to 19.9 percent in 1985. These funding reductions have led to a significant erosion of the services in the community mental health system and a shifting of people with mental disorders and chemical addiction into other service settings.

This trend has contributed to another, though not altogether negative, change: out of necessity, clinical social work has been expanded into settings that traditionally have not had such services. A prime example is the placement of clinical social workers in the primary care setting, often as part of the patient centered medical home model that is beginning to redefine our system of healthcare (Starfield, 2010). The majority of those with treatable mental illnesses will never encounter a mental health professional; however, they will often seek *medical* care. This has given rise to a burgeoning body of research and literature on brief behavioral health practices in primary care (see Robinson, Gould, & Strosahl, 2010). Clinical social workers are also being pressed into service in school-based programs, jails, crisis centers, and other settings where sustained, regular contact with clients is unlikely.

Finally, managed care has helped give rise to an upsurge of interest in brief approaches such as solution-focused therapy (De Shazer, 1991), problem-focused therapy (Watzlawick, Weakland, & Fisch, 1974), and narrative therapy (White & Epston, 1990). However, practical adoption of these approaches in clinical social work has waxed and waned over the years. One problem is that the advocates of these models have not adequately conducted the research needed to show they actually work. For example, in the twenty-five years since it was introduced, narrative therapy has been evaluated in just one uncontrolled study (Vromans & Schweitzer, 2010). Brief solution-focused therapy has been examined in several "post hoc" research studies, but never in a randomized trial comparing it with a wait list control group or with another credible treatment. More concerning is that meta-analyses of existing studies suggest that the effect size of solution-focused therapy is weak to modest at best (Gingerich & Eisengart, 2000; Kim, 2008). A consequence of this lack of interest in clinical research is that iterative improvements to these brief methods have not occurred. Even negative research findings lead to positive refinements. This lack of back-and-forth has led to the gradual ossification of the movement. Consequently, there have been few notable innovations in these popular brief therapy approaches since their introduction.

At the same time, institutions are requiring clinicians to use evidence-based treatments, most of which are described in treatment manuals that are dense and hard to follow. An even bigger problem is that contemporary approaches to treatment have emphasized disorder-specific research, such that each mental disorder seems to require a specialized treatment. This places the clinician in a difficult position: so many treatment manuals, so little time! What is needed is a simple, straightforward, evidence-based approach that allows the therapist to apply the same principles across a broad range of problems. Enter focused acceptance and commitment therapy, or FACT.

In this chapter, we will introduce the reader to the basic principles of using acceptance and commitment therapy (Hayes, Strosahl, & Wilson, 1999; chapter 1 of this volume) as a brief intervention. To set the stage, it will first be necessary to reassess some of our cherished assumptions about what clients want in therapy, how the process works, and how people change. In our experience, most of the barriers to embracing brief therapy are psychological. Clinicians can easily get lost in their assumptions about what is possible and what is not, and prematurely dismiss brief interventions as a gimmick (while simultaneously embracing actual gimmicks). Second, we will examine the three core components of the FACT approach: focusing questions, case formulation, and targeting. Finally, we will use a case example to highlight how these components work in the therapeutic conversation.

Cherished Assumptions: Fact or Fiction?

We hear many objections to the idea that clients can fundamentally change in only one or two sessions: "It takes longer to form a therapeutic relationship, and without the relationship, clients don't change." "It takes a couple of sessions just to get to know the client." "Trying to get someone to change before you know a lot about them is dangerous." "People with complex problems developed them over years, and they aren't going to change overnight." These statements are often made with a tone of certainty, as if there is no debate. But if it is our job in some ways to assist clients in modifying maladaptive personal "truths," we must of course be willing to challenge our own assumptions as well. Let's take a look at what the data say.

Fact: Clients Prefer Parsimonious Treatment

Clients enter therapy because they are distressed, and as their distress dissipates, they are less inclined to return for additional sessions (Brown & Jones, 2005). This suggests that their primary motives in seeking help are to receive emotional reassurance and to get practical problem-solving advice. These two outcomes are easily achieved for most clients within the first few sessions of therapy. A startling fact is that most clients will end therapy quickly. Between 30 and 40 percent of clients drop out of treatment without consulting their therapist (Olfson et al., 2009; Talmon, 1990). In one study of more than nine thousand clients, over 85 percent had ended treatment by the fifth session. Most importantly, the modal (i.e., the most frequently occurring result in the sample) number of psychotherapy visits is *just one* (Brown & Jones, 2005). In traditional psychotherapy, the first session is usually devoted to taking a history and preparing a treatment plan. Interventions are usually reserved for later sessions because we assume they must be designed around a protracted initial evaluation. The reality is that a sizable number of clients will not return for a second visit. Furthermore, the most robust predictor of whether a client will stay in therapy is continued high levels of psychological distress (Brown & Jones, 2005). In other words, clients in long-term therapy are not necessarily getting better; they may be staying in therapy because *it isn't working*. On the other hand, there is increasing evidence that even one session of therapy can have substantial impact with a surprisingly wide range of mental health problems (Campbell, 2012).

Interestingly, a quality-improvement study involving several hundred clients conducted at the second author's mental health center showed no differences in outcomes between clients who dropped out of therapy versus those who stayed in. In addition, there were no outcome differences between clients seen once versus clients who had multiple therapy sessions. The only difference was that clients who dropped out reported lower levels of satisfaction with their therapist and their overall care experience. So if we are to be guided by the preponderant evidence, it appears that most clients prefer brief therapy. It is worth recognizing that although a therapy session takes only an hour of the therapist's time, it consumes far more for the client, who may have to hire a babysitter, take unpaid time from work, commute to and from the appointment, and pay for gas on top of it all. In reality, therapy is an inconvenience for most clients.

Fiction: The Benefits of Therapy Are Dependent on the Number of Sessions

This assumption means that the benefits of therapy accrue over time. In other words, the more therapy, the better the outcome. This is sometimes referred to as the "dose effect." The seminal study in this area was published more than twenty-five years ago (Howard, Kopta, Krause, & Orlinsky, 1986) and continues to impact many managed care certification and case review policies. First, approximately 15 percent of clients experience improvements before they arrive for the first session. It appears that the decision to seek help is itself helpful. The most important finding was that 50 percent of the total therapeutic benefit is achieved by the eighth session. It is indeed the case that additional benefits are received in longer treatment, but after the eighth session, progress slows so much that therapy ceases to be cost-effective. A more recent study showed that clients who underwent brief treatments experienced relatively rapid rates of change compared with clients who received longer-term treatment. Interestingly, the number of therapy sessions was not a significant predictor of amount of clinical change (Baldwin, Berkeljon, Atkins, Olsen, & Nielsen, 2009).

Fiction: Longer Therapies Produce More Durable Benefits

A related assumption is that longer-term treatment is superior in preventing relapse; for example, sixteen sessions of cognitive therapy should produce longer-lasting improvements than eight sessions. A recent test of this assumption showed that the degree of symptom-reduction and long-term improvement in social functioning was just as great in an eight-session treatment as in a sixteen-session treatment (Molenaar et al., 2011). Similar results have been found in studies comparing short- and long-term family therapy for anorexia (Lock, Agras, Bryson, & Kraemer, 2005), short- and long-term family-based treatments for childhood behavior problems (Smyrnios & Kirkby, 1993), and brief and longer-term cognitive behavioral therapy for post-traumatic stress disorder (Sijbrandij et al., 2007). This finding has also been observed with depression and a wide range of anxiety disorders (see Cape, Whittington, Buszewicz, Wallace, & Underwood, 2010 for a review).

Fact: Brief Interventions Produce Wide Spectrum Change

Treatments that reduce symptoms of distress but fail to alter longer-term patterns of maladaptive behavior will create a revolving-door problem. Clients have to seek therapy repeatedly to address new problems created by underlying and often long-standing issues. A well-researched and respected model of change in psychotherapy holds that there are three distinct changes associated with therapy that occur at different points in the process (Howard, Lueger, Maling, & Martinovich, 1993). The first phase, remoralization, involves a subjective sense of improvement as the client starts to do something about the problem. In the second phase, remediation, clinical symptoms are reduced to low levels. In the final phase, rehabilitation, stable improvements in functioning begin to appear. Since rehabilitation is the slowest benefit to develop, the argument could be made that brief interventions will have little impact on long-term functional status.

However, in a recent study of a brief intervention program in a primary care clinic, clients receiving two or more sessions showed significant change in all three phases (Bryan, Morrow, & Appolonio, 2009). Another recent study examined the effectiveness of a two- to four-session cognitive behavioral intervention for regular amphetamine users and found a significant increase in the probability of abstinence (Baker et al., 2005). These studies suggest that even brief interventions can have a substantial and lasting impact.

Fiction: Rapid Gains Are a Rare Event in Therapy

The most likely single outcome of therapy is that the client will exhibit marked improvements within the first four sessions. It is estimated that 40 to 45 percent of depressed clients exhibit sudden large gains within the first two to four treatment sessions (Doane, Feeny, & Zoellner, 2010; Tang, DeRubeis, Hollon, Amsterdam, & Shelton,

2007). Similarly impressive results have been seen in clients receiving therapy for post-traumatic stress disorder (52 percent; Doane, Feeny, & Zoellner, 2010), binge eating (62 percent; Grilo, Masheb, & Wilson, 2006), and irritable bowel syndrome (30 percent; Lackner et al., 2010). Furthermore, rapid clinical response is associated with long-term improvements in functioning as well as a long-term protection against relapse (see Aderka, Nickerson, Boe, & Hoffman, 2012 for a meta-analysis of the rapid response research). Rapid gains in therapy are not the exception, but the rule.

Principles of Focused Acceptance and Commitment Therapy

As the preceding section suggests, there is plenty of reason for optimism about the impact of very brief interventions. At the same time, our field needs an approach that can produce significant change in a large percentage of clients in almost any situation. FACT is a condensed version of acceptance and commitment therapy and is intended for use where brief interventions are preferred. In this section, we will provide a short overview of the core principles underlying FACT.

An Overview of FACT

One of the undeniable facts of human existence is that it is so hard for us to be happy. This is because our capacity for language is a double-edged sword. For example, on one hand it allows us to imagine a variety of futures so that we may problem solve, plan, and organize to achieve desired ends. On the other hand, we can also imagine a better life, determine that it is not achievable, and fall into helpless passivity. This and other language processes that help us transcend life's difficulties cause suffering when misapplied. And so happiness is not the natural resting state of human existence. Rather, suffering is ubiquitous because language and cognition are both essential and destructive.

THE SIRENS OF SUFFERING

In FACT, there are three processes related to the "dark side" of language: fusion, rule-following, and avoidance. Simply stated, *fusion* means losing perspective on thoughts, feelings, memories, and sensations. We cease to see thoughts as just thoughts, memories as memories, and so on. Instead, these inner experiences begin to dominate our conception of ourselves. We look inside at what we assume to be our own identity, and it does not look pretty. To paraphrase the comic strip character Pogo, "I have met the enemy and it is me."

The second siren, *rule-following*, like other language processes, is handy in many contexts. When in peril, we should seek safety. If hungry, we should find food. Rules such as these and countless others help us navigate everyday decisions efficiently. But then we come upon negative thoughts, feelings, and memories. Because we are socialized to believe that being healthy is to be free of such things, we identify them as threats to our well-being. This sets off rules that say that we should analyze what is going on and then control or eliminate it in the service of achieving wellness. Even though we all have ample personal evidence to show that painful, unwanted private experiences are *not* subject to voluntary control, we remain "law-abiding citizens," as it were, adhering to impossible rules rather than learning from experience.

The third siren, *avoidance*, stems from the other two. To lead a full life, one with meaning, we inevitably encounter experiences that are distressing: challenge, failure, rejection, physical pain, loneliness, and so forth. If this is all seen as threatening and we are unwilling to tolerate it, we must then restrict our range of activity. This is behavioral avoidance. Its counterpart, emotional avoidance, may come in a variety of forms: distraction, worrying about trivial concerns, attempting to suppress thoughts, emotions, or memories, endlessly ruminating about past failures and why we can't be happy like others, and so on. As we attempt to free ourselves from distressing, unwanted private experiences, the paradoxical result is that they become more intrusive and dominant. In order to avoid something, we must be vigilant for it, and darn if it isn't there every time we check!

In this way, suffering and emotional and behavioral avoidance act in a self-perpetuating cycle that can take many forms. We withdraw from activity suspected of causing distress, and as we become less engaged with the world, we have more opportunity to ruminate, thus magnifying the distress and prompting more avoidance. We find ourselves less involved with meaningful pursuits. We may escalate avoidance in ways that compound the problem, perhaps making rash decisions, perhaps avoiding decisions altogether. We look for numbing or escape with chemicals, food, self-harm, and suicidal thinking and behavior. Even television can provide this numbing and escape. Like alcohol, television in moderation is benign for most of us, but the "dosage" may begin to displace physical, intellectual, and social activity, allowing us the vicarious experience of rich lives while making our own lives seem impoverished in comparison.

In FACT, it is not painful private experience that is unhealthy. Rather, what is unhealthy is the attempt to avoid, control, or suppress such experience. Emotion control is not the solution; it is the problem. When we do things that really matter—when we broaden rather than constrict our lives—failure, rejection, reminders of trauma, and a host of other unwanted experiences await us. However, it is precisely in these situations where vitality, purpose, and meaning are achieved. Pain may be inevitable, but it is dignified when we do what matters. Unfortunately, most clients enter therapy with the opposite view—that painful private experiences are the "enemy" of health and must be vanquished. They hope that the clinician will help them with an unachievable goal.

THE ROAD TO VITALITY

In FACT, we quickly help the client reframe the problem as following rules that invite failure (e.g., not having anxiety in a situation that is by definition anxiety producing) and divert the focus away from what really matters (e.g., participating in the situation because it is important). This is achieved using a sequence of focusing questions, described below, that bring clients into contact with the futility of their struggle. Once they recognize that their rules do not produce the results they expect, they are able to try something different. For many, this is all they need to begin to explore new options.

Other clients will be "stuck" and will require more skills to escape their unworkable patterns. We teach them to make room for distressing private experience, to stand in the presence of socially programmed rules and self-generated narratives without being dominated by them, and to pursue what they value. This is achieved by teaching skills that promote acceptance, mindfulness, and values-based living. To this end, there are a variety of FACT-case formulation and treatment-planning tools available. Space allows us to describe just a few here, but the interested reader can learn much more from a recent text describing the approach in detail (Strosahl, Robinson, & Gustavsson, 2012).

Practicing FACT: Focused Interviewing

The first step in promoting radical change in just a few sessions starts with the social worker rapidly focusing the therapeutic conversation on the core themes of rule following, emotional avoidance, and the unworkable results the client is getting. We will demonstrate with a case example.

- ### Case Example: Madrigal

Madrigal is an eighteen-year-old single Latina who was referred by her primary care doctor for treatment of depression. Her depression screening score at her medical visit was in the "moderately severe" range. Madrigal stated that her depression started about six months earlier following the suicide of her cousin, Gilberto. Prior to that, she had done very well in high school, getting As and Bs. She was involved in after-school clubs and activities and was in line to get a college scholarship. Since the suicide, her grades had plummeted and she had withdrawn from most of her extracurricular and social activities. Madrigal's family immigrated to the United States when she was six years old. Both of her parents are monolingual and work in the orchards.

Madrigal had been very close to her cousin since childhood. As they reached early adolescence, Gilberto began to have legal problems and did poorly in school. Even though he was struggling, they always remained friends. As Gilberto developed a reputation as a gang "homie," Madrigal's father prohibited him from coming to visit her. This led to intense anger on her part, and she began fighting with her parents over little things.

Gilberto eventually got involved with a woman who was a few years older than him. Madrigal thought she was unsuitable for Gilberto. This led to Madrigal and Gilberto having a falling out just a few months before his death. Sadly, Gilberto killed himself after discovering that his girlfriend was sleeping with someone else.

FACT Focusing Questions: Determining Workability

The purpose of focusing questions is to rapidly pinpoint the "problem" as the client sees it and then to redefine the problem as being the result of repeated efforts to control thoughts and feelings. The goal is to help clients appreciate that their coping strategies are counterproductive, regardless of what their rules tell them.

The sequence of questions is as follows:

1. What are you seeking in coming here, and what would "better" look like?

2. What have you tried already to get better?

3. How have these strategies worked up to now?

4. What has this cost you?

CLINICAL DIALOGUE: THE WORKABILITY INTERVENTION

Early in this first meeting, Madrigal's social worker establishes a focus by tying her behavior directly to the unwanted results.

Social Worker: Madrigal, tell me what you hoped to gain from coming here today. What would tell you that our meeting had been helpful and that you were doing better?

Madrigal: I just feel bad inside all the time. I don't want to be around my friends. I don't care about doing anything. I feel like I can't be who I was before. I used to laugh a lot and always was the one my friends came to for advice. My grades used to be good. Now it's just…just not like that at all.

Social Worker: So, tell me, what have you tried to get back to your old self, to the way you were?

Madrigal: I try to make myself busy and it helps for a little bit, and then I start to feel bad again. I just tell myself to be positive and act happy. I don't let myself think about Gilberto. When my parents try to talk to me about my problem, I don't want to talk with them. They kicked him out so there is no way they would understand.

Social Worker: So, it sounds like you try to stay active as one strategy. You also try to convince yourself to feel differently. You don't let yourself think about what happened to Gilberto and the effect it has had on you. And you don't talk to your parents about this because you are still mad at them. Do you feel that these strategies are working, not working, or somewhere in between?

Madrigal: I've been feeling worse, so…I don't know… I guess, like, they're not working?

Social Worker: Is it possible that some of these strategies might actually be making things worse? For example, trying not to think about Gilberto's death: how is that working?

Madrigal: (*Becoming tearful.*) I can't stop thinking about it. It just comes over me. Like when I'm sleeping and I wake up, it is the first thing on my mind. Then I try to push it out of my mind because I have to go to school.

Social Worker: Does it work to push it out of your mind?

Madrigal: Not really. I can't concentrate at school. I just start remembering things Gilberto and I did when we were young. I think about why he didn't call me, why he didn't let me help him. I think that maybe I let him down—that I wasn't there for him when he needed me, you know?

Social Worker: So, I guess what you are saying is that you can't really push this away, even though you want to; and the effort you have to put into pushing this away is taking all of your energy away from school, your friends, and the things you enjoy doing. Is that right?

Setting the Stage: What Kind of Life Would You Choose, If You Could Choose?

There are two primary tasks in FACT. One is helping bring about a new definition of the problem, such that the client sees it in a different light and feels empowered to approach it from a new angle. Second, since the antidote to emotional avoidance is emotional approach, the client has to have a powerful motivating reason for being willing to experience pain. FACT is not about stewing in emotions for the sake of stewing. It is the pursuit of valued living that justifies accepting and tolerating distressing private experience.

CLINICAL DIALOGUE: THE LIFE PATH ASSESSMENT

Social Worker: So it sounds like there is something going on here. On the one hand (*gestures with her left hand*), you have this life that you want to have where you do good in your studies, you are trusted and sought out by your friends, and you are on track to go to college. On the other hand (*gestures with her right hand*), you have the pain of losing Gilberto and you have the desire not to feel this pain. So you don't let yourself think about it, you retreat from your friends, you don't talk to your parents, you stay in your room—things like that.

Madrigal: (*Confirms with a nod.*)

Social Worker: So, let's imagine that this is a life path you are walking on (*spreads hands out in front of Madrigal*). On this end is the life you would like to be living, and on this end is your desire to control or stop your sadness, your anger, and your guilt. And let's say that you get to pick where you want to be on this life path, and you also get to pick the direction you are moving in every day. If you can, put your finger somewhere between the one hand and the other hand to tell me where you think you are. (*Madrigal places her hand very close to the "control" hand.*) Now, point in the direction you are moving in today. (*Madrigal points in the direction of control.*) So, my question is, do you want to be here and head in the direction you are headed?

Madrigal:	No, I want to be over here (*gestures toward the "vital living" hand*).
Social Worker:	Because the only way you can keep from feeling sad, mad, and guilty is to stay over here (*points to the control hand*). But to do that means you can't go over here (*points to vital living hand*). So, if you could choose, would you choose to go in this direction (*points to vital living hand*), knowing that you would no longer be able to avoid feeling sad, mad, or guilty about Gilberto's death?
Madrigal:	Yeah, it would be scary for me. I'm not sure how I'd react or what would happen to me. I think I might just fall apart.
Social Worker:	Exactly! Because you've never really "done" these feelings before, so how could you know how you will react?

Case Formulation in FACT: The Four Square Analysis

The next step is to condense the information that has been gathered in a way that informs treatment. The Four Square Analysis fits this purpose. The Four Square is a 2 by 2 matrix: the horizontal axis is divided between behaviors that are working and behaviors that are not working; the vertical axis is divided between public behaviors (those behaviors that can be seen by others) and private behaviors (such as thoughts, feelings, memories, or physical sensations). The social worker can either complete a four square analysis mentally, or take a few minutes to sketch out the analysis on a notepad or whiteboard. Either way, this analysis helps determine the best "leverage points" with the client.

Madrigal's Four Square Analysis

Madrigal's dilemma is a common one for clients who have fallen into the trap of emotional and behavioral avoidance. To begin moving in the direction of vital living, Madrigal must be able to make voluntary contact with what is being avoided. She needs some help learning to *accept* the presence of her painful thoughts and emotions without struggle or judgment. This will require her to be able to see her emotions as just emotions and her thoughts as just thoughts, as if she were simply observing them.

For example, Madrigal has developed a narrative about Gilberto's suicide that is an emotional land mine: she blames her parents for forcing Gilberto out of her life, but blames herself for not disobeying her parents and maintaining regular contact with him. When her mind starts "chattering" to her about the suicide, it is important that she see this chatter as simply a story her mind has created to make some sense of the suicide and to assign blame and responsibility for such an unthinkable act. So, in addition to feeling sad and mad, Madrigal must also be able to adopt an *observer role* when her mind begins to tell this story.

		Workability	
Behavior		Not working (do less)	More workable (do more)
	Public	• Avoiding friends at school • Not doing school work and letting grades go down • Dropping out of school activities • Not discussing her anger with parents	• Willing to seek help • Does have social connections available to her at school • Has shown ability to organize herself if she is motivated
	Private	• Avoids connecting with sadness, grief, and anger • Identified with her "story" that she is responsible for Gilberto's suicide	• Ability to observe and report on her thoughts and emotions • Ability to get some perspective on her avoidance • Has strong values about education and improving herself • Has strong pro-social motives

Figure 7.1   Madrigal's four square analysis.

Clinical Dialogue

The social worker is now in a position to use the information derived from the four square analysis to help Madrigal engage in more workable behaviors—or in other words, to really *engage* in her life.

Social Worker: That's cool! You want to start moving in that direction. Now, what step could you take, no matter how small, that would tell you that you were moving in the direction of the life you want to live?

Madrigal: Umm…let's see….I have a friend, Jennifer, who I used to talk to about everything. I've been avoiding her for weeks, always making up some kind of excuse when she wants to do something with me. Now she has stopped talking to me; I think I hurt her feelings or something. So, I could go up to her and say, you know…something….I could tell her what I've been going through because no one at school knows about any of this.

Social Worker: So, let's say you did that, which sounds good to me, but what do you think will happen inside when you open up to her about this?

Madrigal: I'm afraid I might just start sobbing or something. The pain might be more than I can handle. I would be embarrassed if this happened around other people. Um…she might ask me about why Gilberto and I weren't talking. Then I'd feel really guilty.

Social Worker: Okay, so in order to take even a small step in that direction, you might end up face to face with all this stuff you are carrying around. Would it be okay for you just to let it be there and do nothing to try to change it? If your mind starts yakking at you about how you let Gilberto down, could you just notice that it's just your mind talking? It isn't like truth handed down from God; it is just your mind's story about all this.

Madrigal: But I *did* let him down! When he needed me the most, I wasn't there for him.

Social Worker: I know you are devastated that he killed himself and that you are feeling sad and guilty that he did that without reaching out to you. And at the same time, your mind is just telling a story about what you did or didn't do. Your mind has no way of knowing what Gilberto was going through, or even whether he thought of you or thought you could help him. But when your mind says, "But I *did* let him down," it can be persuasive.

Madrigal: You mean that I'm not the same as my mind…? Um…this is kind of different from what I always thought.

Social Worker: You have a mind, but you are not the same as your mind. You have sadness here, but you are not the same as your sadness. You have guilt here, but you are not the same as your guilt. You are the human being who experiences these things. You are the one who hears your mind's story about letting Gilberto down. You are not the same as the story.

Madrigal: I think I get what you are saying. I don't know how much of it I'll remember to use when I start feeling bad.

Social Worker: Good point. It is easy to talk about this stuff, but in practice, it is hard to do because your mind is tricky. It will try to rope you into believing that the story *is* real and you *are* guilty. So, if you get lost in this, here's something you can do: close your eyes and imagine that you're lying on your back in the sun watching the clouds move around in the sky. Try to put each emotion, thought, or memory on a cloud and just let it move to the horizon the way clouds do. You can just notice each cloud and allow it to do its thing. Let's practice this a little before we wrap up

> today. (*A short guided imagery exercise ensues, in which the worker leads Madrigal through a process of relaxing and then adopting an objective stance toward all thoughts and feelings that arise.*)

Case Outcome

Madrigal returned for her first and only follow-up visit two weeks later. Her depression screening showed she was in the "normal" range. She had followed through with her plan to talk with Jennifer. She had a variety of emotional "moments" but did not run from them. She discussed her guilt, and Jennifer reminded her that Gilberto chose to end his life and that Madrigal had no power to influence him. In effect, Jennifer had added new "content" to Madrigal's story, an added bonus that would not have occurred if she had not been willing to take the step of opening up. She and Jennifer had continued hanging out together. Now, Madrigal was considering sitting down and hashing out her angry feelings with her parents.

Summary: Walking Through the Door

In this chapter, we have briefly described the core operating assumptions and principles of FACT. The approach can be applied to any number of life situations because the themes of acceptance, mindfulness, and valued living are all intimately tied to the human condition. When clients get wind of an alternative to the unworkable outcomes of rule following and avoidance, they are in a position to pursue life in a new, more robust way. As we like to say, the FACT therapist opens the door, but it is the patient who walks through. This is the essence of brief therapy for radical change.

References

Aderka, I., Nickerson, A., Boe, H., & Hoffman, S. (2012). Sudden gains during psychological treatments of anxiety and depression: A meta-analysis. *Journal of Consulting and Clinical Psychology, 80,* 93-101.

Baker, A., Lee, N., Claire, M., Lewin, T., Grant, T., Pohlman, S., et al. (2005). Brief cognitive behavioural interventions for regular amphetamine users: A step in the right direction. *Addiction, 100,* 367-378.

Baldwin, S., Berkeljon, A., Atkins, D., Olsen, J., & Nielsen, S. (2009). Rates of change in naturalistic psychotherapy: Contrasting dose-effect and good-enough level models of change. *Journal of Consulting and Clinical Psychology, 77,* 203-211.

Brown, G., & Jones, E. (2005). Implementation of a feedback system in a managed care environment: What are patients teaching us? *Journal of Clinical Psychology, 61,* 187-198.

Bryan, C., Morrow, C., & Appolonio, K. (2009). Impact of behavioral health consultant interventions on patient symptoms and functioning in an integrated family medicine clinic. *Journal of Clinical Psychology, 65,* 281-293.

Campbell, A. (2012). Single-session approaches to therapy: Time to review. *Australian & New Zealand Journal of Family Therapy, 33,* 15-26.

Cape, J., Whittington, C., Buszewicz, M., Wallace, P., & Underwood, L. (2010). Brief psychological therapies for anxiety and depression in primary care: Meta-analysis and meta-regression. *BMC Medicine, 8,* 38.

De Shazer, S. (1991). *Putting difference to work.* New York: W. W. Norton.

Doane, L., Feeny, N., & Zoellner, L. (2010). A preliminary investigation of sudden gains in exposure therapy for PTSD. *Behaviour Research and Therapy, 48,* 555-560.

Gingerich, W., & Eisengart, S. (2000). Solution-focused brief therapy: A review of outcome research. *Family Process, 39,* 477-498.

Grilo, C. M., Masheb, R. M., & Wilson, G. T. (2006). Rapid response to treatment for binge eating disorder. *Journal of Consulting and Clinical Psychology, 74,* 602-613.

Hayes, S. C., Strosahl, K., & Wilson, K. G. (1999). *Acceptance and commitment therapy: An experiential approach to behavior change.* New York: Guilford Press.

Howard, K., Kopta, S., Krause, M., & Orlinsky, D. (1986). The dose-effect relationship in psychotherapy. *American Psychologist, 41,* 159-164.

Howard, K., Lueger, R., Maling, M., & Martinovich, Z. (1993). A phase model of psychotherapy: Causal mediation of outcome. *Journal of Consulting and Clinical Psychology, 51,* 1059-1064.

Kim, J. (2008). Examining the effectiveness of solution-focused brief therapy: A meta-analysis. *Research on Social Work Practice, 18,* 107-116.

Lackner, J., Gudleski, G., Keefer, L., Krasner, S., Powell, C., & Katz, L. (2010). Rapid response to cognitive behavior therapy predicts treatment outcome in patients with irritable bowel syndrome. *Clinical Gastroenterology and Hepatology, 8*, 426-432.

Lock, J., Agras, S., Bryson, S., & Kraemer, H. (2005). A comparison of short- and long-term family therapy for anorexia nervosa. *Journal of the Academy of Child and Adolescent Psychiatry, 44*, 632-639.

Molenaar, P. J., Boom, Y., Peen, J., Schoevers, R. A., Van, R., & Dekker, J. J. (2011). Is there a dose-effect relationship between the number of psychotherapy sessions and improvement of social functioning? *British Journal of Clinical Psychology, 50*, 268-282.

Olfson, M., Mojtabai, R., Sampson, N. A., Hwang, I., Druss, B., Wang, P. S., et al. (2009). Dropout from outpatient mental health care in the United States. *Psychiatric Services, 60*, 898-907.

Robinson, P., Gould, D. & Strosahl, K. (2010). *Real behavior change in primary care: Improving patient outcomes and increasing job satisfaction.* Oakland, CA: New Harbinger.

Sijbrandij, M., Olff, M., Reistsma, J., Carlier, I., de Vries, M., & Gersons, B. (2007). Treatment of acute posttraumatic stress disorder with brief cognitive-behavioral therapy: A randomized controlled trial. *American Journal of Psychiatry, 164*, 82-90.

Smyrnios, K., & Kirkby, R. (1993). Long-term comparison of brief versus unlimited psychodynamic treatment of children and their parents. *Journal of Consulting and Clinical Psychology, 61*, 1020-1027.

Starfield, B. (2010) Reinventing primary care: Lessons from Canada for the United States. *Health Affairs, 29*, 1030–1036.

Strosahl, K., Robinson, P. & Gustavsson, T. (2012). *Brief interventions for radical change: Principles and practice of focused acceptance and commitment therapy.* Oakland, CA: New Harbinger.

Substance Abuse Mental Health Services Administration (SAHSA). (2010) *Mental health, United States, 2010.* Available from US Department of Health and Human Services, Washington, DC.

Talmon, M. (1990). *Single session therapy: Maximizing the effect of the first (and often only) therapeutic encounter.* San Francisco: Jossey-Bass.

Tang, T., DeRubeis, R., Hollon, S., Amsterdam, J., & Shelton, R. (2007). Sudden gains in cognitive therapy for depression and depression relapse/recurrence. *Journal of Consulting and Clinical Psychology, 75*, 404-408.

Vromans, L., & Schweitzer, R. D. (2010). Narrative therapy for adults with major depressive disorder: Improved symptom and interpersonal outcomes. *Psychotherapy Research, 19*, 1-12.

Watzlawick, P., Weakland, J., & Fisch, R. (1974). *Change: Principles of problem formation and problem resolution.* New York: W. W. Norton.

White, M., & Epston, D. (1990). *Narrative means to therapeutic ends.* New York: W. W. Norton.

CHAPTER 8

In Pursuit of Excellence: Developing Competencies for Delivery of Brief Interventions

Patricia J. Robinson, PhD

Mountainview Consulting Group, Inc.
Zillah, WA

Brian Mundy, LCSW

Institute for Community Living
New York, NY

Social workers deliver services to a broad range of clients in many settings. The number of children, families, and adults of all ages in need of social work services is increasing faster than the rate of available resources, and social work values suggest the importance of the principle of "the greatest good" in directing practice. In community mental health, primary care, and other practice settings such as correctional facilities, hospitals, and hospice care, there is an increasing demand for social workers to revise their practice toward a brief intervention model in order to provide more services to more people at the time of need. The introduction of managed care into behavioral health has also asked social workers to revise their practice and to see more clients in less time with better results (Aaronwitz, 2012).

All too often, academic training in Masters level social work does not prepare clinicians for the challenges of today's health care world. Most newly graduated social workers receive a "crash course" in the realities of clinical work during their field placement or at their first employment. It is at this point that many social workers identify gaps between their graduate preparation and the demands of the practice setting. The experienced social worker may also struggle with discrepancies between practice habits that worked well for many years and the demands of today's world of health care. Preparation gaps, in combination with high caseloads and higher productivity standards, lead many social workers to experience job dissatisfaction. Without further skill training, they become vulnerable to burnout.

Ongoing competency training is an integral part of career development (Boyd-Franklin, 2003). Competency in brief intervention work, in particular, is fundamental to social workers' success. Social workers who take a systematic approach to learning brief intervention skills are more likely to form a strong and enduring connection to the values that led to their choice of social work as a career. With a strong value connection, social workers exude passion for their work and a strong sense of hope. This empowers clients to also experience great hope and stamina in pursuing more meaningful lives, even with substantial challenges such as poor health and financial problems. A commitment to learning naturally brings us together into communities, and these communities promote self-care, an ethical responsibility for social workers (Hunter and Schofield, 2006). In writing this chapter, our intention is to assist social workers with planning career development activities that enhance success in health care work, improve resilience, and strengthen connection to the larger social work community.

We offer readers a tool for enhancing understanding and developing a broad range of skills supportive of excellence in brief practice.

The Brief Intervention Competency Assessment Tool, or "BI-CAT" (a copy of which can be found at the end of this chapter), asks social workers to self-assess level of competence in twenty areas. Along with the BI-CAT, we present behavioral anchors to help readers better understand levels of low, adequate, and exceptional competency. After reading this chapter, we hope that our readers can (1) use the BI-CAT for self-assessment with confidence, (2) select specific areas for improving competence, and (3) recruit colleagues with greater competence in brief work to provide assistance through modeling and coaching. Indeed, it is through being "watched" and guided by an exceptional brief clinician that the new, exceptional brief intervention social worker evolves.

In concluding our chapter, we present a case example of a social worker struggling to meet the challenges of working briefly. Mary uses the BI-CAT as a career development tool. A coworker introduces her to focused acceptance and commitment therapy (FACT). She achieves greater job satisfaction and develops a more rewarding connection with other social workers. We encourage our readers to read chapter 7 in this book, which introduces FACT, as it offers many useful clinical strategies for brief work.

Prior to launching into the BI-CAT, we briefly describe the population-based care perspective, as it contrasts with the case perspective that social workers often learn first. The case perspective typically suggests a focus on members of a caseload, and this, for social workers, often means the most vulnerable members of the community. We will also introduce the primary care behavioral health (PCBH) model, which provides direction for social workers who are moving into work settings that require a population-based care perspective. The PCBH model describes a new role for social workers and provides tools for brief intervention work in a team treatment context. While the PCBH model was specifically developed to guide delivery of behavioral health services in the primary care setting, many of its features apply equally well to other settings where social workers need to practice briefly.

The Population-Based Care Perspective

Population-based health care suggests that much is to be gained in clinical and cost outcomes when we focus resources on helping all people maintain optimal health as long as possible, rather than attending exclusively to people in acute need of services. When we focus interventions on all members of a population, we are able to prevent development and progression of disease and, over time, reduce the number of people who become substantially disabled and require very expensive care. Population-based care also suggests that we may realize better outcomes by changing the way we care for people who are most disabled by health problems. Providing disease management programs to members of this small but costly group involves offering evidence-based interventions that support the development of self-management skills, emotional health, a social support base and, in general, a higher quality of life. By saving money spent caring for the most vulnerable, we create a pot of money for intervening with members of the population who are still healthy or less impaired by disorder and disease than the most severely impaired members.

Principles of population-based health apply to people of all ages and may be addressed in almost any health care delivery venue. For example, a primary care clinic might develop a program that targets parents of infants with the intention of providing information about the time and course of colic behaviors and strategies for intervening should these occur. This program would ideally prevent secondary problems associated with uninformed parental responses to this somewhat common problem (such as more frequent medical visits, decline in parent functioning due to sleep and mood problems, increased conflict between parents, and, in a worst case scenario, parental harm to the infant). Another example could be the decision of a mental health service to target healthy weight and healthy lifestyle behaviors among clients taking psychotropic medications that cause weight gain by initiating ongoing support to members of this group in person and by telephone. In both examples, developers of the population-based health program would define outcomes, measure them over time, and revise the program as indicated.

Over the past two decades, population-based care principles have increasingly been applied to the primary care setting. This trend has created a positive environment for redesigning the delivery of both medical and mental health care in primary care. With this we have seen the development of the patient centered medical home (PCMH) and the primary care behavioral health (PCBH) models. The PCMH attempts to deliver services to the patient at the time of need, including those services that enhance the development of skills necessary to maintain health and prevent disease as long as possible. The PCBH model describes procedural details for implementing, maintaining, and evaluating delivery of behavioral health services in primary care.

The Primary Care Behavioral Health (PCBH) Model

The PCBH model (Robinson & Reiter, 2007; Strosahl, 1994a, 1994b) evolved from early randomized control trials demonstrating improved clinical, satisfaction, and cost outcomes for integrated behavioral health care relative to the usual practice of primary care providers referring clients to outpatient mental health clinics (e.g., Katon et al., 1996). Large health care organizations, such as the United States Air Force, and numerous Federally Qualified Health Centers have implemented this model. A procedural manual is fundamental to PCBH dissemination efforts and to the realization of anticipated outcomes. With increasing frequency, research findings indicate that behavioral health services delivered in the context of the PCBH model result in improved symptoms, better quality of life, and higher life satisfaction for most clients; that most clients benefit from an average of four or fewer visits; that gains made by clients are maintained for several years; and that clients and primary care providers prefer this model to usual care (Bryan et al., 2012; Bryan, Morrow, & Appolonio, 2008; Cigrang, Dobmeyer, Becknell, Roa-Navarrete, & Yerian, 2006; Corso et al.,

2012; Ray-Sannerud et al., 2012; Simon et al., 1998; Smith, Rost, & Kashner, 1995). Numerous resources are now available to support behavioral health and primary care providers in implementing the model (Hunter, Goodie, Oordt, & Dobmeyer, 2009; O'Donohue, Byrd, Cummings, & Henderson, 2005; Oordt & Gatchel, 2003; Robinson, 1996; Robinson, Del Vento, & Wischman, 1998; Robinson, Gould, & Strosahl, 2010; Robinson & Reiter, 2007; Robinson, Wischman, & Del Vento, 1996; Rowan & Runyan, 2005; Runyan, Fonseca, & Hunter, 2003; Strosahl, 1997; Strosahl, Robinson, & Gustavvson, 2012).

The PCBH model describes the role and responsibilities of primary care behavioral health providers, primary care providers (PCPs), and nursing staff working together in the context of the PCMH. Typically, the term "behavioral health consultant" (BHC) is used to describe the services of the primary care behavioral health provider working in the PCBH model. The BHC functions as a consultant to clients and providers and delivers brief intervention services and PCBH pathway services. The BHC offers brief intervention services to children, youth, and adults, often on the same day of the client's visit with the referring PCP or nurse. The BHC uses evidence-based interventions adapted to the brief context of primary care (see, for example, Robinson, 2005; 2008; Robinson et al., 1995; Goodie, Isler, Hunter, & Peterson, 2009) and translates these to even briefer versions that BHCs can teach PCP and nurse members of the team. This allows the PCP, the BHC's primary customer, to support client efforts to practice new strategies and skills over time and in this way sustain gains in functioning. The BHC is considered to be a primary care provider rather than a specialist and charts in the medical record rather than a separate mental health record. The BHC does not have a caseload, does not "open" or "close" cases, and is easily accessed by clients and family members on an intermittent basis over the course of their lifetime.

BHC pathway services involve consistent involvement of the BHC with specific members of a particular client population. Clinics develop PCBH pathways in order to improve outcomes to high-impact client groups. The targeted group may be that of a healthy population (such as children coming for well-child visits) and the focus may be primary prevention (for example, identifying parent-child relationship problems and providing brief, same-day interventions to improve relating skills). Alternatively, pathway services may target clients with mental and/or physical health problems (such as depression, diabetes, or chronic pain) and the focus is on teaching self-management skills. Whatever the target, the goal of pathway services is to increase the healthy lifespan of members of the targeted group by consistently adding the expertise of the BHC to client care. Specific BHC pathway services may include assessment and intervention visits in individual, family, or group contexts. In some cases, services may involve delivery of monthly group services to clients (for example, those with chronic disease) for as long as they receive care at the clinic.

Brief Intervention Competency Assessment Tool

We developed the brief intervention competency assessment Tool (BI-CAT, see figure 8.1) with the intention of providing social workers a feasible method for self-assessing knowledge and skill levels in the daily practice of activities that support working briefly with clients. (A copy of the BI-CAT is available for download at http://www.newharbinger.com/28906. See the back of the book for more information.) The BI-CAT is a brief tool and not intended to be comprehensive, but instead to suggest twenty fundamental competencies for brief practice in a broad range of settings where social workers provide service, ranging from inpatient units and jails to mental health clinics and primary care settings. The BI-CAT taps into competencies in four domains: practice context, intervention design, intervention delivery, and outcomes-based practice. In constructing the BI-CAT, we did not assume that social workers would use only one psychotherapeutic approach but that they would draw from an array of evidence-based interventions. Social workers with greater training in brief psychotherapies (such as solution-focused therapy, motivational interviewing, and focused acceptance and commitment therapy) are likely to have higher competence in intervention design and delivery and outcomes-based practice domains, and workers with training in brief therapies and the primary care behavioral health model are likely to have higher competencies in all four domains.

BI-CAT Behavioral Anchors

In the following section, we offer descriptions for each of the competencies, along with three behavioral anchors defining low, adequate, and exceptional levels of competence. The BI-CAT asks respondents to use a scale of 0-10 in self-assessing competence. Low competence ratings are scores of 0-3, adequate ratings are associated with scores of 4-6, and exceptional levels of competence with scores of 7-10. The behavioral anchors describe both knowledge and skill competencies. We recommend that social workers use this tool to self-assess and to strategically plan activities to develop stronger levels of competence in identified areas of weakness. We encourage social workers who are new to brief work to go beyond reading and seek training from colleagues and/or coworkers with higher levels of competence in brief work. Such input will likely include skill training through modeling, observation, guided rehearsal, and ongoing coaching in the context of daily practice. Increasingly, organizations will need to identify providers who have strong competencies for brief work and create protocols to guide their provision of mentoring services for staff who are new to brief treatment.

Domain 1: Practice Context. This domains taps into knowledge and skills related to applying brief interventions tailored to the social worker's practice context. Skillful application of brief interventions involves understanding the population you serve so that you are able to reach out to them, address barriers to their use of services, provide transparent interventions amenable to support by non-social-worker colleagues, and change routine practices to improve services to clients. Table 8.1 provides a description of low, adequate, and exceptional competency levels for the four areas in this domain.

Table 8.1. BI-CAT Practice Context Domain Items and Behavioral Anchors for Low, Adequate, and High Competence

1. Understand the most common problems of clients in your setting and promote their access to your services for these problems.	
Low	Has no have specific information about potential and actual clients' most common complaints; unable to use this information as a basis for outreach
Adequate	Has information about top five problems/requests/diagnoses and knowledge of how to address these
High	Has information about top five problems/requests/diagnoses and action plan for outreach that describes these services to potential and actual clients
2. Address barriers to client access of your service (e.g., minimize stigma, select optimal location).	
Low	Cannot identify specific barriers that clients often experience in attempts to access services
Adequate	Can describe specific access barriers that clients experience and attempts to address some of these on a case-by-case basis (e.g., attempts to lessen stigma, provides bus tokens)
High	Periodically surveys clients about access barriers and feasible strategies for addressing these; makes changes to routine practices to reduce barriers (e.g., moves practice to more accessible location, offers services at preferred times, etc.)
3. Work to share your skills with other members of your team so that they can support your interventions.	
Low	Attends all staff meetings but does not report on any specific brief intervention activities beyond linkage and referral activities, and does this only when requested to do so

Adequate	Attends all staff meetings; reports on resources and linkage activities as requested; attends workshops on evidence-based brief interventions and provides brief summary of learning at staff meetings
High	Adapts brief interventions for use by team members who have less time with clients (e.g., adapting five-minute breathing exercise to a two-minute version) and teaches these through half-page handouts and presentations at staff meetings; creates one-page client education handouts and makes these available to other team members
4. Define the demands of your practice setting and make necessary adjustments to your practice (e.g., numerous clients and limited providers or shortened visit times).	
Low	Continues to ask clients to attend one-hour initial and one-hour follow-up appointments, even when evidence for such is lacking and other clients receive no services and continue without care on long waiting lists
Adequate	Tracks number of days that clients wait for service and attempts to provide same-day service for acute clients and service for non-acute clients within one week; makes changes to appointment length as needed to reach access standards
High	Tracks number of days that clients wait for service and attempts to provide same-day service for all clients requesting it by adjusting appointment time to what is required to serve clients (e.g., averaging thirty minutes per client)

Domain 2: Intervention Design. This area suggests competency levels for designing interventions supportive of brief work with clients, beginning with providing a standard introduction that suggests that the client may benefit from a single appointment. Table 8.2 provides behavioral descriptors for low, adequate, and high competence on each of the nine areas in this important domain.

Table 8.2. BI-CAT Intervention Design Domain Items and Behavioral Anchors for Low, Adequate, and High Competence

5. Introduce yourself and your services in ways that promote change (e.g., My job is to help you help yourself—I may only see you once; we will come up with one or more strategies to help you today).	
Low	Introduction suggests that the focus on the initial visit will be limited to assessment
Adequate	Introduction suggests that the initial visit will include assessment and recommendations regarding behavior change
High	Introduction suggests that the initial visit will include assessment, behavior change recommendations, and skills training and that many clients benefit from a single appointment
6. Target problem of concern to client at time of visit.	
Low	Obtains lengthy psychosocial history in initial visit
Adequate	Obtains brief psychosocial history and inquires about problem concerning client at time of visit
High	Obtains psychosocial information within five minutes and focuses assessment and brief intervention on problem of concern to client at time of visit
7. Identify and use client strengths in intervention design.	
Low	Does not routinely ask questions that help identify client strengths to use in intervention design; focus of assessment is on client weaknesses, deficits, and pathological symptoms; designs intervention to reduce or eliminate symptoms
Adequate	Assessment includes questions that help identify client strengths and weaknesses; focus of assessment is on identifying client skill deficits and remediation strategies, as well as reducing symptoms

High	Assessment includes questions that help identify client strengths and weaknesses; conceptualizes intervention design in terms of client strengths, including ability to identify and accept current symptoms/problems as signals of the need for behavior change and willingness to learn new skills

8. Normalize the client's problem or avoid pathology explanations of the problem.

Low	Routinely works to establish a specific diagnosis, communicates diagnosis to client, and then sees client through the lens of a "diagnosed" person
Adequate	While understanding and being guided by a client's diagnosis, communicates understanding of the context of client's diagnostic symptoms and expresses view that symptoms emerge in a biological, psychological, and social context
High	While understanding a client's diagnosis and using it as needed for billing purposes, communicates to client that problem or symptoms are understandable in the client's life context and that change in that context is possible

9. Complete assessment prior to beginning behavior change planning.

Low	Blends assessment and behavior change planning, often returning to assessment after development of a behavior change plan
Adequate	Attempts to complete assessment prior to beginning behavior change planning
High	Consistently completes assessment and summarizes findings to client prior to beginning behavior change planning

10. Offer client a case conceptualization in a problem summary statement.

Low	Does not provide a problem summary statement with a case conceptualization

Adequate	Provides problem summary statement with weak (or no) case conceptualization in it
High	Provides problem summary statement with strong case conceptualization ("So, you've been staying in your room more and you notice thoughts about 'failing' more. Staying in your room doesn't change those thoughts, and you notice that your mood worsens when you don't go out, so some change in that behavior might make sense?")

11. Focus on small changes ("one step at a time").

Low	Works from extensive treatment plan with multiple goals
Adequate	Targets client's priority among treatment plan goals
High	Targets client's target problem as well as specific change plans designed to improve that problem

12. Frame intervention as "an experiment to see what happens" (i.e., create permission to fail).

Low	Frames behavior change as a request ("Will you do X?")
Adequate	Frames behavior change as a plan ("So our plan is X?")
High	Frames behavior change as an experiment ("So our plan is X, and we both agree that this is just an experiment to see what happens, right? If it doesn't work, we'll know we need to try something different.")

13. Assess confidence in behavior change plan at all visits.

Low	Does not ask about client's level of confidence in behavior change plan
Adequate	Asks about client's level of confidence in behavior change plan ("How confident are you in our plan?")
High	Asks about client's level of confidence in behavior change plan in every visit, using a rating scale question ("On a scale of 1 to 10, where 1 is 'not confident' and 10 is 'very confident,' how confident are you in our plan?")

14. Identify and address barriers to client's follow through with behavior change plans.	
Low	Expresses concern that client did not follow through on a change plan and attributes this to a lack of motivation; requests that client try plan again
Adequate	Identifies barriers to client's follow-up, sees barriers as challenges, encourages continued effort
High	Identifies and addresses barriers to follow-up (e.g., "So you went to the park and saw your friends and forgot that you planned not to drink at the park. I have an idea about how to help you learn to stay more aware in situations like that—want to hear about that?")
15. Encourage client to take ownership of behavior changes.	
Low	Focuses on client compliance ("So, you did follow through with our plan this time?")
Adequate	Focuses on client compliance and acknowledges client's role in following through with behavior change plans ("Good for you; you followed through. How did it work for you?")
High	Normalizes lack of compliance, is curious about barriers, and sees barriers as an opportunity for clinician and client to learn. Also inquires about behavior changes client made other than the planned change that had a positive impact on client status. Attributes positive outcomes to client's ability to be aware, choose, and take action ("Awesome. You did the plan and parts of it worked for you, and you found some other things that were helpful, too.")

Domain 3: Intervention Delivery. These competencies tap into skills involved in visit-by-visit delivery of brief interventions. They guide social workers into greater adoption of the population-based care perspective described earlier in this chapter and, by so doing, empower social workers to serve more clients. Table 8.3 provides behavioral anchor descriptions for the two items in this domain.

Table 8.3. BI-CAT Intervention Delivery Domain Items and Behavioral Anchors for Low, Adequate, and High Competence

16. Establish a care pathway (or routine procedure) for consistent delivery of acceptable, effective interventions for common client problems (e.g., skill groups for clients with depression, lifestyle problems, or chronic disease; workshops for clients with high stress, parenting concerns, or sleep problems).	
Low	Does not understand the concept of a care pathway
Adequate	Understands what a care pathway is and works with colleagues to develop an initial care pathway to improve multiple outcomes (e.g., client or provider satisfaction, clinical outcomes, more optimal use of resources)
High	Implements and evaluates multiple care pathways that improve outcomes and participates in revisions to pathways as suggested by outcome information
17. Offer open-access groups to clients to enhance access to skill practice and social/emotional support.	
Low	Does not offer group or class services
Adequate	Offers closed-group services to a select group of clients (e.g., a seven-session class for depressed clients)
High	Offers open-access groups and workshops with topics that are relevant to clients with a variety of problems (e.g, a five-session "Life Satisfaction" class that teaches a variety of strategies that are relevant to clients with many different kinds of problems, with each class as a stand-alone unit open to client self-referral)

Domain 4: Outcomes-Based Practice. Use of feasible outcomes to plan, evaluate, and make intervention plan changes provides a strong foundation for brief intervention work. Data needs to guide case-by-case work as well as overall effectiveness of a social worker's (or clinic's) brief intervention practice. Skills in this domain apply to delivery of services to all units, including individuals, families, and groups. Table 8.4 describes the behavioral anchors for these three competencies.

Table 8.4. BI-CAT Outcomes-Based Practice Domain Items and Behavioral Anchors for Low, Adequate, and High Competence

\multicolumn{2}{l}{18. Use outcomes tailored to delivery of brief interventions (e.g., problem severity rating).}
Low	Does not collect outcome information
Adequate	Collects outcome information at beginning and end of treatment
High	Collects outcome information at all visits (e.g., "On a scale of 1 to 10, where 1 is 'not a problem' and 10 is 'a very big problem,' how big of a problem is parenting your son/managing your diabetes/doing what you choose to do when you feel anxious at this point in time?")
\multicolumn{2}{l}{19. Demonstrate willingness and ability to change intervention based on assessment results (e.g., confidence rating).}
Low	Tends to encourage client to implement behavior change plan even when client seems uninterested or under-committed to it
Adequate	When client indicates a lack of confidence, makes an effort to change behavior change plan (e.g., "Let's take this plan off the list; you didn't seem interested in that one. Okay?")
High	When client indicates a confidence level of 6 or less, asks client what changes can be made to the behavior change plan to increase client confidence, and then makes these changes
\multicolumn{2}{l}{20. Use outcomes in aggregate to evaluate the effectiveness of your practice (e.g., client change in mental health or health-related quality of life scores from initial to last follow-up visits).}
Low	Does not have aggregate outcome information to help with evaluating practice effectiveness or is not interested in available information
Adequate	Reviews available aggregate information and participates in discussions about data with other team members
High	Actively uses available aggregate information to plan and make changes to service delivery

BI-CAT Evaluation

Our evaluation of the BI-CAT is preliminary. We have results from a survey of twenty behavioral health clinicians. All clinicians worked in a setting that encouraged them to complete treatment with clients in six or fewer contacts, and all were trained in acceptance and commitment therapy, as well as other cognitive behavioral approaches. Clinicians varied in level of competency, and those with higher competence tended to see clients more briefly. All clinicians made gains in average competency ratings after a one-day training in focused acceptance and commitment therapy (Strosahl, Robinson, & Gustavvson, 2012) and use of techniques from *Real Behavior Change in Primary Care: Improving Outcomes and Increasing Job Satisfaction* (Robinson, Gould, & Strosahl, 2011). In the future, we plan more systematic evaluation of the BI-CAT, including collection of survey, observation, and behavioral event interview data.

• *Case Example: Mary*

Mary is a twenty-seven-year-old licensed Masters level social worker and behavioral health consultant (BHC). She is working in her home state. She graduated from a state university two years ago. Though Mary's training in school included courses on brief therapy, she feels frustrated trying to employ her skill set to the truly brief, team approach required at her PCMH clinic. She became worried when she noticed that she was less excited about going to work, spent more time daydreaming during visits with clients, and became easily irritated by colleagues. Mary even wondered if she had chosen the wrong career.

Mary went to her supervisor and asked for help. She explained that she wanted to learn whatever she could in order to provide better BHC services and that she desperately wanted to feel more effective. Her supervisor introduced her to the BI-CAT and suggested that she use it as a self-assessment tool. Once Mary completed her ratings, she and her supervisor mapped out a career development plan. This plan included Mary's reading more about brief intervention work in primary care (see, for example, chapters presenting case examples with children, adults, and older adults in Robinson & Reiter, 2007) and reviewing what she had learned in graduate school about solution-focused therapy (Miller, Hubble, & Duncan, 1996). Her supervisor also arranged for her to go to another clinic to shadow a more experienced BHC.

About six months later, a colleague from graduate school told Mary that he'd attended several trainings on acceptance and commitment therapy (ACT) and found its trans-diagnostic approach supportive of working briefly with clients. Mary decided to attend the Association for Contextual and Behavioral Sciences (ACBS) world conference with her friend. At the conference, Mary attended a workshop on using ACT in primary care (Robinson, Gould, & Strosahl, 2010) and applying the principles of focused acceptance and commitment (FACT) (Strosahl, Robinson, & Gustavsson, 2012) to the context of brief intervention work. She was impressed by the strong evidence base for ACT interventions. Upon returning from the conference, Mary incorporated "workabililty questions" and values-clarification exercises into her clinical work and noted better client engagement immediately.

Mary joined one of the many ACBS listservs (see http://www.contextualpsychology.org) and spearheaded a learning cohort for PCMH social workers. She continued to use her BI-CAT results to develop her skill set and administered a survey to her PC colleagues in an effort to identify a population for development of a PCBH pathway. Results suggested that improved treatment of chronic pain was a top priority. With a small group of colleagues, Mary developed a pathway pilot that relied on use of the primary care Bull's-Eye Plan to improve psychological flexibility and quality of life for clients with chronic pain (for instructions, see http://www.newharbingeronline.com/real-behavior-change-in-primary-care.html). In order to meet the needs of this large group of clients, Mary started several monthly groups to serve them. Outcomes from the chronic pain class included improved satisfaction with care for clients and for primary care providers and nurses as well. Scaled scores on the Duke Health Profile (Parkerson, Broadhead, & Tse, 1990) suggested improvement in social health among group participants. Mary is planning a series of five-to-ten-minute presentations on the Bull's-Eye Plan at provider and nursing meetings. She continues to meet monthly with the small group of staff who are evaluating the chronic pain pathway.

Mary is on her way to developing exceptional competencies in delivery of brief interventions in several areas where her initial ratings were low. She is now completing ten client visits per day, and her outcome data suggest that most clients are improving. Several of her colleagues have asked to come and shadow her individual work with clients and her group work with clients with chronic pain. She suggested that they read this chapter and complete the BI-CAT before their visit to her clinic so that they would be better able to see ways to address identified skill gaps.

Conclusion

The BI-CAT offers readers an opportunity to better describe their strengths and weaknesses in relation to providing brief interventions. With vigilance and with the support of others, the BI-CAT is a useful career development tool that can help new and experienced professionals develop fundamental skills for succeeding in today's health care world. When social workers demonstrate adequate and exceptional skill levels in brief intervention work and apply interventions consistent with FACT, they are likely to experience greater job satisfaction as well as better outcomes with clients.

References

Aaronwitz, E. (2012). A brief (but explosive) history of pay-per-session social work practice in mental health clinics. *Social Work Currents 57*. New York City: NASW-NYC.

Boyd-Franklin, N. (2003). *Black families in therapy: Understanding the African American experience* (2nd ed.). New York: Guilford.

Bryan, C. J., Corso, M. L., Corso, K. A., Morrow, C. E., Kanzler, K. E., & Ray-Sannerud, B. (2012). Severity of mental health impairment and trajectories of improvement in an integrated primary care clinic. *Journal of Consulting and Clinical Psychology, 80*, 396-403.

Bryan, C. J., Morrow, C.E., & Appolonio, K.A. (2008). Impact of behavioral health consultant interventions on patient symptoms and functioning in an integrated family medicine clinic. *Journal of Clinical Psychology, 65*, 1-13.

Cigrang, J. A., Dobmeyer, A. C., Becknell, M. E., Roa-Navarrete, R. A., & Yerian, S. R. (2006). Evaluation of a collaborative mental health program in primary care: Effects on patient distress and health care utilization. *Primary Care and Community Psychiatry, 11*, 121-127.

Corso, K. A., Bryan, C. J., Corso, M. L., Kanzler, K. E., Houghton, D. C., Ray-Sannerud, B., & Morrow, C. E. (2012). Therapeutic alliance and treatment outcome in the primary care behavioral health model. *Families, Systems, & Health 30*, 87-100.

Goodie, J., Isler, W., Hunter, C., & Peterson, A. (2009). Using behavioral health consultants to treat insomnia in primary care: A clinical case series. *Journal of Clinical Psychology, 65*, 294-304.

Hunter, C. L., Goodie, J. L., Oordt, M. S., & Dobmeyer, A. C. (2009). *Behavioral health in primary care: A practitioner's handbook*. Washington, DC: American Psychological Association.

Hunter, S. V., & Schofield, M. J. (2006). How counselors cope with traumatized clients: Personal, professional and organizational strategies. *International Journal for the Advancement of Counselling, 28*, 121-138.

Katon, W., Robinson, P., Von Korff, M., Lin, E., Bush, T., Ludman, E., et al. (1996). A multifaceted intervention to improve treatment of depression in primary care. *Archives of General Psychiatry, 53*, 924-932.

Miller, S. D., Hubble, M. A., & Duncan, B. L. (1996). *Handbook of solution-focused brief therapy*. San Francisco: Jossey-Bass.

O'Donohue, W. T., Byrd, M. R., Cummings, N. A., & Henderson, D. A. (Eds.). (2005). *Behavioral integrative health care: Treatments that work in the primary care setting*. New York: Brunner-Routledge.

Oordt, M. S., & Gatchel, R. J. (2003). *Clinical health psychology and primary care: Practical advice and clinical guidance for successful collaboration*. Washington, DC: American Psychological Association.

Parkerson, G. R., Broadhead, W. E., & Tse, C. J. (1990). The Duke health profile: A 17-item measure of health and dysfunction. *Medical Care, 28*, 1056-1072.

Ray-Sannerud, B. N., Dolan, D. C., Morrow, C. E., Corso, K. A., Kanzler, K. W., & Corso, M. L. (2012). Longitudinal outcomes after brief behavioral health intervention in an integrated primary care clinic. *Families, Systems, & Health, 30,* 60-71.

Robinson, P. (1996). *Living life well: New strategies for hard times.* Reno, NV: Context Press.

Robinson, P. (2005). Adapting empirically supported treatments to the primary care setting: A template for success. In W. T. O'Donohue, M. R. Byrd, N. A. Cummings, & D. A. Henderson. (Eds.), *Behavioral integrative care: Treatments that work in the primary care setting* (pp. 53-71). New York: Brunner-Routledge.

Robinson, P. (2008). Putting it on the streets: Homework in cognitive and behavioral therapy. In W. O'Donohue (Ed.), *Cognitive behavior therapy* (2nd ed.), Hoboken, NJ: John Wiley & Sons, Inc.

Robinson, P., Bush, T., Von Korff, M., Katon, W., Lin, E., Simon, G., et al. (1995). Primary care provider use of cognitive behavioral techniques with depressed patients. *Journal of Family Practice, 40,* 352-357.

Robinson, P., Del Vento, A., & Wischman, C. (1998). Integrated treatment of the frail elderly: The group care clinic. In A. Blount. (Ed.), *Integrated primary care: The future of medical and mental health collaboration.* New York: W. W. Norton.

Robinson, P. J., Gould, D., & Strosahl, K. D. (2010). *Real behavior change in primary care: Strategies and tools for improving outcomes and increasing job satisfaction.* Oakland, CA: New Harbinger.

Robinson, P. J., & Mundy, B. (2014). In pursuit of excellence: Developing competencies for delivery of brief interventions. In M. S. Boone (Ed.). *Mindfulness and acceptance in social work: Evidence-based practices and emerging applications.* Oakland, CA: New Harbinger.

Robinson, P., & Reiter, J. (2007). *Behavioral consultation and primary care: A guide to integrating services.* New York: Springer.

Robinson, P., Wischman, C., & Del Vento, A. (1996). *Treating depression in primary care: A manual for PCMs and therapists.* Reno, NV: Context Press.

Rowan, A. B., & Runyan, C. N. (2005). A primer on the consultation model of primary care behavioral health integration. In L. C. James & R. A. Folen (Eds.), *The primary care consultant: The next frontier for psychologists in hospitals and clinics* (pp. 9-27). Washington, DC: American Psychological Association.

Runyan, C. N., Fonseca, V. P., & Hunter, C. (2003). Integrating consultative behavioral healthcare into the Air Force Medical System. In W. T. O'Donohue, K. E. Ferguson, & N. A. Cummings (Eds.), *Behavioral health as primary care: Beyond efficacy to effectiveness* (pp. 145-163). Reno, NV: Context Press.

Simon, G. E., Katon, W., Rutter, C., Von Korff, M., Lin, E., Robinson, P., et al. (1998). Impact of improved depression treatment in primary care on daily functioning and disability. *Psychological Medicine, 28,* 693-701.

Smith, G., Rost, K., & Kashner, T. (1995). A trial of the effect of a standardized psychiatric consultation on health outcomes and costs in somaticizing patients. *Archives of General Psychiatry, 52,* 238-243.

Strosahl, K. (1994a). Entering the new frontier of managed mental health care: Gold mines and land mines. *Cognitive and Behavioral Practice, 1,* 5-23.

Strosahl, K. (1994b). New dimensions in behavioral health primary care integration. *HMO Practice, 8,* 176-179.

Strosahl, K. (1997). Building primary care behavioral health systems that work: A compass and a horizon. In N. A. Cummings, J. L. Cummings, & J. N. Johnson (Eds.), *Behavioral health in primary care: A guide for clinical integration.* Madison, CT: Psychosocial Press.

Strosahl, K. D., Robinson, P. J., & Gustavsson, T. (2012). *Brief interventions for radical change: Principles and practice of focused acceptance and commitment therapy.* Oakland, CA: New Harbinger.

Brief Intervention Competency Assessment Tool (BI-CAT)

Competency means "adequacy; possession of required skill, knowledge, qualification, or capacity." This tool is designed to help you assess your competence in skills involved in the effective delivery of brief interventions. Specific competencies are grouped in four domains: Practice Context, Intervention Design, Intervention Delivery, and Outcomes-Based Practice. Use this scale of 0 to 10 to assign a "rating" to your competence level at this time. Scores between 0–3 suggest "low" competence, 4–6 "adequate" competence, and 7–10 "exceptional" competence. Use results to formulate a career development plan to further your competence.

Low				Adequate					Exceptional
0	1	2	3	4	5	6	7	8	9	10

PRACTICE CONTEXT. This area concerns your ability to consistently promote optimal behavior change opportunities for your clients in the setting where you work. Do you...

Competency	Rating
1. Understand the most common problems of clients in your setting and promote their access to your services for these problems?	
2. Address barriers to client access of your service (e.g., minimize stigma, select optimal location)?	
3. Work to share your skills with other members of your team so that they can support your interventions?	
4. Define the demands of your practice setting and make necessary adjustments to your practice (e.g., numerous clients and limited providers/shorten visit times)?	

INTERVENTION DESIGN. This area concerns your ability to design strong brief interventions. Do you...

Competency	Rating
5. Introduce yourself and your services in ways that promote change (e.g., My job is to help you help yourself—I may only see you once; we will come up with one or more strategies to help you today)?	
6. Target problem of concern to client at time of visit?	
7. Identify and use client strengths in intervention design?	
8. Normalize the client's problem or avoid pathology explanations of the problem?	
9. Complete assessment prior to beginning behavior change planning?	
10. Offer client a case conceptualization in a problem summary statement?	
11. Focus on small changes ("one step at a time")?	
12. Frame intervention as "an experiment to see what happens" (i.e., create permission to fail)?	
13. Assess confidence in behavior change plan at all visits?	
14. Identify and address barriers to client's follow-through with behavior change plans?	
15. Encourage client to take ownership of behavior changes?	

INTERVENTION DELIVERY. This area concerns your ability to integrate brief interventions into your system of care so that more clients benefit from your brief services. Do you…

Competency	Rating
16. Establish a care pathway (or routine procedure) for consistent delivery of acceptable, effective interventions for common client problems (e.g., skill groups for clients with depression, lifestyle problems, or chronic disease; workshops for clients with high stress, parenting concerns, or sleep problems)?	
17. Offer open access groups to clients to enhance access to skill practice and social/emotional support?	

OUTCOMES-BASED PRACTICE. This area concerns your ability to use outcomes to plan and evaluate treatment. Do you…

Competency	Rating
18. Use outcomes tailored to delivery of brief interventions (e.g., problem severity rating)?	
19. Demonstrate willingness and ability to change intervention based on assessment results (e.g., confidence rating)?	
20. Use outcomes in aggregate to evaluate the effectiveness of your practice (e.g., client change in mental health or health-related quality of life scores from initial to last follow-up visits)?	

See Robinson & Mundy (2013) for BI-CAT behavioral anchors to assist you in making discriminations between three general levels of competence: low, adequate, and exceptional.

PART III

The Client in Context: Addressing Broader Systems

CHAPTER 9

Mindfulness and Engaged Buddhism: Implications for a Generalist Macro Social Work Practice

Michael Uebel, PhD, LCSW

Clayton Shorkey, PhD, LCSW

University of Texas at Austin

Before the turn of the twentieth century, Chicago's 19th Ward, the home of Jane Addams's Hull House, faced an ecological crisis. Garbage had been piling up, obscuring sidewalks with compact refuse several feet high, and the spread of disease borne by flies and vermin among the poor immigrant families living there left the 19th Ward with the third highest mortality rate in the city (Elshtain, 2002). In a collective and socially-engaged response to this crisis, the Hull House Women's Club, transcending the traditional and expected roles of women in late nineteenth-century Chicago, began to research the roots of the waste problem and to collect the garbage that was polluting the neighborhood themselves. As a result of this activism, the mayor was compelled to appoint Addams as garbage inspector for her ward, and waste-collection reform ascended to the top of the city's civic agenda.

Addams's efforts, as Elshtain (2002) emphasizes, were not narrowly political in nature—that is, satisfied with merely placing social reformers in positions of some authority. Rather, her project was broader in scope: "working to ensure that those who took on civic tasks—even chores as humble yet necessary as garbage collection—realized their importance to the whole, and saw their efforts as a vital part of the wider challenge to make the city more livable and beautiful" (p. 169). Addams and her settlement coworkers embody what we will discuss in this essay as the core principles of ecologically-engaged macro practice as expressed in specific Buddhist traditions—namely, the creation of change within both humans themselves and the physical environment (natural and built) through the recognition and realization of the interdependence of humanity, nature, and the nonliving.

Three years after Addams became the first woman appointed Sanitary Inspector of the 19th Ward, Edward Ricketts, the founder of the discipline of marine ecology, was born in an immigrant neighborhood in northwest Chicago. Ricketts's careful observations and collections of marine life on the Pacific coastline—his 1939 handbook *Between Pacific Tides* remains unsurpassed—provided rich opportunities to reflect on the radical interconnectedness of human and animal environments. As he developed it in his philosophical writings of the 1930s, observable interconnectedness represented the strongest evidence that the world is best understood "nonteleologically," that is, by abandoning the search for single causes in favor of acceptance and empathy simply with "what is" (Ricketts, 2006). For Ricketts, teleological thinking was moralizing and didactic, whereas nonteleological approaches were beyond categorical understandings of the world. "The whole is necessarily everything" (p. 133), he posited, since "everything impinges everything else, often into radically different systems, although in such cases faintly.... I doubt very much if there are any teleologies" (p. 128).

Among Ricketts's most cherished books was a copy of D. T. Suzuki's *Essays in Zen Buddhism*, which, when it appeared in 1933, was one of the first texts to introduce Zen to an English-speaking audience. Ricketts deeply appreciated Zen's radical empiricism, its direct experience of "the whole picture...portrayed by *is*, the deepest word of deep ultimate reality, not shallow or partial as reasons are, but deeper and participating, possibly encompassing the oriental concept of 'being'" (2006, p. 133, emphasis in original). To understand the holistic "is" of existence means experiencing it as interdependent, free of the impulse to categorize and hierarchize, which, as we will see, often distances us from the realities we are trying to change. Ricketts, along with Addams, furnishes macro social work with a model for thinking and practice, one that appreciates the deep interrelation between all organisms and their complex, changing environments.

This essay will suggest that the attitudinal thrust of engaged Buddhism furnishes generalist macro social work practice with tools to cultivate the "ecology of mind" (Bateson, 2000) upon which environmental and social justice vitally depend. Engaged Buddhism, alternatively known as socially engaged Buddhism, refers to the social and political application of the core teachings of Buddhist ethics and philosophy, including the idea that all things are dynamically interdependent; that suffering issues from separateness and duality; and that mindful, clear, and compassionate understanding of the present situation and the suffering it generates is the basis for wisdom (*prajna*). Engaged Buddhism strives to create new social conditions that nurture positive personal change and the possibility of awakened action.1

Buddhist Perspectives: Suffering, Interdependence, Impermanence

Recent work in mindfulness and engaged Buddhist psychology (Loy, 2008; Nichtern, 2007; Olendzki, 2010; Spellmeyer, 2010) has underscored the importance of large-scale social change as rooted in the overcoming of our illusion of separateness, the cherished but mistaken notion that we exist as autonomous, independent agents in a world that can be degraded precisely because it is other, or "not us." At the foundation of generalist macro social work practice is the recognition that approaching people as autonomous, divorced from their social context, is always partial at best and hazardous at worst. This recognition stipulates that the practitioner move fluidly between client systems of varying sizes while always respecting that the values supporting generalist practice are, from the perspective developed here, as much tied to the local as to the transcendent. In other words, we see traditional social work values such as acceptance, self-determination, dignity, and intrinsic self-worth informing practice not only with localized selves embedded in larger concentric systems but with the changing totality itself—persons, systems, and environments—where boundaries fade and the self as process or function comes to the foreground. This is the point where *ego* becomes *eco*.

Before unpacking this from a Buddhist perspective, we acknowledge at the outset that Buddhism is not monolithic, that it consists of multiple streams of philosophy and spiritual tradition with wide historical, geographic, cultural, and linguistic differences. Our approach will be "generically" Buddhist, attending mainly to elements "common" to forms of Buddhism as practiced in the Mahayana tradition, especially Zen (Chinese *Chan*) Buddhism and the important Chinese school, *Hua-yen*, that profoundly influenced Zen in Japan. These forms will anchor our inquiry into the role of engaged Buddhism in macro social work. Later it will be observed that the Zen tradition, in particular, is concerned with ecological and environmental issues at the most fundamental levels of practice.

To return then to our comment about values related to the local and the transcendental, where the latter implicates a non-dual approach to persons and the systems with which they interact, it is important to grasp a fundamental Buddhist notion concerning the self or, for that matter, any isolatable entity, living or nonliving. The idea is this: suffering (*duhkha*, the first so-called mark of existence) ceases when we experience *anātman* (no-self or no-thing, the second mark of existence), which is the lack of independent selfhood, and which, seen from the other side, is interdependence with all other things. In the experience of *anātman*, separation from the rest of the world is denied, shown to be an illusion, such that "the psycho-social construction of a separate self *in here* is at the same time the construction of an 'other' *out there*, that which is different from me" (Loy, 2008, p. 105). The coconstruction of self and other means that as one changes or comes into being, the other necessarily does, or, as the Buddha expressed it in book three of the *Khuddaka Nikaya*: "from the arising of this, comes the arising of that" (*Udāna*, 2012, p. 26). Awareness of this dependent arising (*pratītya-samutpāda*) is simultaneously awareness of *anātman* since all things are radically interrelated and thus cannot be said to exist apart or alone as delimited "selves" or "things." The last of the three "marks of existence"—impermanence (*anitya*)—stresses that, since everything is in fact ceaselessly changing and permanence is illusory, the self and all its "others" are groundless, more like processes or forms than things. Yet, in the face of impermanence, we struggle to ground ourselves, often through overconsumption and accumulation, only to get caught in more suffering, more garbage—real and psychological—as Addams and the early settlement workers knew too well. For Buddhism and, we argue, macro social work practice, the most profound solution to suffering is to realize our non-duality with all "others" such that our own well-being is inseparable from their well-being.

Social Work and Sociological Perspectives: PIE Revisited

Generalist social work practice, we suggest, can accommodate the development of mindfulness- and acceptance-based approaches by superseding the well-known person-in-environment (PIE) approach and its tie to systems theory through the cultivation of the Buddhist philosophical notion of *ānātman*, or what we might call *person-as-environment*, that is, the ecological and holistic view that the duality of person and her social and natural world is a false one. This shift in perspective seems important given the more recent ratification of the person-in-environment focus by the Council on Social Work Education (CSWE, 2001), but less important when we return to the origins of social work practice and the pioneering visions of women such as Jane Addams and Mary Richmond. Discussions of the history of the person-in-environment framework consistently invoke Addams or Richmond (e.g., Cornell, 2006), presumably for their holistic understanding of environment, while later conceptualizations of PIE, as Zapf (2005; 2010) has pointed out, tend strongly to elide the physical environment by restricting environment to the *social* environment only. From another angle, Dominelli (2012) has argued that the PIE approach, while largely ignoring the physical environment, is not sufficiently political since it fails to provide a framework for fully "integrating considerations and consequences of physical environments, the biosphere, and human needs" (p. 126), the central mission of what she calls "green social work." Zapf (2010) has proposed that, given the emergence—and emergency—of global environmental threat to human existence, the old metaphor of PIE should be revised to convey the coincidence of persons and environment, namely, people *as* place.

Very rarely, however, do discussions or even critiques of PIE attempt to recover what is most radical about the early social work perspectives. Richmond (1922), for example, is usually taken to be a proponent of case work *in* the social environment; and, indeed, her *What Is Social Case Work?* (1922) can be read in this light. After all, she emphasizes gaining equal insight into individual personality and into the social environment as well as taking indirect action through that environment (e.g., pp. 101-2), and she discusses case work in terms of adjusting the individual to it. Yet, a closer reading of her seminal book reveals that Richmond's "social case work in being" (p. 90), as she calls it, depends upon a holistic and ecological sense of the self, involving values seen from multiple points of view, which all contribute to an expansive perspective of "life as a whole":

> It is easy to be pleased with the results of social service when we measure them just after the first changes for the better, or when we see them from one angle and no more. But when we dare to examine them from the point of view of life as a whole, with the permanent welfare of the individual and of society in mind, we are applying a much severer test of values. (p. 90)

For Richmond, "life as a whole" constitutes the wide-angle view of the person and her society. Person in social environment is thus "one angle and no more" for assessing and creating change. Richmond appears to aim at something more expansive, what she terms a "theory of the wider self": "We all need to get rid of whatever vestige of an idea still remains with us that a man's mind is somewhere in his head, or that it has any location in space whatever" (p. 131). This view of the decentered mind/ego closely resembles the Buddhist notion of the "empty" self, or no-self, the relinquishing of our delusion of a rooted singular and locatable self or mind. In the terms of generalist social work practice, the emergence of this unlocatable self radically transcends the "bracketing" of ego undertaken in the name of the principle "professional use of self" wherein one's own judgments or biases are not to obtrude upon the worker-client relationship. The self, from the Mahayana Buddhist perspective, is always potentially "wider," precisely because awakening entails realizing the emptiness of our self-being, which is the same as realizing our simultaneous difference from and oneness with the world.[2]

The Buddhist explanation of the human condition—that the worst anguish results from clinging to the delusion of our separateness from the world—can be extended into social theory and practice by drawing upon the conceptual underpinnings of generalist macro social work practice, specifically, the force field perspective as developed by Kurt Lewin (1997). Lewin posited very simply that the achievement of change goals depends upon the mindful awareness of potential barriers. Less a form of anticipation than of clear vision of the present situation or "macro reality" (Kirst-Ashman & Hull, 2006, p. 172), the force field perspective is the conceptual foundation of macro social work practice (Brueggemann, 1996). The steps of mindful macro action include identifying and assessing the strength of barriers and advantages (restraining and driving forces, respectively), identifying actors who influence these forces, and, finally, formulating strategies for change. An additional concept of Lewin's, that of *life space*, adds a component to the macro social work model that brings it in closer alignment with the practices of engaged Buddhism. The life space, Lewin's term for the total environment as individuals or groups perceive it and in turn how this perceived environment affects their actions, resonates with a mindfulness-based approach attuned to the interdependent nature of reality. Naturally, perceptions of events are not always accurate or complete, and thus the social worker is called upon to observe with equanimity (*upekṣhá*)—an awakened capacity to see things as they emerge and change, for better or worse, with nonreactive, open, and balanced presence—the dynamics of the force field with its multiplicity of life spaces. Because the macro social worker positions herself as a change agent precisely in "the transactional area where the actual interchanges between people and environments occur, where qualities of the person intersect with qualities of the environment, with positive or negative consequences for both" (Germain, 1981, p. 325), a mindful attitude of equanimity is essential.

Toward a Culture of Awakening: Social Work in Being

The development of social workers as macro change agents depends, in our view, upon the cultivation of ethical practices related to social activism, for example, the ancient *brahma-vihara* (sublime abidings) meditation, a meditation involving four practice components, known together as the Four Immeasurables: beginning with loving-kindness (*metta*) extended to oneself, to a friend, to a stranger, and to an enemy, and extended successively to include the virtues of compassion (*karuna*), sympathetic joy (*mudita*), and, in this context, the most crucial one, equanimity. These elements of the ethical life are the heart of personal transformational processes upon which the well-being of the social, natural, and material orders depends. They comprise a true *mindful art of living*.[3]

We highlight equanimity for, in our view, this is the attitude most constructive for *social work in being*, to modify slightly Richmond's (1922) evocative neologism. The attitude of equanimity, furthermore, rounds out the rather bare-bones definition of mindfulness as nonjudgmental awareness of the present moment by underscoring the active, and potentially activist, components of the state of accepting awareness. Here, Langer & Moldoveanu (2000) are helpful since they see mindfulness as an active drawing of novel distinctions, as opposed to a cool cognitive process. For these authors, "the process of drawing novel distinctions can lead to a number of diverse consequences, including (1) a greater sensitivity to one's environment, (2) more openness to new information, (3) the creation of new categories for structuring perception, and (4) enhanced awareness of multiple perspectives in problem solving" (p. 2). The points of commonality with the most distinctive elements of generalist social work practice are striking. Schatz, Jenkins, and Sheafor (1990) identify five foundational elements of generalist practice: (1) "use of a multilevel problem-solving methodology," (2) "a multiple, theoretical orientation, including an ecological systems model that recognizes an interrelatedness of human problems, life situations, and social conditions," (3) "a knowledge, value, and skill base that is transferrable between and among diverse contexts, locations, and problems," (4) "open assessment unconstricted by any particular theoretical or interventive approach," and (5) selection of strategies and interventions based upon "the problem, goals, and situation of attention and the size of the systems involved" (p. 223).

From the perspective of mindfulness- and acceptance-based approaches, the essential elements of generalist practice aim at an openness and spontaneity in response to the uniqueness of each present condition, situation, or problem. Cultivating flexible and mobile modes of thinking and seeing, rooted in an appreciation of the reality of change and difference, the generalist practitioner exemplifies "beginner's mind," as summarized in the famous opening line of Shunryu Suzuki's *Zen Mind, Beginner's Mind* (2011): "In the beginner's mind there are many possibilities, but in the expert's there are few" (p. 1). The beginner's mind is open and spontaneous; it is the equanimous mind *par excellence*. Further, the *generalist mind*, not constricted by any single intervention approach, and requiring eclecticism and spontaneity, is usefully aligned with the mindfulness idea of *ehipassika*, or "come and see, come and experiment for yourself."

Ehi-passika animates Buddhism, which is founded on looking to one's own experience rather than on believing a single authority, and is neatly condensed in Zen master Sengcan's warning: "Do not search after the truth, only cease to cherish opinions" (Jones, 2003, p. 62). Buddhism thus provides to social work an emphasis on the experience-based diagnosis of the full human condition, along with trust in the eventual solution or cure. Between diagnosis and cure there is of course the intervention(s), and here, according to the Buddhist analogy, intervention is only a raft for crossing the river of *duhkha*. Once the other side is reached, one may abandon the raft rather than carry it further, identifying with accomplishment, for there are inevitably other rivers to ford. Dropping attachment to method, humility arises, a foundation stone for awakening.

What do we mean by "awakening," and what are the implications for macro social work practice of what Jones (2003), writing about engaged Buddhism, calls a "radical culture of awakening" (p. 72)? Awakening begins with recognizing how awareness is organized, and here Erich Fromm (1960) is most clear:

> [E]xperience can enter into awareness only under the condition that it can be perceived, related, and ordered in terms of a conceptual system and its categories. The system is in itself a result of social evolution. Every society, by its own practice of living and by the mode of relatedness, of feeling, and perceiving, develops a system of categories which determines the forms of awareness. This system works, as it were, like a *socially conditioned filter*; experience cannot enter awareness unless it can penetrate this filter. (p. 99; emphasis in original)

Fromm draws our attention to the social constructionist view that objects of experience are products of socially sanctioned modes of perception and the categories that structure them. Zen Buddhism, in particular, has stressed that our very notion of self is socially conditioned, and so Rinzai Zen monks, for example, spend a significant portion of their training doing meditative exercises, such as *koans* (statements or stories, defying logical or conceptual understanding, developed by masters in order to modify students' conscious awareness), in order to cut through the conditioning filters. Participants in a recent qualitative study of the phenomenological effects of *koan* study reported "better awareness of prejudices and biases with the ability to suppress those types of habitual associations, and a new relation to and acceptance of spiritual questions and doubts" (Grenard, 2008, p. 151). *Koans* build and enhance the mindfulness required "to recognize habitual or conditioned patterns of behavior which can be avoided or modified as required by a particular situation" (Grenard, 2008, p. 184). Exhausting the logical activity of the mind, *koans* awaken consciousness by compelling it to abandon conditioned views of reality.

When directly engaging with the operations of their own minds using, for example, *koan* practice, Zen students are able to see the extent to which their minds are conditioned and their perceptions of reality normally organized according to categories that obscure the nature of reality. From the perspective of engaged Buddhism, awakening means letting go of attachment to the categories of thinking that reinforce our separateness from the interdependent world as a whole. Our conditioned categories tend to take the form of binaries, such as self/other, observer/observed, interiority/exteriority, nature/mankind, human/nonhuman, wilderness/built world, and so on. The problem resides not in either term of the binary, but rather in the relationship of one to the other. Binaries always conceal hierarchies; that is, judgments are implicit—sometimes explicit—concerning each duality so that one term is valued more than the other or is taken to have power over the other. This is one aspect, the hierarchical, of the socially conditioned filtering that the awakened mind and the awakened culture work to undo through rendering it absolutely transparent and recontextualizing it within the model of deep interdependence. The difference of one term in the duality from the other can be recognized and accepted at the same time that the terms are understood to be inseparable, continuous, and dependent upon one another.

As a consequence of dualistic and hierarchical thinking, we become estranged from the environment, from other humans and nonhumans, and from the physical world itself. In a fascinating essay analyzing the experience of being an ecotourist at a marine park in Australia, Halsey (1999) demonstrates how the park's regulatory structures, e. g., its gates, roadways, signs, and checkpoints, actually interrupt the flow of tourists, as bodies and as perceivers, and ultimately disrupt the "production of an intense and diverse 'eco-experience'" (p. 228). Halsey attends to the dichotomies that are reinforced by park regulation: human/environment, observer/observed, and marine/terrestrial. Turning nature into an "other," such binaries are inimical to any awareness of interdependence, with potentially grave consequences: "Ecologically, the ocean is not separate to the observer—it is an extension of their body. If the ocean suddenly dries up so will human bodies" (p. 230). They also potentially foreclose the very affective responses of the tourist to her natural environment. Drawing upon French philosopher Gilles Deleuze, Halsey offers a revaluation of the centrality of affect in the experience of and relation to the environment, and concludes that "the important aspect of conceiving experience in terms of affects is that 'no-one knows ahead of time the affects one is capable of; it is a long affair of experimentation, requiring a lasting prudence' (Deleuze, 1992, p. 627). When a space has been pre-packaged and (re)presented the capacity to engage in such experimentation is somewhat diminished" (p. 233). Macro social workers are certainly familiar with the often rigid, dogmatic, and authoritarian nature of requirements for service in human service agencies. From the Buddhist perspective, what are precisely diminished are the affects inhering in the attitudinal foundations of mindful and engaged macro practice—the joy (and sorrow) of experiential and experimental openness (*ehi-passika*) and the calm of interdependence.

It is no surprise, then, that ecological social workers (e.g., Besthorn, 2002; Heinsch, 2012)—social workers who pay special attention to the social, cultural, and institutional contexts of person-environment relations—have urged an unmediated experience of the natural world through nature-based activities and direct engagements such as wilderness programs and even pet ownership in order to foster a healthier sense of self and world that is at once holistic, communal, and balanced. Since its origins in the 1980s, however, ecological social work has fallen short of specifying ways to cultivate the ecological value systems and conceptions of self that the literature generally agrees upon as crucial to reforming social work's commitment to the environment. Despite limited conceptual alliances with deep ecology and transpersonal psychology (Besthorn, 2001; 2002; 2012), ecologically informed social work rarely discusses Buddhist approaches. To foster dialogue, we are signaling here the cultivation of what may be called an "eco-mind" (Japanese *daishin* or, literally, "big mind") through mindfulness practices of equanimity, which in turn support attitudes of interdependence or interbeing (Nhat Hanh, 1993), openness through the beginner's mind (Suzuki, 2011), and awareness of impermanence (Chah, 2005). Before we turn to specific Zen practices of mindfulness and acceptance with which the social work practitioner can build and enhance her generalist practice in larger settings, we will briefly discuss the conceptual outlines of an ancient culture of awakening as expressed in *Hua-yen* Buddhism, which profoundly influenced the later flourishing of Zen and engaged Buddhism.

First appearing in systematic form in seventh-century China, the *Hua-yen* philosophical school offered a way of looking at human existence as a vast web of interdependence in which the disturbance of one strand wobbles the whole web (Cook, 1977). The school's fondness for the following image, mentioned many times in its literature, reveals an attempt to symbolize a cosmos in which the relationship of all its members is one of simultaneous mutual identity and mutual intercausality. In the heavenly dwelling of the great god Indra, there is a net that, extending endlessly in all directions, is adorned with glittering jewels hung in each node of the net. Inspection of a single jewel reveals that in its polished surface all other jewels are reflected there, infinite in number, and each jewel reflected in this single one is itself reflecting all other jewels. This limitless reflecting process is the essence of one of the most commonly used metaphors in Buddhist environmental ethics to emphasize that direct experience of, and action upon, just one facet of the environment is action upon the cosmos. This universal experience comprises the awakened ecologist's worldview. Thus Zen Buddhists, who emphasize direct experience of reality and understanding of the self, possess a confidence that indifference even to, say, one leaf of cabbage, as a famous story in the literature dramatizes it, can upset peace and affinity with the total environment (Graef, 1990).

Zen Earth, Zen Water

Zen master Dōgen (1200-1253), the founder of the Japanese Sōtō Zen sect, very often employed nature metaphors in his teachings on self, mind, and the ethical life. Especially in his teachings on non-duality, Dōgen, inspired by the Taoist emphasis on the harmony of nature and human nature, relied upon concrete imagery for illustration:

> If you yourself, who are the valley streams and mountains, cannot develop the power that illuminates the true reality of the mountains and valley streams, who else is going to be able to convince you that you and the streams and the mountains are one and the same? (Dōgen, 2002, p. 80)

The equanimous mind—what we have termed the eco-mind—unsurprisingly bears resemblance to nature itself: "Magnanimous Mind [or *daishin*] is like a mountain, stable and impartial. Exemplifying the ocean, it is tolerant and views everything from the broadest perspective" (Dōgen & Uchiyama, 2005, p. 37). Through *daishin*, the non-dual mind emerges and forms the basis for an inclusive ethical view of nature as possessing intrinsic value. Harvey (2000), in his book on Buddhist ethics, notes that for Dōgen "each aspect of nature has an intrinsic value as part of ultimate reality, and to let go of oneself in full awareness of the sound of the rain or the cry of a monkey is to fathom this in a moment of non-dual awareness" (p. 177). Letting go of the ego that interferes with non-dual awareness and interbeing affords us the existential ground upon which to question the ego's attachments to the three basic "poisons," as Buddhist ethics conceptualizes them, destroying the natural environment. Overconsumption (the traditional poison of greed) and wastefulness (the poison of aversion) combine with the poison of delusion, here collective repressions such as denial of our own role in the depletion and destruction of natural resources. Harming the environment, seen from an awakened perspective, is nothing other than self-harm.

When we associate overconsumption, dependency, waste, greed, pollution, and the like, with a natural resource, the one that springs to mind is probably oil. Yet there is a far greater natural and human crisis in our midst, one related to another natural resource—water. That we are in the midst of a global freshwater crisis has been well-known for decades, and, around the world, lakes, rivers, and aquifers are being depleted far faster than their natural replenishment. Goldman Sachs estimates that global water consumption is doubling every twenty years, and the United Nations foresees demand exceeding supply by more than 30 percent by 2040 (Interlandi & Tracy, 2010). Precisely because water in this country is taken for granted, used so mindlessly, it calls for our mindful attention; and, as a potential object of mindful and equanimous macro social work, it is important to understand not just all the jaw-dropping statistics concerning its use and waste (e.g., the amount of freshwater used per day to irrigate golf courses worldwide would, per day, support 4.7 billion people at the UN daily minimum), but the global frame in which it is embedded. Global climate change, massive death due to poor sanitation, the unchecked privatization of water sources and distribution, the decaying water infrastructure, and rising social inequities (the coming division between the water haves and have-nots) are just some of the crucial issues demanding a perspective that can be effective only if it is fully interdependent.

A macro social worker employing the eco-mind would approach a crisis such as the US droughts with a refusal to make the alliances that are typical of the social justice paradigm, where the most vulnerable systems receive the most attention. The multifaceted problem of water shortages calls for strategies that are expansive temporally (short-term solutions like drought restrictions and long-term ones like fighting unchecked urban sprawl) and spatially, across environments, including attention to wildlife devastation (the threat of fires), reservoir preservation, and protecting the rights of those who share water sources (farmers, fishermen, and energy plants).

In Zen Buddhism, especially, conservation is traditionally emphasized, and novices are instructed not to waste water. The water used to wash rice can be filtered, and then used in the cooking pot, and the *tenzo* (cook) handles water according to the saying, "See the pot as your own head; see the water as your lifeblood" (Dōgen & Uchiyama, 2005, p. 6). At the main entrance to the precincts of Eiheiji monastery, where Dōgen resided, a pair of large stone pillars commemorates a well-known legend. Here it is told that when Dōgen used a ladle of water to wash his face at Eiheiji, which is deep in the mountains where there is abundant water, he used only half of it and returned the remaining water to the stream for the sake of the people following him (see Narasaki, 1983, pp. 135-38). Dōgen's act is more than mere conservation; it embodies an ethics and "economics of generosity" (Nichtern, 2007, p. 82) that guide and exemplify responsible stewardship based on understanding interdependence and the intrinsic value of the environment itself.

While mindfulness of breath meditation may itself express rudimentary ecological awareness, specific meditative practices are available that incorporate nature imagery or environmental themes. For example, the following verse, from Vietnamese Zen master Thich Nhat Hanh's writing on mindful living, enjoys wide use by his students, who recite it mentally in seated meditation:

> Breathing in, I know that I am breathing in.
>   Breathing out, I know that I am breathing out.
>   Breathing in, I see myself as a flower.
>   Breathing out, I feel fresh.
>   Breathing in, I see myself as a mountain.
>   Breathing out, I feel solid.
>   Breathing in, I see myself as still water.
>   Breathing out, I reflect things as they are.
>   Breathing in, I see myself as space.
>   Breathing out, I feel free. (Nhat Hahn, 1992, pp. 11-12)

Nhat Hanh (1990) also popularizes another method of mindful practice, the recitation of short verse meditations (*gatha*) that not only prompt us to maintain awareness and equanimity in daily life, but also recall us to our interconnectedness with the earth. These verses may be memorized or posted in strategic locations, and recited, for instance, when turning on a water faucet:

> Water flows from high in the mountains.
> > Water runs deep in the Earth.
> > Miraculously, water comes to us,
> > and sustains all life. (Nhat Hanh, 1990, p. 9)

Washing one's hands can become an occasion for renewing dedication to the physical world through skillful means (*upaya*):

> Water flows over these hands.
> > May I use them skillfully
> > to preserve our precious plane. (Nhat Hanh, 1990, p. 10)

With Zen insights, ethics, and practices as a model, macro social workers are in a position to skillfully—which is to say mindfully and with equanimity—respond to the interlinking of individual suffering and collective suffering, unable to avoid the conclusion that the great ecological, social, and cultural crises of our time are also spiritual challenges. Thus, any response calls for a spiritual dimension.

Notes

1. For the historical evolution of engaged Buddhism and its principal figures, see Queen (2000); for a wide-ranging set of examples of how socially engaged Buddhism can be put into practice, thought, and action, see McLeod (2006); for a rich rationale of Buddhist social theory, see Jones (2003); and for a fine example of how Buddhism and ecology intersect, see Tucker & Williams (1998).

2. There is a certain philosophical affinity between no-self and self as context in acceptance and commitment therapy (ACT). Self as context, like no-self, is the featureless perspective from which a person acts, perceives, and remembers. In mindfulness meditation, an awareness of a spacious, interconnected, and timeless or changeless sense of oneself arises, providing the naturalistic basis for transcendent and spiritual experience (Hayes, 1984). Hayes (1984),

describing the Eastern conception of no-self/no-thing, summarizes self as context: "the only events that are without edges (they are not things) are nothing and everything. Experientially, we are everything/nothing" (p. 105). See also Hayes (2002), where the similarities between self as context and Buddhism are more extensively, but tentatively, discussed.

3. We refer the reader to highly accessible Buddhist teachers such as Kornfield (1993; 2009), Salzberg (1995), and Brach (2013) for specific practices to enhance additional attitudinal strengths and virtues.

References

Bateson, G. (2000). *Steps to an ecology of mind*. Chicago: University of Chicago Press.

Besthorn, F. H. (2001). Transpersonal psychology and deep ecological philosophy: Exploring linkages and applications for social work. *Social Thought, 20*, 23-44.

Besthorn, F. H. (2002). Radical environmentalism and the ecological self: Rethinking the concept of self-identity for social work practice. *Journal of Progressive Human Services, 13*, 53-72.

Besthorn, F. H. (2012). Deep ecology's contributions to social work: A ten-year retrospective. *International Journal of Social Welfare, 21*, 248-259.

Brach, T. (2013). *True refuge: Finding peace and freedom in your own awakened heart*. New York: Bantam.

Brueggemann, W. G. (1996). *The practice of macro social work*. Chicago: Nelson-Hall.

Chah, A. (2005). *Everything arises, everything falls away: Teachings on impermanence and the end of suffering* (P. Breiter, Trans.). Boston: Shambhala.

Cook, F. H. (1977). *Hua-yen Buddhism: The jewel net of Indra*. University Park, PA: Pennsylvania State University Press.

Cornell, K. L. (2006). Person-in-situation: History, theory, and new directions for social work practice. *Praxis, 6*, 50-57.

Council on Social Work Education (CSWE). (2001). *Educational policy and accreditation standards*. Alexandria, VA: Author.

Deleuze, G. (1992). Ethology: Spinoza and us. In J. Crary & S. Kwinter (Eds.), *Incorporations* (pp. 625-633). New York: Zone.

Dōgen (2002). The sounds of the valley streams, the forms of the mountains. In F. D. Cook, (Ed. & Trans.), *How to raise an ox: Zen practice as taught in Zen Master Dogen's Shobogenzo* (pp. 69-80). Somerville, MA: Wisdom Publications.

Dōgen, & Uchiyama, K. (2005). *How to cook your life: From the Zen kitchen to enlightenment* (T. Wright, Trans.). Boston: Shambhala.

Dominelli, L. (2012). *Green social work: From environmental crises to environmental justice*. Cambridge, MA: Polity Press.

Elshtain, J. B. (2002). *Jane Addams and the dream of American democracy: A life.* New York: Basic Books.

Fromm, E. (1960). Psychoanalysis and Zen Buddhism. In D. T. Suzuki, E. Fromm, & R. De Martino, *Zen Buddhism and psychoanalysis* (pp. 77-144). New York: Harper & Brothers.

Germain, C. B. (1981). The ecological approach to people–environment transactions. *Social Casework, 62,* 323–331.

Graef, S. (1990). The foundations of ecology in Zen Buddhism. *Religious Education, 85,* 42-50.

Grenard, J. L. (2008). The phenomenology of koan meditation in Zen Buddhism. *Journal of Phenomenological Psychology, 39,* 155-188.

Halsey, M. (1999). Environmental discontinuities: The production and regulation of an eco-experience. *Criminal Justice Policy Review, 10,* 213-255.

Harvey, P. (2000). *An introduction to Buddhist ethics.* Cambridge: Cambridge University Press.

Hayes, S. C. (1984). Making sense of spirituality. *Behaviorism, 12,* 99-110.

Hayes, S. C. (2002). Buddhism and acceptance and commitment therapy. *Cognitive and Behavioral Practice, 9,* 58-66.

Heinsch, M. (2012). Getting down to earth: Finding a place for nature in social work practice. *International Journal of Social Welfare, 21,* 309-318.

Interlandi, J., & Tracy, R. (2010). The new oil. *Newsweek, 156,* 40-46.

Jones, K. (2003). *The new social face of Buddhism: An alternative sociopolitical perspective.* Boston: Wisdom.

Kirst-Ashman, K. K., & Hull, Jr., G. H. (2006). *Generalist practice with organizations and communities.* Belmont, CA: Thompson Brooks/Cole.

Kornfield, J. (1993). *A path with heart: A guide through the perils and promises of spiritual life.* New York: Bantam.

Kornfield, J. (2009). *The wise heart: A guide to the universal teachings of Buddhist psychology.* New York: Bantam.

Langer, E. J., & Moldoveanu, M. (2000). The construct of mindfulness. *Journal of Social Issues, 6,* 1-9.

Lewin, K. (1997). *Resolving social conflicts and field theory in social science.* Washington, D.C.: American Psychological Association.

Loy, D. R. (2008). *Money, sex, war, karma: Notes for a Buddhist revolution.* Boston: Wisdom.

McLeod, M. (Ed.) (2006). *Mindful politics: A Buddhist guide to making the world a better place.* Boston: Wisdom.

Narasaki, I. (1983). *Un, shin, sui, i* (Cloud, heart, water, mind). Tokyo: Pantaka Shuppan.

Nhat Hanh, T. (1990). *Present moment, wonderful moment: Mindfulness verses for daily living.* Berkeley, CA: Parallax Press.

Nhat Hanh, T. (1992). *Touching peace: Practicing the art of mindful living.* Berkeley: Parallax Press.

Nhat Hanh, T. (1993). *Interbeing.* Berkeley, CA: Parallax Press.

Nichtern, E. (2007). *One city: A declaration of interdependence.* Boston: Wisdom.

Olendzki, A. (2010). *Unlimiting mind: The radically experiential psychology of Buddhism.* Boston: Wisdom.

Queen, C. S. (Ed.) (2000). *Engaged Buddhism in the West.* Boston: Wisdom.

Richmond, M. E. (1922). *What is social case work? An introductory description.* New York: Russell Sage Foundation.

Ricketts, E. (2006). Essay on non-teleological thinking. In K. A. Rodger (Ed.), *Breaking through: Essays, journals, and travelogues* (pp. 119-133). Berkeley: University of California Press.

Salzberg, S. (1995). *Lovingkindness: The revolutionary art of happiness.* Boston: Shambhala.

Schatz, M. S., Jenkins, L. E., & Sheafor, B. W. (1990). Milford redefined: A model of initial and advanced generalist social work. *Journal of Social Work Education, 26,* 217-231.

Spellmeyer, K. (2010). *Buddha at the apocalypse: Awakening from a culture of destruction.* Boston: Wisdom.

Suzuki, S. (2011). *Zen mind, beginner's mind.* Boston: Shambhala.

Tucker, M. E., & Williams, D. R. (Eds.). (1998). *Buddhism and ecology: The intersection of dharma and deeds.* Cambridge, MA: Harvard University Press.

Udāna: Exclamations. (2012). Trans. G. DeGraff (Thanissaro Bhikkhu). Retrieved June 1, 2013, from http://www.accesstoinsight.org/lib/authors/thanissaro/udana.pdf.

Zapf, M. K. (2005). The spiritual dimension of person and environment: Perspectives from social work and traditional knowledge. *International Social Work, 48,* 633-642.

Zapf, M. K. (2010). Social work and the environment: Understanding people and place. *Critical Social Work, 11*(3), n. p. Retrieved June 10, 2013, from http://www1.uwindsor.ca/criticalsocialwork/social-work-and-the-environment-understanding-people-and-place.

CHAPTER 10

Thinking Functionally and Contextually About Cultural Diversity in Mindfulness-Based Treatments

Akihiko Masuda, PhD
Georgia State University

Matthew S. Boone, LCSW
University of Arkansas at Little Rock

Mary L. Hill, MA
Georgia State University

Rebecca M. Pasillas, PhD
Texas Tech University Health Sciences Center, Paul L. Foster School of Medicine

Social work in the United States has many points of origin, but one that has often been identified is the settlement house movement spearheaded by Jane Addams in the late nineteenth century. Affluent men and women moved into poor neighborhoods hoping to elevate the moral and intellectual capacities of their neighbors. For all its strengths, including planting the seed of an entire profession devoted to serving those most marginalized in our society, this model of helping contained at least one point of tension which would manifest itself in various ways throughout the history of social work: one group of people, usually one with financial means and power, defining what counts as helping for other groups of people.

Beginning in the late 1960s and early 1970s, this tension, and similar tensions in other disciplines such as psychology and counseling, gave rise to efforts to make service provision more attuned to the unique needs and perspectives of those being served. Since then, what has become known as "cultural competence" has become an integral part of the ethical practice of many health professions. It is generally accepted—if not always optimally put into practice—that social workers must account for the dynamic influence of ethnicity, gender, socioeconomic status, and other domains on clients, social workers, and the helping relationship itself. The NASW (National Association of Social Workers) Standards for Cultural Competence in Social Work Practice, published in 2001, identifies a broad spectrum of practice areas in which social workers should pursue competence: ethics and values, self-awareness, cross-cultural knowledge, cross-cultural skills, service delivery, empowerment and advocacy, creating a diverse workplace, professional education, language diversity, and cross-cultural leadership.

At the same time that cultural competence has taken root in the helping professions, mindfulness and acceptance have become hot topics in clinical research and practice (Baer, 2006; Hayes, Follette, & Linehan, 2004). What have been called "contextual" (Hayes, Levin, Plumb-Vilardaga, Villatte, & Pistorello, 2013; Jacobson, 1997) or "third wave" (Hayes, 2004a, 2004b; Hayes, Masuda, Bissett, Luoma, & Guerrero, 2004) cognitive behavioral therapies have emerged, each with a central emphasis on open and nonjudgmental contact with the "here and now"—in other words, mindfulness and acceptance. Although they differ from one another in various ways, treatments such as dialectical behavior therapy (DBT; Linehan, 1993), mindfulness-based cognitive therapy (MBCT; Segal, Williams, & Teasdale, 2002, 2013), acceptance and commitment therapy (ACT; Hayes, Strosahl, & Wilson, 1999, 2012) all focus, to some degree, on changing one's relationship to inner experiences (e.g., thoughts and feelings) rather than directly changing the experiences themselves, when doing so serves full and vital living. For example, rather than challenging negative thoughts, as one would in Beck's cognitive therapy (Beck, Rush, Shaw, & Emery, 1979), these therapies might encourage the client to simply observe and acknowledge them without being unduly influenced by them.

As researchers and practitioners have introduced mindfulness- and acceptance-based approaches to diverse populations, some have wondered whether they are culturally competent. For example, Hall and his colleagues (Hall, Hong, Zane, & Meyer, 2011) argued that even though these approaches resonate with East Asian philosophies and therefore appear promising for Asian-Americans, they carry Western conceptions of mental health that may undermine their effectiveness. Woidneck and her colleagues (Woidneck, Pratt, Gundy, Nelson, & Twohig, 2012) noted the dearth of ACT studies conducted with samples that include at least 20 percent non-Caucasian subjects. However, Fuchs and her colleagues (Fuchs, Lee, Roemer, & Orsillo, 2013) suggested that the emphasis on context, dialectics, metaphors, values, psychoeducation, and skills building in many mindfulness- and acceptance-based treatments may make them more relevant to clients from marginalized and underserved backgrounds. Conducting a meta-analysis of thirty-two studies with nondominant populations, Fuchs et al. concluded that there is preliminary support for the inclusion of these treatments in culturally competent practice.

Because the evidence is still limited, it is premature to make a strong case for the broader applicability of mindfulness- and acceptance-based approaches. However, given the existing evidence (Fuchs et al., 2013; Hayes, Luoma, Bond, Masuda, & Lillis, 2006; Hayes, Villatte, Levin, & Hildebrandt, 2011), it is plausible to speculate that the conceptual framework behind these interventions may help shed light on the broad range of clinical issues with which individuals from diverse sociocultural backgrounds present. At the same time, like other treatment models, DBT, MBCT, ACT, and other mindfulness- and acceptance-based therapies can easily be conducted in culturally insensitive ways. This is especially true when they are presented as merely collections of techniques (Hayes, Muto, & Masuda, 2011; Masuda, 2014), rather than as conceptual models on which individually tailored clinical work is based.

In this chapter, we argue for the importance of practicing mindfulness- and acceptance-based approaches in ways that take into the account the historical, cultural, and situational contexts in which therapeutic work takes place. To do so, we first present an overview of our philosophical and conceptual worldview. Acknowledging our worldview is important because it identifies the position from which the present topics (e.g., cultural competency, acceptance- and mindfulness-based therapies) are discussed, a position that may be different from—and relative to—the perspectives of others. Next, we examine the implications of this worldview for three areas that are important to culturally attuned social work practice: clinical effectiveness, the therapeutic relationship, and cultural competence. As discussed elsewhere (S. Sue, Zane, Hall, & Berger, 2009), these concepts have different meanings for different scholars and practitioners, and they can be discussed at multiple levels (e.g., individual, organizational, professional, societal). Acknowledging this variability, we focus primarily on the individual level to explore the client-social worker interaction. Finally, using our discussion of clinical effectiveness, the therapeutic relationship, and cultural competence as a jumping off point, we examine key considerations in the cultural adaptation of mindfulness- and acceptance-based approaches.

The View from Where We Are Standing: Functional Contextualism

Our worldview is grounded in a philosophical position called functional contextualism (Biglan & Hayes, 1996; Hayes et al., 2013; see also chapter 11). Functional contextualism, like other contextual theories from which social work draws, such as feminist theory, postmodernism, and systems theory (Howe, 2009), starts with the assumption that a person cannot be fully understood without understanding the unique historical and situational context he or she inhabits. In addition, functional contextualism explicitly seeks to predict and influence human behavior (i.e., anything we do and say), not merely understand it contextually.

There are a few notable features of functional contextualism that are relevant to this chapter. First, functional contextualism is said to be *functional* because it focuses on the impact of a given behavior on the context in which it occurs. Take, for example, a social worker's therapeutic relationship with a client. A functional contextual perspective focuses on how the social worker's actions both *influence* and *are influenced by* the therapeutic context in any given moment. The emphasis is not necessarily on what the behavior of the social worker looks like (e.g., saying "I care about you"), but on how his or her action interacts with or influences the client (the client may be more likely to talk about painful events in her past), and, in turn, how the client's response influences the social worker (the worker may feel encouraged to ask deeper and more probing questions). Stated another way, functional contextualism focuses on the function of a behavior rather than its "form."

Second, a functional contextual approach is said to be *contextual* because it views the function of one's behavior as shaped by the reciprocal relationship between the behavior and the context in which it occurs. "Context" here refers to the dynamic interplay of one's personal history (e.g., learning history, genetic heritage) and the current environment (Biglan & Hayes, 1996). Because one's personal history and current environment are constantly evolving, changing, and influencing one another, the function of one's behavior can change depending on the context in any given moment.

Third, because an individual has his or her own unique history, this focus on function and context naturally leads to an idiographic understanding of therapeutic interactions—that is, an understanding focused at the individual level (Hayes, Muto, et al., 2011; Hayes & Toarmino, 1995). When the social worker leans in, nods gently, and shows by his facial expression that he is moved by what the client is saying, the client's personal history influences whether or not she experiences these actions as empathy. In other words, the client's history determines whether the social worker's actions function as they are intended. Does the client come from a family where empathy is expressed in this way? Does she come from a neighborhood where it is safe to reveal vulnerability? Does she have a history of romantic relationships in which she has been supported and loved? Does she come from a culture in which overt expressions of feeling are valued? Is this the beginning phase of treatment or have they been working for a while? All of these elements of the client's personal history, and many more, may influence whether the social worker's actions function as an empathic response. Thus, there is no way to create a "rule" of how a social worker is supposed to interact with any given client from any given cultural domain. Instead, functional contextualism highlights the importance of sensitivity and openness to moment-by-moment changes in therapeutic interaction. These features of functional contextualism parallel the *process* model of clinician's cultural competency proposed by López (1997).

Fourth, functional contextualism is essentially pragmatic (Biglan & Hayes, 1996; Hayes, Hayes, & Reese, 1988). Rather than merely trying to understand a phenomenon of interest (e.g., why a client cuts himself in response to painful emotions), it also seeks to predict and influence that phenomenon (determine what maintains cutting and prevent it from occurring in the future). From a functional contextual perspective, it is not sufficient to merely understand a behavior; understanding is the beginning of influencing the behavior. Consequently, in the realm of cultural competence, a functional contextualist is not only interested in understanding what cultural competency is, but also how we can influence and promote it (Hayes, 2005).

Finally, the pragmatism of functional contextualism extends to its view of truth; something is "true" only if it works toward a given goal (Hayes, Barnes-Holmes, & Wilson, 2012). This is very different from other philosophies that assume that the world can be discovered as it truly is. Though functional contextualism does not dispute that there is a "real world," it has no investment in trying to uncover it. Rather, it attempts to generate useful ways of speaking about the world (e.g., scientific theories), and these ways of speaking are considered "true" if they serve the purpose of prediction and influence.

Acceptance and Commitment Therapy: A Functional and Contextual Approach to the Promotion of Vital Living

Acceptance and commitment therapy (ACT, see chapter 1) is a mindfulness- and acceptance-based behavior therapy that is grounded in functional contextualism. The tenets of functional contextualism described above, such as its pragmatism, its approach to truth, and its commitment to understanding the function of behavior in its context, are embedded in ACT theory and interventions. Though an extensive analysis of the influence of functional contextualism on ACT is beyond the scope of this chapter, a brief description will suffice to set the stage for the rest of our discussion about acceptance, mindfulness, and cultural diversity. (See Hayes, Strosahl, & Wilson, 2012, and Hayes et al., 2013, for recent in-depth explorations.)

ACT seeks to build psychological flexibility—the ability to be open to one's internal experience without needlessly struggling and to choose effective actions in the service of one's values (Hayes et al.,

2006). A social worker practicing ACT would help a client explore how unwanted behaviors (e.g., bingeing and purging, ruminating, arguing with one's spouse) are responses to particular circumstances—in other words, how they function in various contexts. The social worker would hone in on one specific function of behavior that is thought to be a core component in psychopathology and human suffering in general: *experiential avoidance*, or attempting to avoid or control internal experiences (thoughts, feelings, memories) and the situations that give rise to them (Hayes, Wilson, Gifford, Follette, & Strosahl, 1996). The social worker would encourage the client to examine whether avoiding and controlling painful experiences serves the purpose of building a meaningful life. If not, then the social worker would teach the client to let go of struggling with those thoughts and feelings (i.e., acceptance) and engage in actions that are driven by his or her values (i.e., commitment). To do so, the social worker would enlist mindfulness, experiential exercises, values clarification exercises, and traditional behavior therapy interventions to facilitate greater flexibility in the presence of painful thoughts and feelings.

This focus on building patterns of action in the service of personally chosen values is where ACT is especially pragmatic. No behavior is "good" or "bad" in ACT; behavior is either "workable" or "unworkable" in the service of building a life worth living. This extends to behavior such as thinking, where social workers and clients are often tempted to look for truth. In other cognitive behavioral therapies, the client might be encouraged to examine the evidence for and against a distressing thought like "I always fail" or "I'm a burden." In ACT, the client would be encouraged to mindfully notice these thoughts, neither engaging them nor pushing them away, and decide whether they are useful for guiding behavior. Or, stated in terms of function, the client would be helped to change the function of his or her distressing thoughts from organizing behavior (e.g., thinking "I'm a failure" and then putting no effort into succeeding) to being merely a part of the endless stream of internal experiences, nothing more or less. Personally chosen values are then identified to organize behavior in place of those distressing thoughts.

Some Implications of this Perspective for the Practice of Social Work

The functional contextual perspective, and what follows from it (e.g., ACT), have implications for practicing social work in a way that is culturally attuned and contextually specific. In this section, we will briefly review these implications in the interrelated domains of clinical competence, the therapeutic relationship, and cultural competence.

Clinical Competence

Clinicians and researchers have yet to reach a consensus on what defines a therapy as clinically competent (S. Sue et al., 2009; Whaley & Davis, 2007). From a functional and contextual perspective, the question of clinical competence should be pragmatic: prediction and influence. Since it is intended to promote psychological flexibility and vital living (Hayes et al., 2006), ACT is competent only if it does so. By this standard, a growing body of literature suggests that ACT is generally effective (i.e., clinically competent) for a diverse group of individuals with a wide range of problems and that it achieves this effectiveness by promoting psychological flexibility and its components (Hayes et al., 2006; Hayes, Villatte, Levin, & Hildebrandt, 2011; Ruiz, 2010). However, these data do not show that ACT is effective for every person in every situation. At the individual level of analysis, it is crucial to evaluate whether ACT provided by a given social worker is effective for this client, with this sociocultural background, in this situation, with this issue, and in this interaction. In other words, asking whether ACT is clinically competent largely ignores the contextual nature of social work and other helping professions (Luoma, Hayes, & Walser, 2007).

The Therapeutic Relationship

As noted above, to work functionally and contextually, the social worker must assess the impact of his or her actions on the client—and vice versa—from moment to moment. Such awareness allows the social worker to choose effective interventions and to adjust the course of the work as necessary. Therefore, at least theoretically, the social worker must practice mindfulness. For example, the social worker could focus externally by paying attention to small changes in the client's affect and tuning in to the pitch and pace of the client's speech (Wilson & Dufrene, 2008). Or the social worker could focus internally by observing both positive and negative thoughts about the client and bringing gentle awareness to urges to intervene when doing so is not clinically useful.

The goal of prediction and influence also shapes how the social worker intervenes. For example, ACT usually stresses experiential learning over intellectual learning. However, if experiential interventions such as metaphors and mindfulness exercises do not move the client toward psychological flexibility, they have not met the "influence" part of the goal. Similarly, if providing intellectual learning, such as giving a lecture—something usually discouraged in ACT and most treatment models—promotes psychological flexibility, then it *has* met the goal.

Cultural Competence

From a functional contextual perspective, asking whether ACT, or any other treatment model, is culturally competent is too broad a question and one that is perhaps misleading. Whether a social worker's actions are culturally competent is determined functionally, contextually, and pragmatically. As such, a more appropriate question would be to ask if the actions of the social worker, grounded in a particular treatment model, are culturally competent in the context of a particular therapeutic relationship with a particular client. The social worker might have the appropriate awareness, knowledge, and skills—three domains of cultural competence outlined by D. W. Sue (2006)—but if his or her actions do not help to move the client toward a particular therapeutic goal (insight, self-actualization, symptom reduction, psychological flexibility, or whatever the treatment hopes to achieve), then that social worker's interaction with the client is not culturally competent. Thus, clinical competence is essential to cultural competence. This perspective parallels the perspective of Stanley Sue and colleagues (2009): cultural competence is a multidimensional process of "scientific mindedness" (i.e., forming and testing hypotheses), dynamic sizing (flexibility in generalization and individuation), and culture-specific resources (having knowledge and skills to work with other cultures) in response to different kinds of clients" (p. 529).

Implications for the Culturally Competent Practice of Mindfulness- and Acceptance-Based Treatments in Social Work

In this final section, we will briefly explore the implications of a functional contextual perspective to specific areas of cultural competence. Note that though these topics are important to the practice of mindfulness and acceptance-based treatments such as ACT, they are likely to be relevant to other treatment approaches as well.

Cross-Cultural Empathy

We never fully understand others, but we can choose to make efforts to do so. In any treatment model, the social worker must make sincere attempts to understand the client's experience through his or her eyes—to see what the client sees and feel what the client feels. Working functionally and contextually, however, requires using these perspective-taking skills to understand the reciprocal influence of the client and his or her environment. This is crucial to identifying how the client's problems are expressed and maintained as well as collaboratively developing and evaluating realistic solutions.

One practical way for the social worker to build a functional and contextual understanding is to go outside the office and meet the client in his or her real life context. Home visits are particularly useful for this purpose, especially for social workers who usually serve their clients in inpatient or outpatient settings. Seeing the client outside allows the social worker to see and feel the issues and concerns that the client experiences. For example, if the client reports financial difficulty, home visits will help the social worker to see the client's living conditions (e.g., members in the household, interpersonal interactions and roles played by each of the household members, resources the client has or needs) and to feel what it is like to live in the environment. Through the home visit, the social worker may see details of the client's life that otherwise may remain hidden, such as additional problems to be solved, previously unidentified strengths of the client and the environment, and realistic priorities for what needs to be done.

Cultural Bias of Treatment Models

It is difficult to state conclusively whether mindfulness- and acceptance-based interventions such as ACT or DBT are culturally biased; nevertheless, it is safe to say that they are not bias-free. Like all approaches, they draw on specific philosophical and conceptual perspectives (e.g., dialectics and behaviorism in DBT, functional contextualism in ACT). However, from a functional contextual point of view, following a particular perspective is not necessarily problematic if doing so allows the social worker to be effective for a wide range of concerns experienced by people with diverse sociocultural backgrounds (Hayes, 2005). In other words, the goal of a culturally competent intervention is not to be bias free, but to be idiographically effective across diverse populations of clients (Masuda, 2014). To be effective, however, it is important to make efforts to reduce the negative influence of biases that both the clinician and client hold. One way to do this is for the social worker to develop an awareness of his or her own biases.

Awareness of the Social Worker's Own Bias

Judging what is clinically relevant for a given client is not always an easy task. Our professional and personal histories inevitably shape our notions of mental health and wellness. Throughout the course of our work, we must be cautious not to rigidly adhere to our assumptions about various sociocultural factors, like what constitutes a family, what defines a meaningful life, and what is the optimal amount of self-disclosure in a close relationship. We find it useful to touch on the inevitability of biases and the potential impact of these biases on the therapeutic work as early as possible. For example, the first author informs clients that he makes the best effort to be culturally sensitive and competent, but that he nevertheless may offend the client without knowing it. He asks the client to let him know when he comes across as culturally insensitive so that he can address any ruptures to the therapeutic alliance and be more attuned in the future.

Taking a mindful and open stance toward one's biases is also crucial for separating the client's problem behaviors from the social worker's internal reactions (Hayes, Strosahl, & Wilson, 2012). Just as the client must learn to engage flexibly with thoughts and feelings in a given life context, the social worker must also learn to act flexibly in the presence of any personal biases that emerge in the therapeutic relationship. Ideally, when the social worker encounters a thought, feeling, or urge that could negatively impact the work, he or she can draw on the psychological flexibility model itself for guidance. Hayes, Strosahl, and Wilson (2012) suggest that ACT therapists do the following: "acknowledge the issue (privately at first [and] then to the client if that seems clinically useful); be more open with it psychologically; and focus on the values-based actions that can be taken in the service of the client" (p. 160).

For example, the second author relies on ACT techniques when he encounters thoughts or feelings that threaten to pull him away from being present with clients who are culturally different from him. When he has an occasional racially biased thought, or a sense of disconnection based on the client's "otherness" (according to his mind), he welcomes these experiences as naturally occurring phenomena. How could they *not* show up for a person who grew up in the United States, with its history of racial division? At the same time, he does not give them any weight, neither shaming himself for having them nor fighting their existence. Instead, he simply imagines "making space" for them, treating them like invited guests, while not allowing them to have any sway over his actions in the moment. Instead, he centers himself on his breath and tunes in again to the lived experience of the person in front of him.

Adaptation of Treatment Techniques

From a functional and contextual standpoint, structural modifications of treatment techniques are always expected in practice (Hayes, Muto, et al., 2011; Masuda, 2014). The right structure, form, and style of treatment are determined at an individual level depending on, for example, the needs of the client, the capabilities of the social worker, and the quality and developmental stage of the therapeutic relationship (Lee, 2010; Luoma et al., 2007). Modifications may include changing the content or length of mindfulness exercises, metaphors, and experiential exercises or altering the style of the working relationship, such as being more or less directive or didactic (Drossel, McCausland, Schneider, & Cattivelli, 2014). While interventions can vary greatly in ACT, any modifications should be made in the service of achieving vital and meaningful living.

Functional adaptations of treatment techniques are especially important for cultural competence (Drossel et al., 2014; Masuda, 2014). Simply adhering to a treatment protocol—for example, presenting a mindfulness exercise *exactly* as it is written in a manual—is likely to fall short of truly supporting change in a client's life (Hall et al., 2011). When the social worker becomes caught up with the content of a therapeutic technique (e.g., the exact words of the metaphor or experiential exercise) rather than its function (e.g., facilitating acceptance or the identification of values), he or she is likely to be less aware of the actual impact of delivering that technique. For example, the "Chessboard Metaphor" often used in ACT (Hayes, Strosahl, & Wilson, 2012, pp. 231-233) is designed to promote an experience of the self that is distinct from the events the person experiences (i.e., thoughts and feelings). In the metaphor, the pawns, rooks, and other chess pieces are the "good" and "bad" thoughts that fight an endless war with one another; the self is the board that simply observes the war without becoming invested in the outcome. In many ACT texts (e.g., Hayes, Strosahl, & Wilson, 2012), the black chess pieces are presented as the "bad" thoughts and the white pieces are presented as the "good" thoughts. For many clients, especially those who come from an ethnic background commonly identified as "black" or "brown" in a given culture, this exercise could elicit strong countertherapeutic responses, such as a sense of being invalidated or even violated. Adapting it to deemphasize the color of the pieces may be necessary. As another example, the word "mindfulness" has different connotations in different cultural contexts. Clients who come from evangelical Christian traditions that discourage them from engaging in what are perceived as "New Age" or alternative religious practices—lest they leave themselves open to satanic influence (see, for example, Peretti, 1986)—will likely benefit from alternative terminology, such as "becoming aware" or "noticing." Though therapeutic mistakes and periods of "cultural incompetence" are inevitable, we encourage social workers to be mindful of the *intended* function as well as the *actual* function of every intervention and adapt their actions accordingly.

The Role of Language

What is essential about the role of language in clinical practice is not necessarily which language(s) the client and the social worker speak, but how language maintains problem behavior or facilitates values-based living. Language is a two-edged sword. It causes suffering unique to humans, and at the same time, it can promote a full and flexible life (Hayes, Strosahl, et al., 2012). For example, we can be tyrannized by thoughts like "I'll never amount to anything" or guided by values statements like "I want to build close relationships and pursue a meaningful career" (see chapters 1 and 7). As such, it is crucial for social workers to pay close attention to see where language leads the client in any given moment.

In the therapeutic interaction, it is ideal for the social worker to use the language(s) that promote the vital living of the client. It is also important for the social worker to be aware of other aspects of language, such as the client's level of literacy and how comfortable the client is with putting words to thoughts and feelings. Knowing these aspects of language helps the social worker adapt and alter therapy techniques and exercises in order to optimize treatment (Fuchs et al., 2013). Take, for example, a thirteen-year-old bilingual client who speaks both English and Spanish. When she is with her mother, she uses Spanish to express her emotions and thoughts, not necessarily because she is more proficient in Spanish but because she feels more connected with her mother when she does so (Marian & Kaushanskaya, 2008). If the therapeutic goal is to promote the quality of the mother-daughter relationship, Spanish may be the preferred choice of language in the clinical work.

However, the social worker is not always capable of speaking the client's preferred language. For example, an English-speaking social worker and a first-generation Japanese client may have to rely on English to communicate. (This is likely the more common situation in cross-cultural social work in North America.) In this case, what is important is not necessarily to use the language with which the client is most comfortable (i.e., Japanese), but to make an effort to maximize treatment effectiveness using the language the client and social worker have in common. However, even when doing so, words from the client's primary language can be incorporated into treatment interventions. For example, if the social worker invites the client to mindfully notice a difficult thought without engaging it, the client could choose an English thought (e.g., "I'm stupid"), its Japanese equivalent (e.g., "*Ore ha bakada*"), or both, depending on which choice would best facilitate undermining the thought's influence on the client's behavior.

The Role of Significant Others in the Client's Life Context

Western mental health often stresses the importance of confidentiality and secrecy, and social workers usually make every effort to keep the client's experience in therapy *within* the therapy context. As such, clinicians tend to focus exclusively on the client, leaving the client's life context untouched. However, there are times when involving significant others in treatment may be beneficial (Pasillas & Masuda, in press). These may be family members, partners, neighbors, and spiritual leaders who share the same cultural background as the client and who act as facilitators to the treatment, translating concepts and interventions into a form that is more culturally relevant. Gaining support from significant others increases the likelihood that an intervention will be a success. Important considerations should include the client's willingness to involve a significant other, whether it is possible to bring the person into the session, whether the person is willing to support the interventions of the social worker, and how the significant other can assist the client in pursuing values.

The Role of Religion and Spirituality

There has historically been tension between religion and psychotherapy (Cummings, O'Donohue, & Cummings, 2009), and psychotherapy has too often disregarded the legitimacy of religion and spirituality in its theories and interventions. In many cases, however, religion and spirituality are essential parts of a client's values, and promoting valued living requires that the social worker explore and understand their role in the client's life (Murrell, Schmalz, & Sinha, 2014) and, where appropriate, incorporate them into the therapeutic work. From a functional contextual perspective, the role of belief, ritual, and practice in both the therapeutic work and the client's life is a functional issue, not an ontological one. In other words, neither the treatment nor the social worker needs to take a position on the existence of a God or gods. The social worker only needs to understand the purpose and meaning of religion and spirituality in the client's life and, if possible, harness these to build values-driven actions. For example, the second author of this chapter, who grew up as an Episcopalian, once worked with a Muslim couple seeking help for their explosive arguments. One session they arrived saying they had not fought in the previous two weeks, a notable exception. When asked about this, they said they had not been fighting because it was Ramadan, the Muslim month of fasting, and they were doing their best to work things out more calmly. This demonstrated not only the power of the couple's religious beliefs to influence their behavior, but also that under the right circumstances, they already possessed the skills to work through conflict peacefully. Thereafter, channeling the spirit of Ramadan was woven into conversations about values in therapy, and doing so allowed them to organize their behavior in a way that their reactive emotions had previously done. The intensity and frequency of their arguments decreased as they began to accept their reactions to each other without giving into them, something that was supported and dignified by their values.

Conclusion

As ACT and similar treatments have been extended to a wide range of populations and clinical contexts, cultural competency and cultural adaptations have become imperative. It is important to highlight that cultural competency does not exist by itself, and that it cannot be separated from the context in which it occurs. Similarly, mindfulness- and acceptance-based treatments do not exist in a vacuum; they occur in a given context. Social workers and clients always bring their unique histories to the therapeutic encounter. With this in mind, we hope this chapter evokes thoughtful questions and greater awareness to help social workers and clients come into the present and pursue what matters.

References

Baer, R. A. (2006). *Mindfulness-based treatment approaches: Clinician's guide to evidence base and applications*. San Diego, CA: Elsevier.

Beck, A. T., Rush, A. J., Shaw, B. F., & Emery, G. (1979). *Cognitive therapy of depression*. New York: Guilford Press.

Biglan, A., & Hayes, S. C. (1996). Should the behavioral sciences become more pragmatic? The case for functional contextualism in research on human behavior. *Applied & Preventive Psychology, 5*, 47-57.

Cummings, N., O'Donohue, W., & Cummings, J. (2009). *Psychology's war on religion*. Phoenix, AZ: Zeig, Tucker & Theisen.

Drossel, C., McCausland, C., Schneider, N., & Cattivelli, R. (2014). Functional adaptation of acceptance- and mindfulness-based therapies: An ethical imperative. In A. Masuda (Ed.), *Mindfulness and acceptance in multicultural competency: A contextual approach to sociocultural diversity in theory and practice*. Oakland, CA: New Harbinger.

Fuchs, C., Lee, J. K., Roemer, L., & Orsillo, S. M. (2013). Using mindfulness- and acceptance-based treatments with clients from nondominant cultural and/or marginalized backgrounds: Clinical considerations, meta-analysis findings, and introduction to the special series: Clinical considerations in using acceptance and mindfulness-based treatments with diverse populations. *Cognitive and Behavioral Practice, 20*, 1-12.

Hall, G. C. N., Hong, J. J., Zane, N. W. S., & Meyer, O. L. (2011). Culturally competent treatments for Asian Americans: The relevance of mindfulness and acceptance-based psychotherapies. *Clinical Psychology: Science and Practice, 18*, 215-231.

Hayes, S. C. (2004a). Acceptance and commitment therapy and the new behavior therapies: Mindfulness, acceptance, and relationship. In S. C. Hayes, V. M. Follette & M. M. Linehan (Eds.), *Mindfulness and acceptance: Expanding the cognitive-behavioral tradition* (pp. 1-29). New York: Guilford Press.

Hayes, S. C. (2004b). Acceptance and commitment therapy, relational frame theory, and the third wave of behavioral and cognitive therapies. *Behavior Therapy, 35*, 639-665.

Hayes, S. C. (2005). Eleven rules for a more successful clinical psychology. *Journal of Clinical Psychology, 61*, 1055-1060.

Hayes, S. C., Barnes-Holmes, D., & Wilson, K. G. (2012). Contextual behavioral science: Creating a science more adequate to the challenge of the human condition. *Journal of Contextual Behavioral Science, 1*, 1-16.

Hayes, S. C., Follette, V. M., & Linehan, M. M. (2004). *Mindfulness and acceptance: Expanding the cognitive-behavioral tradition*. New York: Guilford Press.

Hayes, S. C., Hayes, L. J., & Reese, H. W. (1988). Finding the philosophical core: A review of Stephen C. Pepper's world hypotheses: A study in evidence. *Journal of the Experimental Analysis of Behavior, 50*, 97-111.

Hayes, S. C., Levin, M. E., Plumb-Vilardaga, J., Villatte, J. L., & Pistorello, J. (2013). Acceptance and commitment therapy and contextual behavioral science: Examining the progress of a distinctive model of behavioral and cognitive therapy. *Behavior Therapy, 44,* 180-198.

Hayes, S. C., Luoma, J. B., Bond, F. W., Masuda, A., & Lillis, J. (2006). Acceptance and commitment therapy: Model, processes and outcomes. *Behaviour Research and Therapy, 44,* 1-25.

Hayes, S. C., Masuda, A., Bissett, R., Luoma, J., & Guerrero, L. F. (2004). DBT, FAP and ACT: How empirically oriented are the new behavior therapy technologies? *Behavior Therapy, 35,* 35-54.

Hayes, S. C., Muto, T., & Masuda, A. (2011). Seeking cultural competence from the ground up. *Clinical Psychology: Science & Practice, 18,* 232-237.

Hayes, S. C., Strosahl, K. D., & Wilson, K. G. (1999). *Acceptance and commitment therapy: An experiential approach to behavior change.* New York: Guilford Press.

Hayes, S. C., Strosahl, K. D., & Wilson, K. G. (2012). *Acceptance and commitment therapy: The process and practice of mindful change* (2nd ed.). New York: Guilford Press.

Hayes, S. C., & Toarmino, D. (1995). If behavioral principles are generally applicable, why is it necessary to understand cultural diversity? *The Behavior Therapist, 18,* 21-23.

Hayes, S. C., Villatte, M., Levin, M., & Hildebrandt, M. (2011). Open, aware, and active: Contextual approaches as an emerging trend in the behavioral and cognitive therapies. *Annual Review of Clinical Psychology, 7,* 141-168.

Hayes, S. C., Wilson, K. G., Gifford, E. V., Follette, V. M., & Strosahl, K. (1996). Experiential avoidance and behavioral disorders: A functional dimensional approach to diagnosis and treatment. *Journal of Consulting and Clinical Psychology, 64,* 1152-1168.

Howe, D. (2009). *A brief introduction to social work theory.* Basingstoke, UK: Palgrave Macmillan.

Jacobson, N. S. (1997). Can contextualism help? *Behavior Therapy, 28,* 435-443.

Lee, E. (2010). Revisioning cultural competencies in clinical social work practice. *Families in Society, 91,* 272-279.

Linehan, M. M. (1993). *Cognitive-behavioral treatment of borderline personality disorder.* New York: Guilford Press.

López, S. R. (1997). Cultural competence in psychotherapy: A guide for clinicians and their supervisors. In C. E. Watkins, Jr. (Ed.), *Handbook of psychotherapy supervision* (pp. 570-588). Hoboken, NJ: John Wiley & Sons.

Luoma, J. B., Hayes, S. C., & Walser, R. D. (2007). *Learning ACT: An acceptance and commitment therapy skills-training manual for therapists.* Oakland, CA: New Harbinger.

Marian, V., & Kaushanskaya, M. (2008). Words, feelings, and bilingualism: Cross-linguistic differences in emotionality of autobiographical memories. *The Mental Lexicon, 3,* 72-90.

Masuda, A. (2014). Psychotherapy in a cultural context. In A. Masuda (Ed.), *Mindfulness and acceptance in multicultural competency: A contextual approach to sociocultural diversity in theory and practice*. Oakland, CA: New Harbinger.

Murrell, A., Schmalz, J., & Sinha, A. (2014). Acceptance, mindfulness, and spirituality. In A. Masuda (Ed.), *Mindfulness and acceptance in multicultural competency: A contextual approach to sociocultural diversity in theory and practice*. Oakland, CA: New Harbinger.

National Association of Social Workers. (2001). *NASW standards for cultural competence in social work practice*. Washington, DC: Author.

Pasillas, R. M., & Masuda, A. (2014). Cultural competency and acceptance and commitment therapy. In A. Masuda (Ed.), *Mindfulness and acceptance in multicultural competency: A contextual approach to sociocultural diversity in theory and practice*. Oakland, CA: New Harbinger.

Peretti, F. E. (1986). *This present darkness*. Wheaton, Illinois: Crossway Books.

Ruiz, F. J. (2010). A review of acceptance and commitment therapy (ACT) empirical evidence: Correlational, experimental psychopathology, component and outcome studies. *International Journal of Psychology & Psychological Therapy, 10*, 125-162.

Segal, Z. V., Williams, J. M. G., & Teasdale, J. D. (2002). *Mindfulness-based cognitive therapy for depression: A new approach to preventing relapse*. New York: Guilford Press.

Segal, Z. V., Williams, J. M. G., & Teasdale, J. D. (2013). *Mindfulness-based cognitive therapy for depression* (2nd ed.). New York: Guilford Press.

Sue, D. W. (2006). *Multicultural social work practice*. Hoboken, NJ: John Wiley & Sons.

Sue, S., Zane, N., Hall, G. C. N., & Berger, L. K. (2009). The case for cultural competency in psychotherapeutic interventions. *Annual Review of Psychology, 60*, 525-548.

Whaley, A. L., & Davis, K. E. (2007). Cultural competence and evidence-based practice in mental health services: A complementary perspective. *American Psychologist, 62*, 563-574.

Wilson, K. G., & Dufrene, T. (2008). *Mindfulness for two: An acceptance and commitment therapy approach to mindfulness in psychotherapy*. Oakland, CA: New Harbinger.

Woidneck, M. R., Pratt, K. M., Gundy, J. M., Nelson, C. R., & Twohig, M. P. (2012). Exploring cultural competence in acceptance and commitment therapy outcomes. *Professional Psychology: Research and Practice, 43*, 227-233.

CHAPTER 11

Contextual Behavioral Science and Social Work: A Natural and Effective Partnership?

Joanne Steinwachs, LCSW
Private Practice, Denver, Colorado

Matthew S. Boone, LCSW
University of Arkansas at Little Rock

This chapter explores the possibility that social work and contextual behavioral science are a natural and effective partnership. Contextual behavioral science (CBS; Hayes, Barnes-Holmes, & Wilson, 2012) is an emerging scientific tradition rooted in behaviorism. CBS weaves together a clearly articulated philosophy of science—functional contextualism—with behavioral principles and an extensive program of basic research in human language and cognition (relational frame theory; Hayes, Barnes-Holmes, & Roche, 2001) to develop interventions at the micro, mezzo, and macro levels. In a recent review article describing the foundations, purpose, and possible future directions of CBS, Hayes et al. (2012) describe it as a "strategy of scientific and practical development that gathers together a coherent set of philosophical assumptions and strategies of knowledge development and application" (p. 2) with the goal of creating "a behavioral science more adequate to the challenge of the human condition" (p. 2). "Coherent" means that philosophy, theory, research, practice, and the dissemination of interventions all draw from and inform one another.

This coherence is something social work theory and treatment development has historically lacked (Wakefield, 1996b). Though social work has attempted to tie together its diverse array of theoretical perspectives with higher-order theories like ecosystems theory, doing so has not reconciled these perspectives or led to the development of close links between theory, research, and practice (Wakefield, 1996a). CBS, on the other hand, attempts to link therapeutic interventions to basic principles (e.g., operant and classical conditioning) and a comprehensive theory of language, all of which can be tested and refined to build better interventions. From this effort has emerged acceptance and commitment therapy (ACT, said as one word; Hayes, Strosahl, & Wilson, 2012; see chapter 1), which has a rapidly growing evidence base for a variety of problems. However, CBS fits effectively with many, if not all, of the interventions described in this book.

A truly comprehensive examination of the history, aims, and future directions of CBS could fill an entire book, and readers are directed elsewhere (e.g., Hayes, Barnes-Holmes, & Wilson, 2012; Hayes, Levin, Plumb-Vilardaga, Villatte, & Pistorello, 2013; Hayes, Strosahl, & Wilson, 2012). We will discuss some key features of CBS that we believe are a good fit for social work, including its underlying philosophy, its theory, its comprehensive model of intervention development, and its nonhierarchical values. Both authors give personal accounts to ground the discussion in experiences that may be common to social work practitioners and to demonstrate the personal motivations behind our advocacy of CBS as a good fit for social work.

Social Work and Philosophy: Naming Our Starting Assumptions

Why start with a philosophy of science, as CBS does? Many of us have never taken a philosophy class or thought deeply about the intersection of theory and practice. However, as Healy (2005) observes, "all practicing social workers are social work theorists in that each of us constructs understandings that guide us in identifying who and what should be the focus of our practice and how we should proceed" (xii). Therefore, it is important that we articulate the assumptions from which we are starting.

The practice area for social work is wide, and social work theories are bewilderingly diverse (Hutchison, 2008). However, the dynamic interaction of people and their social and environmental contexts has been at the root of social work since its earliest history. One of the first books on social work practice and theory (Richmond, 1917/1955) describes a focus on both the personality of the client and the client's social setting, which includes family forces, personal forces, neighborhood forces, civic forces, private charitable forces, and public relief forces. Many social work writers have suggested that the only reasonable response to this level of diversity is generalist or eclectic practice (Wakefield, 1996a). However, attending to multiple levels of person/environment interaction can create confusion for the social worker. Where to start?

Social work interventions, when linked only loosely to theory, or linked indiscriminately to a variety of theories, can lead to conceptual incoherence. Lazarus and Beutler (1993) suggest that technical eclecticism—that is, using many techniques from different approaches—while holding a single theoretical stance is the most effective position for clinicians. *Theoretical* eclecticism, in their opinion, is inherently unstable (Lazarus, 1967; Lazarus & Beutler, 1993).

The discussion of the relationship between social work theory and practice is complex and longstanding (Brekke, 2012; Epstein, 1986; Göppner & Hämäläinen, 2007; Johnson, 1947; Kirk & Reid, 2002;

Longhofer & Floersch, 2012), and to address it comprehensively is beyond the scope of this chapter. Ecosystems theory has been offered as an overarching conceptual framework for the profession, but it has shown significant limitations, both in application to direct clinical practice (Wakefield, 1996a) and in resolving the incoherence of social work theory (Wakefield, 1996b). Ecosystems theory may be considered a descriptive contextual perspective (Hayes, 1993) as opposed to a functional contextual one. That is, it is effective in describing the complex web of person and environment but gives little direction in affecting that web (Wakefield, 1996a). Thus, though contextual theories have been important throughout the history of social work (Hutchison, 2008), finding an *applied* contextual theory for social work practice has been elusive.

We would argue that one barrier to applying a contextual perspective like ecosystems theory in practice is that it is not a "theory" in the scientific sense. For example, it cannot be tested or falsified. Without this, it becomes merely a compelling description of the world. CBS emphasizes testable contextual theories (e.g., relational frame theory, described later), but it starts with a philosophy of science that answers questions most of science does not consider necessary to ask, such as "How do we define truth?" and "Are we trying to describe the world as it really is?" This philosophy, functional contextualism, is rooted in behaviorism, to which we turn next.

The Behavioral Tradition in Social Work

Social workers began a relationship with behavioral methods in the 1960s and found radical behaviorism to be a good match for social work values and interests (Gambrill, 1995). At that time, the University of Michigan School of Social Work required all students to take a course in basic behavioral principles (Gambrill, 1995). Contemporary social workers are often misinformed about behaviorism, with many writers stating that behaviorists have no interest in emotion, thoughts, and urges. This is not the case. As Gambrill (1995) observes, "Not only are private events such as thoughts and feelings not dismissed, they are viewed as behaviors that themselves require an explanation (traced to their environmental, evolutionary, and/or psychological origins). They are assumed to have the same functions as public (observable) events. The advantage of viewing thoughts and feelings as behaviors is that they cannot as readily be inaccurately presumed to be the sole cause of behavior" (p. 9). Behavioral interventions by social workers have been used with a wide variety of clients in therapy, prevention, group, and school settings (Gambrill, 1995; Dillenburger, Godina, & Burton, 1997). Social work and behaviorism have a long and robust history, so it is sensible that social work might look again to this approach.

Functional Contextualism: The Philosophical Ground of CBS

Functional contextualism (Hayes, Hayes, & Reese, 1988; also see chapter 10) is a contemporary extension of radical behaviorism that informs CBS at every level, from basic science (e.g., relational frame theory) to treatment development (e.g., ACT). To help ground the reader in functional contextualism, we will give a brief overview. Pepper (1942; reviewed in Hayes, Hayes, & Reese, 1988) describes four philosophical worldviews that may inform scientific thinking: mechanism, formism, organicism, and contextualism. We will focus on only two: contextualism and mechanism. He suggests that each philosophical worldview has a root metaphor and a criterion for determining truth. For mechanism, the root metaphor is a machine made of discrete parts that exist on their own and are driven by a source of energy. The truth criterion, or how we evaluate truth from this perspective, is correspondence: "This is true because it is how this thing really works." Examples from psychology might be the id and ego or schemas. Behavior is propelled by these internal mechanisms, much as a car is propelled by its engine.

Mechanism starts with the assumption that there are real things in the world that can be described and understood. Functional contextualism comes from a different perspective. Functional contextualism does not deny that there might be "real things" in the "real world"; it just does not focus there. Functional contextualism's root metaphor is a process metaphor: the ongoing *act-in-context*. Unlike a machine, which is a "thing," the act-in-context is an interactive process, much like social work's person-in-environment. The term "act-in-context" is hyphenated to underscore that behavior is not separable from its context. For example, for people with different histories, the act of taking the first sip of a cocktail could have many functions: connecting with friends, trying something new, or falling into old self-destructive patterns. The function of the behavior would be determined by its historical and situational context. The past and future are embedded in the present, and events that look the same may have different functions. Functional contextualism's truth criterion is *successful working*: "In this situation, does this behavior lead to the desired outcome?" Something is true if it works to accomplish stated goals.

Successful working is possibly the most challenging conceptual shift for most social workers. Instead of looking at a client from the stance of "healthy" or "correct," the social worker would approach the client's behavior with this question: In this context, what is this behavior in service of? Successful working in the short term might be using alcohol to stay connected to friends. In the long term, that behavior might not "work" for the same purposes. Successful working cannot be determined beforehand. It is determined collaboratively between the social worker and the client.

• *Becoming a Functional Contextualist: a Personal Story*

Functional contextualism is a way of approaching behavior from a counterintuitive perspective, one that differs profoundly from our customary point of view. There are many scholarly discussions of functional contextualism (Hayes et al., 1988; Dymond & Roche, 2013), but I (JS, the first author) will speak about functional contextualism from a personal, clinical, and purely pragmatic place.

Early in my career as a social worker, I found it very difficult to reconcile the overarching principle of person-in-environment with actual interventions with the client. The "problem" always seemed to be some inherent quality of the client that I needed to change. The client was borderline, was depressed, or was attachment disordered, for example. I needed to find a way to make those things go away. As I continued in my career, I found myself becoming more frustrated with the conceptual tools with which I had to work. I found myself becoming more reactive and less responsive to the client's troubles. They needed to just stop being personality disordered, depressed, traumatized, and anxious. We both agreed that I needed to do something to effect that change, and I was at a loss for what to do.

This was illustrated to me one day with a client, Mary, who presented with major depressive disorder and dependent features. In session she was often silent, staring at me and waiting for me to tell her what to do. We spent many hours with me explaining to Mary that her depression had to do with the introjected criticism of her mother and her poor self-esteem. She agreed with me, but continued to be depressed and dependent on me to tell her what to do in session.

The office that I worked in had a large window from which one could see the street two stories below. Mary would often spend the session looking out the window, silent. One day, as I was once again beginning to help Mary understand her low self-esteem and its origins, as she gazed out the window, she gave a sharp gasp, stood, and ran out of the room. I heard her running down the stairs. Curious and shaken, I looked down at the street below, just in time to see Mary dart out into traffic to grab a frightened dog that had wandered onto the street. I watched in amazement as Mary held off traffic, comforted the dog, and then chastised the owner.

Then, I saw Mary turn and look up at the window of my office. By the time she was at my door again, the Mary I knew was back.

It was at this moment that I realized on a profound level how sensitive behavior was to context. The person I saw in the office was just Mary doing her "going to therapy" behavior, and there was a rich and vast repertoire of behaviors that I had never suspected. It was probably on this day that I became a functional contextualist—if not yet in name, then certainly in how I thought about client behavior. But what to do? How could I use this awareness to change Mary's behavior in the therapy office?

With Mary's help I began to do my first fumbling functional analysis. I asked her: What do you think our work is together? How could we bring the Mary I saw through my window into this room? Can I learn more about that brave and strong woman? When does that Mary get to have airtime? These were some of the questions that I began asking—not just Mary, but all of my clients. I began to collaborate with my clients on changing the context of therapy, going out of the office, trying out new things, exploring. The behaviors began to change. This is functional contextualism to me. Everything a human does is behavior, and this behavior is exquisitely sensitive to context. Rather than focusing on changing the behavior, focus on changing the context. Context means what happens before and after the behavior. Context also means the conceptual learning history that is connected to the behavior—the relational framing behavior that the action in question is a part of. (More on this in the next section.)

In functional contextualism, there are no "things." There is no depression, or anxiety, or borderline personality. There is depress-ing, anxiety-ing, borderline personality-ing, and these repertoires are evoked, shaped, and maintained. We are like sea anemones—the ocean surrounds us, and we move flexibly in the water. If something changes in the water, the anemone immediately changes. An anemone without water or water without the anemone is something completely other. In functional contextualism, like person-in-environment, we see the totality of the behaving organism in an interpenetrated, fluidly changing environment.

Relational Frame Theory

It's unlikely that the vast differences in Mary's behavior described above were shaped solely by direct contact with the physical world via her five senses. It's far more likely that this shaping was mediated by something uniquely human: thinking and meaning making. Relational frame theory (RFT; Hayes, Barnes-Holmes, & Roche, 2001; Dymond & Roche, 2013) is a functional contextual theory of language that builds on basic learning principles (e.g., positive reinforcement, classical conditioning) to account for how this happens, and its tenets have been supported in over fifty studies (Dymond & Roche, 2013). What follows is a brief introduction. See Törneke (2010) for a book-length discussion.

Many nonhuman animals can learn to distinguish relationships between objects, such as identifying the bigger of two balls. However, a human being, beginning at a particular point in his or her development, can learn relationships that are based solely on social and cultural convention, like that a dime is "bigger" than a nickel. Eventually, almost anything can be related in this way, including abstractions. For example, with the right history, a human can learn that the Beatles are "bigger" than the Rolling Stones (though other humans might disagree). Because the number of relationships that can be learned is vast (e.g., same/different, bigger/smaller, before/after, here/there), and one need only learn a relation a few times to extend that relation to other phenomena (e.g., if the Beatles can be bigger than the Stones, then Sigmund Freud can be bigger than Carl Rogers), human beings have the potential to relate actual lived experience to concepts, thoughts, meaning, rules, and anything else the mind can create. This explains how an animal, such as a dog, can learn to fear and avoid something literally dangerous, such as a poisonous snake, but a human can also learn to fear and avoid things that are arbitrarily related to poisonous snakes through social and cultural language conventions, such as the word "snake" written on a page, the sound of the word "snake," or the "snake pit" of academia.

Behavior that is influenced by these processes of language is called "verbal behavior" in RFT, and since language is socially and culturally shaped, so is verbal behavior. RFT suggests that verbal behavior is less sensitive to direct experience. This gives human beings the benefit of thinking, planning, predicting, remembering, storytelling, and so on, but also creates suffering when we are unnecessarily guided by our minds. Obsessive-compulsive disorder provides a good illustration. A behavior like hand washing is chosen repeatedly based on inflexible attachment to evaluations, rules, and predictions (e.g., my hands are contaminated, and I must wash them or I will get sick) rather than here and now experience (e.g., I have a feeling in my hands that my mind labels "dirty"). The behavior continues despite the consequences to living life effectively—being late for work, raw skin, more "dirty" feelings. In effect, the behavior is chosen in response to "snakes" when snakes are nowhere to be found. In RFT, psychopathology and psychological well-being are determined by the extent to which a person is sensitive to the here and now and by how flexibly he or she can attend to it, when necessary, to choose effective behavior.

Acceptance and Commitment Therapy

Acceptance and commitment therapy (ACT, see chapter 1) is an intervention designed to rest on a foundation of functional contextualism and RFT. ACT helps clients develop more flexible repertoires of behavioral responding by enlisting six interrelated processes that are collectively referred to as *psychological flexibility*: acceptance (allowing internal experiences to be without trying to change them), defusion (observing the mind rather than engaging its content), contact with the present moment (mindfully noticing experience as it happens), self as context (flexible perspective taking on the self, others, and experience), values (identifying what is important), and committed action (acting in the service of values). The first four processes can be thought of as four facets of mindfulness. Using metaphors, experiential exercises, and mindfulness exercises, all six processes are marshaled to help clients come in direct contact with lived experience when doing so is more workable for their lives. So, in the OCD example above, the social worker would help the client mindfully observe the dirty feeling in her hands, simply notice what the mind says about it, and choose actions that are driven by her values.

Addressing a Broad Array of Human Problems

The scope of social work practice is broad and diverse and requires interventions that are applicable across a wide range of problems. Can CBS applications, built on a foundation of functional contextualism, behavioral principles, and RFT, serve this purpose? Currently, the evidence is promising. The diversity of problems for which ACT, the most visible extension of CBS, has been researched at the micro (individual) and mezzo (group) levels is arguably only rivaled by traditional CBT. As of 2013, there are over seventy randomized controlled trials demonstrating ACT's efficacy for mental health problems, health concerns, and various other problems that are usually outside the province of clinical social work (see chapter 1). ACT has also been researched in organizations, which is important for macro level (organization, community, society) practice, but mostly through interventions with groups of workers within organizations (e.g., Bond & Bunce, 2000), not with the organizations themselves. However, other interventions drawn from the CBS tradition have been applied to mezzo-level issues such as reducing tobacco use and changing community child-rearing norms and to macro level goals such as reducing sexism and changing environmentally harmful practices (Biglan, 1995). An ACT/CBS approach has also been used to inform policy decisions on tobacco taxation and funding support for community interventions (Biglan, 1995; Biglan, Flay, Embry, & Sandler, 2012). For a new analysis of how the CBS approach can be connected to other disciplines in the sciences and possibly have the greatest effect at all levels of practice, see Wilson, Hayes, Biglan, and Embry (in press) and Biglan, Hayes, & Pistorello (2008).

• *How I Stopped Worrying and Learned to Love Science: A Personal Story*

ACT and RFT are both driven by extensive programs of research. I (MB, the second author) know a lot of social workers whose eyes glaze over at the thought of research. What does science really have to do with practice anyway? Aren't people and problems far too complex to be addressed with the scientific method? I think science is vitally important to helping people. Here's why.

Despite having gotten a first-rate social work education, I finished graduate school knowing very little about the role of science in social work. Early in my career, I had a few experiences, two of which I will recount, that made me worry that my pet theories of change, cobbled together from graduate school, my supervisors' practice wisdom, my own experience, and popular culture, needed to be grounded in something more solid.

Shortly after I started my first social work job, I attended a conference on the integration of psychodynamic therapy and CBT. I heard a case presentation on a client with severe OCD who was seeing both a CBT therapist and a psychodynamic therapist. The speaker made a good argument that the psychodynamic therapy was likely getting in the way of the client moving forward: the client ruminated to the point of paralysis, and all the analyzing that occurred in psychodynamic therapy reinforced the avoidance that maintained the client's OCD. This was new to me. I was very fond of analyzing. If the client didn't improve, it wasn't the therapy's fault; it was due to faulty implementation.[1]

At the same time, I was catching up on the repressed memories controversy of the 1990s. I read a number of books and articles written about it, and it appeared that many therapists had not paid any attention to the science of memory as they helped people work through trauma. They had taken the popular idea that painful memories can remain hidden within people and inadvertently created more suffering by trying to draw those memories out. I began to feel anxious that I might make these same kinds of mistakes because of what I didn't know, and my pet theories and methods of change began to seem insufficient and even risky.

Over the next few years I read a lot about "evidence-based practice," a term that was new to me. It meant drawing on research to inform therapy. I quickly discovered that what was considered evidence-based practice for just about any problem was cognitive behavioral therapy (CBT). This simultaneously annoyed me, because I had a hard time believing that most problems arose from inaccurate thinking, and scared me, because I wasn't practicing CBT. I also read about the limits of evidence as we knew it: that CBT research was overly focused on DSM syndromes; that evidence from research settings doesn't always translate to practice settings; that randomized controlled trials (RCTs)—the method of testing most treatments— don't really tell us why a treatment works and that researchers and practitioners are perpetually at odds. However, what nagged at me most was that discussions of evidence-based practice usually positioned science as the royal road to discovering the world as it really is. I wasn't sure how this fit with the social work value of respecting multiple ways of knowing, especially cultural and spiritual ways.

Things changed when I saw Steven C. Hayes give a talk on acceptance and commitment therapy, a newish therapy within the CBT tradition, at a conference on mindfulness and psychotherapy. Mindfulness and acceptance had always been important to me because of their role in my own growth (see the preface in this volume), but I wasn't very good at getting my clients to meditate, and I had no real method besides talking about acceptance for showing them how to be accepting. Hayes jokingly referred to pop psychology's emphasis on positive thinking as "out with the bad thought, in with the good thought" and said that directly targeting inaccurate thinking might not be necessary for change. He also illustrated acceptance by *telling us a touching and instructive story about helping his son deal with imaginary monsters under his bed by making the monsters their own beds.*

On the ACT Internet listserv, which was open to anybody who joined the ACT professional organization, "evidence-based practice" seemed to have a much deeper meaning than I had noticed elsewhere. In ACT and CBS, the program of science behind it, evidence meant going after what drove change in research, not just determining whether change happened. Good science meant avoiding constructs that could not be observed or measured by either scientists or subjects, like "repression." It meant staying away from fuzzy ideas of causality, like the notion that negative feelings are caused by negative thoughts, and fuzzier imperatives for therapy, like the idea that clients must change their negative thoughts to change negative feelings. It also meant looking for better methods of understanding human suffering than holding onto old, tired DSM categories. Furthermore, science wasn't considered the one true way to accessing the real world; it was only a useful way of talking about the world, one of many. And ACT offered a clear model and flexible technology for implementing acceptance in practice, as well as good ideas for where to go once you were more accepting (e.g., identify values, commit to values-driven actions), all of which were grounded in a growing program of basic science. All this information was open to me simply because I was interested—no one took me less seriously because I was a practitioner. This scientific world looked like it was built by social workers: it was nonhierarchical and flexible, and it made it easier to help people in creative ways.

Since I have become an ACT therapist and trainer, I have become more adept at implementing other treatments in the cognitive behavioral tradition, some of which I resisted in the past. One ACT study indicates that ACT can make practitioners more willing to suggest evidence-based interventions, even ones about which they themselves might have doubts (Varra, Hayes, Roget, & Fisher, 2008). In my practice, I do my best to move between treatment models like ACT, traditional CBT, dialectical behavior therapy (DBT; see chapter 2), and cognitive processing therapy for trauma, *hoping to address my clients' problems with interventions that both have adequate evidential support and are acceptable to them. When there is no obvious treatment model, I try to draw on the techniques and principles, like exposure, emotion regulation, behavior activation, acceptance, mindfulness, and values, which are common to these treatment models. And as I go, I do my best to hold the theory undergirding each model lightly. None of them describes the world. They are only as true as they are useful.*

Moving Toward Evidence-Based Principles of Change

Despite the current role of ACT in CBS, CBS is not ACT. CBS is devoted to identifying, testing, and marshaling basic principles to facilitate greater well-being and reduce human suffering. Therefore, it is not necessary that ACT as a discrete, brand-name treatment survive the progression of science (Hayes, Strosahl, & Wilson, 2012). More important for social work's mission to serve individuals, communities, and society is to identify empirically supported principles of change (Rosen & Davidson, 2003). This requires more than simply showing that a treatment makes statistically and clinically significant differences on outcome measures in RCTs, as most outcome research has historically done. It is equally important to ensure that a treatment works according to its theorized processes of change and that specific treatment interventions actually do what the theory suggests they do. Two tools that CBS uses to accomplish this are mediation analyses and laboratory-based component research.

Mediation Analyses

Often we know a treatment "works," but we don't know why. Mediation analyses are statistical tests that demonstrate whether a theorized process of change can account for treatment outcomes.

ACT or another therapy might work better than no treatment, but improvement could be driven by something theorized by the therapy (e.g., improving psychological flexibility) or something else. Psychotherapy research has not always emphasized mediation. In contrast, many ACT studies have included measures of mediation since the first ACT randomized controlled trial (Zettle & Hayes, 1986). Recently, Hayes, Levin, Plumb-Vilardaga, Villatte, and Pistorello (2013) noted the existence of almost two-dozen formal mediation analyses of ACT. (The number continues to grow.) Mediators included psychological flexibility, defusion, values, and other theorized processes. They observed that "in virtually every case, when alternative mediators drawn from other perspectives were applied to ACT interventions, they did not work or did not work as well as those drawn from ACT theory" (p. 11). Mediators theorized by other models (e.g., cognitive therapy) worked less well than mediators based on the psychological flexibility model. This supports the contention that ACT is a distinct treatment, not merely a rehash of other treatments in the cognitive behavioral tradition. Hayes, Villatte, Levin, and Hildebrandt (2011) analyzed all the mediation studies to date and found that "50 percent of the between-group differences in follow-up outcomes can be accounted for by the mediating role of differential post levels in psychological flexibility and its components" (p. 26). In other words, psychological flexibility and its component processes are likely making the difference they are theorized to make.

Laboratory-Based Component Research

In laboratory-based component research, the impact of a single, theoretically-derived treatment component (like a defusion exercise or a metaphor for acceptance) is studied under highly controlled conditions. Though this kind of research cannot demonstrate the efficacy of an intervention in the context of actual clinical practice, it can tell us whether a specific intervention has an impact that is consistent with its theoretical model. For example, ACT's psychological flexibility model is divided into six interrelated processes. If interventions based on these processes make the difference they are theoretically assumed to make, then this lends support to the theoretical model.

For example, Levitt, Brown, Orsillo, and Barlow (2004) compared the impact of a brief acceptance intervention drawn from ACT to both a suppression intervention and no intervention on the effects of breathing CO_2-enriched air, which induces panic-like physiological arousal in patients with panic disorder. Subjects in the acceptance group were significantly less anxious and avoidant than subjects in both the suppression and the no-instruction groups. Interestingly, no group showed significant differences in self-reported panic symptoms or objective physiological measures. In other words, all patients had on average the same symptoms, but those who practiced acceptance were less distressed and more willing to experience additional anxiety. These outcomes are entirely consistent with the ACT/psychological flexibility model, which encourages clients to forgo attempts at controlling private experiences in order to minimize overall suffering and facilitate greater engagement in values-driven actions, even those actions that might incur further pain.

Levin, Hildebrandt, Lillis, and Hayes (2012) conducted a meta-analysis of sixty-six such studies and found significant positive effect sizes for acceptance, defusion, present moment, values, mixed mindfulness, and values plus mindfulness compared to inactive comparisons. (They noted an absence in the literature of studies on self as context.) Larger effect sizes were found for outcomes that were predicted by the psychological flexibility model (e.g., believability of a negative thought rather than its intensity or frequency), and expected differences were found between interventions that the model predicted would be different from one another, such as acceptance and suppression. Furthermore, effect sizes were greater for interventions that incorporated experiential exercises rather than just a rationale (e.g., hearing a metaphor rather than simply having the benefits of an intervention or process explained), which supports the emphasis in ACT on experiential versus intellectual learning. Finally, effect sizes did not differ between distressed and convenience samples, which supports the contention that psychological flexibility and inflexibility are based on normal psychological processes and therefore will be found in both clinical and nonclinical populations.

Mediation analyses and laboratory-based component studies may seem like empirical solipsism to practitioners who are new to research-informed practice. But consider this: when someone tells you that a treatment "works," do you know what that means? Usually it doesn't mean that we know the theory behind the intervention is coherent or that the intervention makes a difference for the reasons it claims. We need something else to go on so that the science of social work can progress in the service of better helping people.

Seeking Out Commonalities in Other Traditions in the Behavioral Sciences

Because CBS is interested in identifying evidence-based principles of change, ACT treatment developers have made efforts to connect ACT and the psychological flexibility model to conceptually similar evidence-based models within the behavioral sciences, many of which are gaining popularity in social work. Hayes, Villatte, Levin, and Hildebrandt (2011) draw together mindfulness-based approaches such as ACT, DBT, and mindfulness-based stress reduction (see chapter 3) with other treatments such as metacognitive therapy (Fisher & Wells, 2009) and motivational interviewing (Miller & Rollnick, 2002) under the umbrella term "contextual cognitive behavioral therapy," noting that all focus on changing the function and context of private events, rather than the events themselves. They fit each model into three meta-categories: open, aware, and active. *Open* processes, such as emotion regulation in DBT and acceptance in most models, are "designed to reduce the automatic behavioral regulatory power of thoughts, feelings, memories, and bodily sensations, but without necessarily first changing the form or frequency of these experiences" (p. 160). *Aware* processes, such as mindfulness, help clients flexibly contact the present and take a more functional perspective on their internal experiences, as well as external events. *Active* processes such as skills training in DBT, values in ACT, and activity scheduling in behavioral activation (see chapter 4) encourage clients to engage in life in more effective and workable ways.

At the level of technique rather than theory, ACT can look like other treatment models outside of the cognitive and behavioral traditions that have influenced social work, such as existential and humanistic approaches (Hayes, Strosahl, & Wilson, 2012), and though the relevant research is yet to be pursued, the six processes of psychological flexibility may offer testable constructs to explain the power of these treatments. For example, the empty chair technique in Gestalt therapy (Congress, 1996), in which the social worker invites the client to interact with an imaginary person or private experience "sitting" in another chair, can easily be explained in ACT terms. This technique can be considered a method for cultivating perspective taking (self as context), building new awareness in the face of aversive feelings (contact with the present moment), and facilitating a more open stance toward rejected private experiences and the situations which give rise to them (acceptance). The second author often uses this technique in his ACT practice.

Bringing Together Researchers and Practitioners

It is common to create a treatment model, test it (or not), and then develop extensive and costly certification processes that limit access, especially for clinicians and clients with fewer resources. CBS takes another path, which we feel fits more closely with social work values. The Association for Contextual Behavioral Science (ACBS), the professional organization of CBS and ACT, makes its resources widely available in the interest of creating an open and nonhierarchical community. ACBS requires that members contribute "values-based dues," which can be as little as $10. In return, members gain Internet access to almost any resource they might need to facilitate their development as an ACT provider (http://www.contextualpsychology.org):

treatment protocols from research studies, PowerPoint presentations by treatment developers, videos of ACT in practice, compendiums of ACT metaphors, podcasts of conversations with researchers and practitioners, and nearly every CBS- and ACT-relevant article in the literature.

The ACBS ACT listserv and the yearly ACBS world conference give practitioners and researchers regular, direct access to one another. It is not uncommon for a brand-new ACT practitioner to seek consultation on the ACT listserv and get a response from not just other ACT therapists, but also treatment developers and basic scientists. It is also not uncommon to see a treatment developer post a new experiential exercise or a passage from an article in progress on the list and get feedback from the entire community.

Perhaps most unusual about the ACT community is that there is no certification process for either practitioners or trainers. Practitioners are provided core competencies against which to evaluate their skills (e.g., Luoma, Hayes, & Walser, 2007) and allowed to call themselves ACT therapists when they themselves feel qualified. Aspiring trainers are encouraged to submit to a peer-review process, and peer-reviewed trainers are simply listed on the ACBS website.

Conclusion

CBS offers coherence of philosophy, theory, research, and applications that social work has been lacking. CBS offers a contextual focus on human suffering, with client values at the center of the approach. CBS is rooted in behaviorism, a model social work has used successfully in many practice domains. The CBS community offers a robust communication between researchers and practitioners and easy access to training. Finally, CBS's focus on intervention overlaps significantly with traditional social work practice areas: micro, mezzo, and, increasingly, macro. In fact, for CBS to continue to extend this breadth of focus, social workers are necessary. Of all the helping professions, social work is arguably the one that is best situated to have an impact with organizations, communities, and cultures.

Notes

1. This is not an indictment of psychodynamic therapy or a claim that CBT is better than psychodynamic therapy. It is meant to illustrate that our assumptions about what works in treatment can be wrong.

References

Biglan, A. (1995). *Changing cultural practices: A contextualistic framework for intervention research.* Reno, NV: Context Press.
Biglan, A., Flay, B., Embry, D., & Sandler, I. (2012). The critical role of nurturing environments for promoting human well-being. *American Psychologist, 67,* 257-271.
Biglan, A., Hayes, S. C., & Pistorello, J. (2008). Acceptance and commitment: implications for prevention science. *Prevention Science, 9,* 139-152.
Bond, F., & Bunce, D. (2000). Mediators of change in emotion-focused and problem-focused worksite stress management interventions. *Journal of Occupational Health Psychology, 5,* 156-63.
Brekke, J. S. (2012). Shaping a science of social work. *Research on Social Work Practice, 22,* 455-464.
Congress, E. P. (1996). Gestalt theory in social work treatment. In F. J. Turner (Ed.), *Social work treatment: Interlocking theoretical approaches.* New York: The Free Press.
Dillenburger, K., Godina, L., & Burton, M. (1997). Training in behavioral social work: A pilot study. *Research on Social Work Practice, 1,* 70-78.
Dymond, S., & Roche, B. (2013). *Advances in relational frame theory: Research and application.* Oakland, CA: New Harbinger.
Epstein, M. (1986). Science and social work. *Social Service Review, 60,* 145-160.
Fisher, P., & Wells, A. (2009). *Metacognitive therapy: Distinctive features.* London: Routledge.
Gambrill, E. (1995). Behavioral social work: Past, present and future. *Research on Social Work Practice, 5,* 460-484.
Göppner, H. J., & Hämäläinen, J. (2007). Developing a science of social work. *Journal of Social Work, 7,* 269-287.
Hayes, S. C. (1993). Analytic goals and the varieties of scientific contextualism. In S. C. Hayes, L. J. Hayes, H. W. Reese, & T. R. Sarbin (Eds.), *Varieties of scientific contextualism* (pp. 11-27). Reno, NV: Context Press.
Hayes, S. C., Barnes-Holmes, D., & Roche, B. (2001). *Relational frame theory: A post-Skinnerian account of human language and cognition.* New York: Kluwer Academic/Plenum Publishers.

Hayes, S. C., Barnes-Holmes, D., & Wilson, K. G. (2012). Contextual behavioral science: Creating a science more adequate to the challenge of the human condition. *Journal of Contextual Behavioral Science, 1,* 1-16.

Hayes, S. C., Hayes, L. J., & Reese, H. W. (1988). Finding the philosophical core: A review of Stephen C. Pepper's *World hypotheses*. *Journal of the Experimental Analysis of Behavior, 50,* 97-111.

Hayes, S. C., Levin, M. E., Plumb-Vilardaga, J., Villatte, J. L., & Pistorello, J. (2013). Acceptance and commitment therapy and contextual behavioral science: Examining the progress of a distinctive model of behavioral and cognitive therapy. *Behavior Therapy, 44,* 180-198.

Hayes, S. C., Strosahl, K., & Wilson, K. G. (2012). *Acceptance and commitment therapy: The process and practice of mindful change.* New York: Guilford Press.

Hayes, S. C., Villatte, M., Levin, M., & Hildebrandt, M. (2011). Open, aware and active: Contextual approaches as an emerging trend in the behavioral and cognitive therapies. *Annual Review of Clinical Psychology, 7,* 141-168.

Healy, K. (2005). *Social work theories in context: Creating frameworks for practice.* Basingstoke, UK: Palgrave Macmillan.

Hutchison, E. (2008). *Dimensions of human behavior: Person and environment* (3rd ed.). Los Angeles: Sage.

Johnson, A. (1947). Science and social work. *Social Science Review, 21,* 297-321.

Kirk, S. A., & Reid, W. J. (2002). *Science and social work: A critical appraisal.* New York: Columbia University Press.

Lazarus, A. A. (1967). In support of technical eclecticism. *Psychological Reports, 21,* 414-416.

Lazarus, A. A., & Beutler, L. E. (1993). On technical eclecticism. *Journal of Counseling and Development, 71,* 381-385.

Levin, M., Hildebrandt, M., Lillis, J., & Hayes, S. C. (2012). The impact of treatment components suggested by the psychological flexibility model: A meta-analysis of laboratory-based component studies. *Behavior Therapy, 43,* 741-56.

Levitt, J., Brown, T., Orsillo, S., & Barlow, D. (2004). The effects of acceptance versus suppression of emotion on subjective and psychophysiological response to carbon dioxide challenge in patients with panic disorder. *Behavior Therapy, 45,* 747-766.

Longhofer, J., & Floersch, J. (2012). The coming crisis in social work: Some thoughts on social work and science. *Research on Social Work Practice, 22,* 499-519.

Luoma, J. B., Hayes, S. C., & Walser, R. D. (2007). *Learning ACT: An acceptance & commitment therapy skills-training manual for therapists.* Oakland, CA: New Harbinger.

Miller, W. R., & Rollnick, S. (2002). *Motivational interviewing: Preparing people for change.* New York: Guilford Press.

Richmond, M. E. (1955). *Social diagnosis.* New York: Russell Sage Foundation.

Rosen, G. M., & Davidson, G. C. (2003). Psychology should list empirically supported principles of change (ESPs) and not credential trademarked therapies or other treatment packages. *Behavior Modification, 27,* 300-312.

Törneke, N. (2010). *Learning RFT: An introduction to relational frame theory and its clinical applications*. Oakland, CA: Context Press/New Harbinger.

Varra, A. A., Hayes, S. C., Roget, R., & Fisher, G. (2008). A randomized control trial examining the effect of acceptance and commitment training on clinician willingness to use evidence-based pharmacotherapy. *Journal of Consulting and Clinical Psychology, 76*, 449-458.

Wakefield, J. C. (1996a). Does social work need the eco-systems perspective? Part 1. Is the perspective clinically useful? *Social Service Review, 70*, 1-32.

Wakefield, J. C. (1996b). Does social work need the eco-systems perspective? Part 2. Does the perspective save social work from incoherence? *Social Science Review, 70*, 183-213.

Wilson, D. S., Hayes, S. C., Biglan, T., & Embry, D. (in press). Evolving the future: Toward a science of intentional change. *Behavioral and Brain Science*.

Zettle, R. D., & Hayes, S. C. (1986). Dysfunctional control by client verbal behavior: The context of reason giving. *Analysis of Verbal Behavior, 4*, 30-38.

Matthew S. Boone, LCSW, teaches acceptance and commitment therapy (ACT) at the School of Social Work at the University of Arkansas at Little Rock and practices ACT, dialectical behavior therapy (DBT), and other cognitive behavioral therapies at the Central Arkansas Veterans Healthcare System. He is an Association of Contextual Behavioral Science (ACBS) peer-reviewed trainer in ACT, a founder of the ACBS Social Work ACT Special Interest Group, and a recipient of the Boston University School of Social Work Alumni Association award for outstanding contributions to the field of social work.

Index

A

about this book, 11–13
acceptance: ACT process of, 34–38; BA process of, 108, 116, 120–121; "both-and" perspective and, 137–139; change based on, 140–141; compassion and, 94–95, 128; definitions of, 127; MBSR process of, 78; nonjudging as integral to, 127; practice of, 10–11; radical, 68, 125–130
acceptance and commitment therapy (ACT), 2, 21–47; acceptance in, 34–38; assessment process in, 32–34; case example illustrating, 32–46; committed action in, 43–46; contact with the present moment in, 41–42; contextual behavioral science and, 258, 267, 271, 274; defusion in, 38–40; descriptive overview of, 22; evidence for effectiveness of, 27, 267; flexible application of, 27–28; functional contextualism and, 47, 241–242, 266; hexaflex diagram for, 30; intervention strategies used in, 31–32; laboratory-based component research on, 272–274; mediation analyses of, 272; model of psychopathology and suffering, 24–26; overview of behavioral processes, 30–31; psychological flexibility in, 23–24, 27, 30–31, 241–242, 266–267; resources related to, 275–276; self as context in, 42–43, 231n; similarities with other models, 274–275; social work and, 26–29, 243–245; values in, 43–46. See also focused acceptance and commitment therapy
act-in-context process, 262

active processes, 274–275
activity scheduling, 112–114
Addams, Jane, 5, 215–216, 220, 236
Art and Science of Mindfulness, The (Shapiro and Carlson), 88
arts-based mindfulness, 148–151
assessment: ACT process of, 32–34; BA process of, 111–112; brief intervention competency, 189, 193–205; FACT life path, 177–178
Association for Contextual Behavioral Science (ACBS), 27, 204, 275
Association for Mindfulness in Education (AME), 80
attitude, choosing one's, 92–93
aversion, working with, 90–92
avoidance: behavioral and emotional, 171–172; experiential, 24–25, 171–172, 242; functional view of, 106; language and, 171; targeted in BA, 102, 115–117
awakening, 224, 225
aware processes, 274–275
awareness: choiceless, 78; of interdependence, 219; nonjudgmental, 223

B

BA. See behavioral activation
Bauer-Wu, Susan, 97
beginner's mind, 223
behavior chain analysis (BCA), 59
behavioral activation (BA), 11–12, 101–121; activity scheduling in, 112–114; approach to change in, 115–116, 118; assessment process in, 111–112; avoidance targeted in, 115–117; behavior defined in, 105–106; case example of, 108–117; contingency management in, 115; dealing with internal reactions in,

107–108; descriptive overview of, 101–103; evidence for efficacy of, 106–107; functional contextualism and, 103–104, 106; mindfulness and acceptance in, 108, 116, 120–121; providing the rationale for, 109–111; skills training in, 114–115; social work theory and, 103–106; stimulus control in, 114; summary of techniques used in, 108–117
behavioral avoidance, 171, 172
behavioral health consultants (BHCs), 192–193, 203
behaviorism, 52–53, 260–261
behaviors: BA perspective on, 105–106; functional view of, 106; life-threatening, 59–61; quality of life–interfering, 62–63; therapy-interfering, 61–62; verbal, 266
being present, 41
Between Pacific Tides (Ricketts), 216
biases: social worker, 247–248; treatment model, 246
BI-CAT. See Brief Intervention Competency Assessment Tool
binary thinking, 137, 138, 225–226
biosocial theory, 55–57
body scan exercise, 77
Boone, Matthew S., 1, 21, 235, 257
borderline personality disorder (BPD): biosocial theory of, 55–57; DBT for treating, 49–50
"both-and" perspective, 137–139
BPD. See borderline personality disorder
Brach, Tara, 127, 128
Brief Intervention Competency Assessment Tool (BI-CAT), 189, 193–205; behavioral anchors, 194–202, 211; case example of using, 203–205; competence ratings, 194; copy for readers, 209–211; intervention delivery domain, 200–201; intervention design domain, 196–200; outcomes-based practice domain, 201–202; practice context domain, 194–196; preliminary evaluation of, 203

brief interventions, 164–165, 187–189; behavioral health consultants and, 192–193; competency assessment tool for, 189, 193–205; facts vs. fictions about, 166–170; lack of research on, 164–165; skills training in, 188; social work trend toward, 187–188. See also focused acceptance and commitment therapy
Buddhism: beginner's mind in, 223; generalist mind in, 223–224; Hua-yen school of, 227; impermanence in, 219; interdependence in, 218–219; mindfulness practice and, 4, 81–82, 83, 157; observing with equanimity in, 222; parable of the mustard seed from, 84; socially engaged, 217–218, 221, 224. See also Zen Buddhism
Bull's-Eye Plan, 204, 205
Butterfly exercise, 35, 36–37

C

Carlson, Linda E., 88
case conceptualization, 112
case examples: of ACT, 32–46; of BA, 108–117; of BI-CAT, 203–205; of FACT, 173–183; of MBSR, 85–87, 94–97
case perspective, 189
CBS. See contextual behavioral science
change: acceptance and, 140–141; BA approach to, 115–116, 118; facts vs. fictions about, 166–170; MBSR and manageability of, 81; self sense and fear of, 93
charity organization societies, 5–6
Chessboard metaphor, 42, 249
children: arts-based activities for, 149–151; group work with, 152–153; HAP groups for, 146–159; mindfulness practice and, 147, 148–149; spiritual issues discussed with, 158–159; strengths perspective for, 147–148, 153–156; working with vulnerable, 146, 159
choiceless awareness, 78
circle sharing exercise, 131, 138–139
clear seeing, 127–128

clinical competence, 243
clinical social work, 6
coaching, intersession, 68–70
cognitive behavioral therapy (CBT), 52, 269
coherence of CBS, 258
Coholic, Diana, 12, 145
committed action, 43–46
community-based treatment programs, 164
compassion: acceptance and, 94–95, 128; Buddhist practice of, 222; effective, 50
competence: brief intervention, 189, 193–205; clinical, 243; cultural, 236, 244–252
confrontational culture, 137
conservation, 230
consultation team, 70–71
consultation-to-the-client, 64
contact with the present moment, 41–42
contemplative silence, 131
contextual behavioral science (CBS), 13, 257–277; ACT and, 258, 267, 271, 274; descriptive overview of, 257–258; functional contextualism and, 257, 261; laboratory-based component research and, 272–274; mediation analyses and, 271–272; philosophy of science in, 259, 260; problems addressed through, 267–268; resources related to, 275–276
contextual cognitive behavioral therapy, 274
contingency management, 115
Cool Minds program, 80
core mindfulness skills, 65–67
Council on Social Work Education (CSWE), 219
Courage to Teach, The (Palmer), 138
creative hopelessness, 34
critical reflection: description of, 126; mindfulness meditation and, 134–137; radical acceptance and, 128–130
critical social work, 126, 134–137, 141
cross-cultural empathy, 245–246
cultural bias, 246
cultural competence, 236, 244–252; adaptation of treatment techniques and, 248–249; cross-cultural empathy and, 245–246; functional contextualism and, 240, 241, 244–245; language issues and, 249–250; personal biases and, 247–248; religion/spirituality and, 251–252; role of significant others and, 251; treatment model bias and, 246

D

DBT. See dialectical behavior therapy
defusion, ACT process of, 38–40
Deleuze, Gilles, 226
depression: behavioral activation for, 103, 104–105, 106–107, 119–120; mindfulness-based cognitive therapy for, 92; social work theory and, 104–105
dialectical behavior therapy (DBT), 2, 49–72; behaviorism and, 52–53; biosocial theory and, 55–57; consultation team in, 70–71; descriptive overview of, 49–51; dialectics and, 53–54; evidence base supporting, 51–52; group skills training in, 65–68; individual therapy in, 64; intersession contact for coaching in, 68–70; life-threatening behaviors and, 59–61; mindfulness and, 54–55, 63, 65–67; modes of treatment in, 63–71; programs informed by, 52; social work values and, 49–51, 71–72; structure of treatment in, 57–58; theoretical foundation of, 52–57; therapy-interfering behaviors and, 61–62; treatment target hierarchy in, 59–63
dialectical dialogue, 53
dialectics, 53–54
diary card, 59, 60
dignity/worth of clients, 28–29
discrimination, 118, 119
distress tolerance, 68
diverse populations, 237–238
D&#014d;gen (Zen master), 228, 230
dose effect, 168
Duke Health Profile, 205

E

eclecticism, 259
ecological awareness, 230–231
ecological social work, 226–227
ecology of mind, 217
ecosystems theory, 260
effective compassion, 50
e-mail/text coaching, 68–70
emotion control, 172
emotion dysregulation, 56–57
emotion mind, 66
emotion regulation, 67, 147
emotional avoidance, 171–172
emotional sensitivity, 56
emotions: critical reflection and, 129; function of, 11
empathy, cross-cultural, 245–246
empowerment approach, 105
empty chair technique, 275
engaged Buddhism, 217–218, 221, 224
environments, invalidating, 56–57
equanimity, 222–223, 228
Essays in Zen Buddhism (Suzuki), 216
evidence-based treatment: ACT as, 27, 270; BA as, 106–107; DBT as, 51–52; FACT as, 165; MBSR as, 79, 95–97
experiential avoidance, 24–25, 171–172, 242
experiential exercises in ACT, 31; Butterfly exercise, 35, 36–37; Observer exercise, 42. See also metaphors in ACT

F

FACT. See focused acceptance and commitment therapy
family therapy approaches, 6
focused acceptance and commitment therapy (FACT), 165, 170–183; case example, 173–183; clinical dialogue, 180–183; focusing questions, 174; Four Square Analysis, 178–180; interview process, 173–178; life path assessment, 177–178; practice of, 173–178; principles of, 170–173; treatment formulation, 178–183; workability intervention, 175–176
focused interviewing, 173–178
focusing questions, 174
Folkman, Susan, 92
force field perspective, 221
Four Square Analysis, 178–180
framing thoughts, 38
Frankl, Viktor, 93
Fromm, Erich, 224
Full Catastrophe Living (Kabat-Zinn), 127
functional contextualism, 239–241; ACT based on, 47, 241–242, 266; behavioral activation and, 103–104, 106; contextual behavioral science and, 257, 261; cultural competence and, 240, 241, 244–245; personal story about, 262–264; philosophical worldview of, 261; relational frame theory and, 265; social work practice and, 243–245
fusion, 25–26, 38, 40, 171

G

Gandhi, 131
generalist mind, 223
generalist social work practice, 223–224
Gestalt therapy, 275
group skills training, 65–68; in core mindfulness, 65–67; in distress tolerance, 68; in emotion regulation, 67; in interpersonal effectiveness, 67

H

HAP. See Holistic Arts-Based Program
Hayes, Steven C., 269
Here for Now: Living Well with Cancer Through Mindfulness (Rosenbaum), 94
hierarchies: binary thinking, 225; DBT treatment, 59–63
Hill, Mary L., 13, 235
Holistic Arts-Based Program (HAP), 145–160; arts-based mindfulness methods in, 148–151; descriptive overview of, 146–148; group work in, 152–153; holistic approach to mindfulness in, 156–159; spiritual issues discussed in, 158–159; strengths perspective in, 147–148, 153–156

homework, MBSR, 78
"how" skills, 65–67
Hua-yen Buddhism, 227
Hull House Women's Club, 215
human relationships, 29

I

impermanence, 219
individual DBT therapy, 64
inside-out approach to change, 115–116
interbeing framework, 130
interdependence, 218–219
interpersonal effectiveness, 67
intersession contact for coaching, 68–70
intervention delivery domain, BI-CAT, 200–201
intervention design domain, BI-CAT, 196–200
invalidating environments, 56–57

J

Jäger, Willigis, 55

K

Kabat-Zinn, Jon, 4, 76, 77, 82, 83, 127, 131, 118
Kanter, Jonathan W., 101
King, Martin Luther, 138
koan practice, 224–225
Koons, Cedar, 49

L

laboratory-based component research, 272–274
language: dark side of, 171–172; double-edged sword of, 170, 249–250; relational frame theory of, 265–266; therapeutic interactions and, 250; used by MBSR instructors, 90
Lazarus, Richard, 92
leverage points, 178
Levine, Ondrea, 125
Lewin, Kurt, 221
life path assessment, 177–178
life space concept, 221–222
life-threatening behaviors, 59–61
Linde, Tom, 163

long-term therapy: facts vs. fictions about, 166–170. See also brief interventions
Love in Action (Nhat Hanh), 138
loving-kindness meditation, 131, 222

M

Macias, Teresa, 131
macro social work practice, 5, 6; engaged Buddhism and, 217–218, 221, 224; force field perspective and, 221; life space concept and, 221–222
managed care, 163–164, 187–188
Man's Search for Meaning (Frankl), 93
Marohn, Felicia, 49
Masuda, Akihiko, 13, 235
MBSR. See mindfulness-based stress reduction
"Me as a River" activity, 150
"Me as a Tree" activity, 150
mechanism, 261–262
mediation analyses, 271–272
meditation: leading in MBSR, 89–90; loving-kindness, 131, 222. See also mindfulness
Merton, Thomas, 80, 131
metacognitive therapy, 274
metaphors in ACT, 31; Chessboard metaphor, 42, 249; Two Mountains metaphor, 28–29. See also experiential exercises in ACT
Meyer, Florence, 80
micro and mezzo social work, 5, 6
mindful art of living, 222
mindfulness: ACT use of, 31; arts-based, 148–151; BA use of, 108, 116; children's practice of, 147, 148–149; core skills in, 65–67; critical social work and, 134–137; DBT use of, 54–55, 63, 65–67; definitions of, 4, 9, 77; ecological awareness and, 230–231; equanimity and, 222–223; holistic approach to, 156–159; MBSR and, 77–78, 81–82, 83, 92; popularization of, 3, 4; practice of, 4–5, 9–10, 13–14; radical acceptance and, 127–128, 141; social work and, 7–9; spirituality and, 157–158; stress

reaction and, 92; traditional origins of, 4, 81–82
mindfulness- and acceptance-based interventions: culturally competent practice of, 245–252; diverse populations and, 237–238; explanatory overview of, 9–11; generalist social work practice and, 223; reasons for utilizing, 14; scenarios illustrating, 1–2; social work and, 7–9, 14
Mindfulness and Social Work (Hick), 8
mindfulness exercises, 31, 77, 84–85
mindfulness-based cognitive therapy (MBCT), 79, 92
mindfulness-based relapse prevention (MBRP), 79
mindfulness-based stress reduction (MBSR), 1–2, 75–97; adaptations of, 79–80; attitude and, 92–93; Buddhism and, 81–82, 83; case examples of, 85–87, 94–97; commitment required for, 77; community of the group in, 84; compassion and acceptance in, 94–95; curriculum used in, 77–79; description of, 76; evidence for effectiveness of, 79, 95–97; instructional language used in, 90; leading meditations in, 89–90; mindfulness exercises in, 84–85; origin and development of, 4, 76, 82; process of investigation in, 87–88; qualities of the teacher in, 88–89; question for participants in, 75–76; research studies on, 79, 95–97; resistance and aversion in, 90–92; social work and, 80–81, 83, 88–89; stress reaction and, 92
motivational interviewing, 274
Mundy, Brian, 187
mustard seed parable, 84

N

Nagy, Gabriela, 101
narrative therapy, 164–165
National Association of Social Workers (NASW), 28, 88–89, 236
natural resources, 229–230
Nhat Hanh, Thich, 131, 138, 230
non-dual approach, 218, 219, 228
nonjudgment, 66, 127, 135–136
nonsuicidal self-injury (NSSI), 59
normality assumptions, 24
Noticing Thoughts That Get You Stuck worksheet, 40
NSSI behaviors, 59

O

Observer exercise, 42
observer role, 179
observing self, 42
obsessive-compulsive disorder, 266
open processes, 274
outcomes-based practice domain, BI-CAT, 201–202
outside-in approach to change, 115–116

P

pain: conventional responses to, 21–22; psychological flexibility and, 23; suffering related to, 24
"Painting on a Line" exercise, 151
parsimonious treatment, 166–167
Pasillas, Rebecca M., 13, 235
pathway services, 193
patient centered medical home (PCMH) model, 191
person-as-environment perspective, 219
person-in-environment (PIE) approach, 219–222; behavioral activation and, 102, 103; Buddhist perspective and, 221–222; early social work and, 220–221
pervasive invalidation, 57
philosophical worldviews, 261–262
philosophy of science, 259, 260
phone coaching, 68–70
polarized thinking, 138
population-based health care, 190–191
power and privilege, 139–140
practice context domain, BI-CAT, 194–196
pragmatism of functional contextualism, 240–241
present moment contact, 41–42
primary care behavioral health (PCBH) model, 189, 191–193

primary care providers (PCPs), 192
primary care settings, 164
primary prevention, 193
private experiences, 24
privilege and power, 139–140
problem-focused therapy, 164
psychodynamic approaches, 6, 268, 277n
psychological flexibility, 23–24, 27, 30–31, 241–242, 266–267
psychological inflexibility, 25
psychopathology, ACT model of, 24–26
psychotherapy. See therapy
Puspitassari, Ajeng, 101

Q

quality of life–interfering behaviors, 62–63
questions: for FACT clients, 174; for MBSR participants, 75–76

R

racism, 118, 119
radical acceptance, 68, 125–130; critical reflection and, 128–130; mindfulness and, 127–128, 141
radical behaviorism, 260, 261
randomized controlled trials (RCTs), 269
rapid clinical response, 170
Real Behavior Change in Primary Care (Robinson, Gould, and Strosahl), 203
reasonable mind, 66
rehabilitation phase, 169
relational frame theory (RFT), 265–266
Relax Kids: The Wishing Star (Viegas), 150
religion: role of, for clients, 251–252; tension between psychotherapy and, 251. See also spirituality
remediation phase, 169
remoralization phase, 169
resistance, working with, 90–92
Richmond, Mary, 220
Ricketts, Edward, 216
Robinson, Patricia, 12, 187
Rogers, Carl, 1
Rosenbaum, Elana, 75
rule-following, 171
Rumi, 140

S

S.T.O.P. acronym, 79
Santos, Maria, 101
Satipatthana Sutta (Nhat Hanh), 128, 130
scheduling activities, 112–114
science: philosophy of, 259, 260; usefulness of, 268–271
self as context, 42–43, 231n
self-assessment: BI-CAT tool for, 189, 193–205. See also assessment
self-disclosure, 29, 88, 247
self-injurious behaviors, 59
settlement house movement, 5, 236
Shapiro, Shauna, 88
Shorkey, Clayton, 13, 215
Siddhartha Gautama, 81
significant others, 251
silent retreat, 131–132
sitting meditation, 89–90
skillful means, 66
skills training: in behavioral activation, 114–115; in DBT groups, 65–68
social conditioning, 224–225
social constructionist view, 224
social justice, 29, 125, 229
social work: ACT and, 26–29, 243–245; BA and, 103–106; behavioral tradition in, 260–261; brief interventions in, 187; clinical competence in, 243; critical, 126, 134–137; cultural competence in, 244–245; DBT and, 49–51, 71–72; ecological, 226–227; ethical values of, 28, 88–89, 222; functional contextualist perspective and, 243–245; generalist practice of, 223–224; HAP methods and, 147–148; historical development of, 5–6; lack of coherence in, 258; MBSR and, 80–81, 83, 88–89; mindfulness and acceptance in, 7–9, 14; philosophy and, 259–260; primary mission of, 101; science and, 268–271; theory and practice of, 5–7; therapeutic relationship in, 243–244; values essential to, 28–29
social work in being, 222–228

social workers: self-awareness of personal biases in, 247–248; therapeutic relationship with, 243–244
socially engaged Buddhism, 217–218, 221, 224
solution analysis, 59
solution-focused therapy, 164, 165
spirituality: children and, 158–159; macro social work and, 231; mindfulness and, 157–158; role of religion and, 251–252; social work and, 130–131, 157
"Spirituality and Critical Social Work" course, 130–140; class format and learning activities, 131–132; course evaluation and interviews, 132–133; student experiences, 133–140
Steinwachs, Joanne, 13, 257
stimulus control, 114
strengths perspective, 147–148, 153–156
stress reaction, 92
stress reduction. See mindfulness-based stress reduction
Strosahl, Kirk, 12, 163
Substance Abuse and Mental Health Services Administration (SAMHSA), 164
successful working, 262
suffering: ACT model of, 24–26; Buddhist view of, 218; pain related to, 24
suicidal behaviors, 59–61
Suzuki, D. T., 216
Suzuki, Shunryu, 223
sympathetic joy, 222
systems perspective, 53

T

technical eclecticism, 259
teleological thinking, 216
theoretical eclecticism, 259
therapeutic relationship: ACT and, 29, 244; awareness of biases in, 247–248; DBT and, 50–51; social work practice and, 243–244
therapy: behaviors interfering with, 61–62; brief approaches to, 164–165, 187–205; facts vs. fictions about, 166–170; tension between religion and, 251
third wave therapies, 237
"Thought Jar" activity, 149
thoughts: defusion from, 38–40; fusion with, 25–26, 38, 40
"Thumbs Up, Thumbs Down" activity, 147
Two Mountains metaphor, 28–29

U

Uebel, Michael, 13, 215

V

Valued Living Questionnaire-2, 44
values: BA assessment related to, 111–112; committed action and, 43–46
verbal behavior, 266
vulnerable children: characteristics of, 146; HAP groups for, 146–159

W

"Warm Fuzzy" notes, 155
water resources, 229–230
What Is Social Case Work? (Richmond), 220
"what" skills, 65
Wherever You Go, There You Are (Kabat-Zinn), 4
willingness, 11, 68
wise mind, 66–67
Wong, Yuk-Lin Renita, 12, 125
workability: ACT perspective on, 26, 34, 242; FACT intervention about, 175–176
worldviews, philosophical, 261–262

Z

Zen Buddhism: conservation in, 230; equanimous mind in, 223, 228; koan practice in, 224–225; radical empiricism of, 216–217. See also Buddhism
Zen Mind, Beginner's Mind (Suzuki), 223

MORE BOOKS from
NEW HARBINGER PUBLICATIONS

MINDFULNESS & ACCEPTANCE IN MULTICULTURAL COMPETENCY
A Contextual Approach to Sociocultural Diversity in Theory & Practice
ISBN: 978-1608827466 / US $58.95
Also available as an e-book
CONTEXT PRESS
An Imprint of New Harbinger Publications, Inc.

MINDFULNESS & ACCEPTANCE FOR ADDICTIVE BEHAVIORS
Applying Contextual CBT to Substance Abuse & Behavioral Addictions
ISBN: 978-1608822164 / US $69.95
Also available as an e-book

ACT MADE SIMPLE
An Easy-To-Read Primer on Acceptance & Commitment Therapy
ISBN: 978-1572247055 / US $39.95
Also available as an e-book

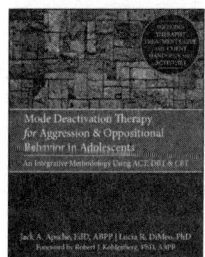

MODE DEACTIVATION THERAPY FOR AGGRESSION & OPPOSITIONAL BEHAVIOR IN ADOLESCENTS
An Integrative Methodology Using ACT, DBT & CBT
ISBN: 978-1608821075 / US $59.95
Also available as an e-book

ACCEPTANCE & COMMITMENT THERAPY FOR THE TREATMENT OF POST-TRAUMATIC STRESS DISORDER & TRAUMA-RELATED PROBLEMS
A Practitioner's Guide to Using Mindfulness & Acceptance Strategies
ISBN: 978-1608823338 / US $58.95
Also available as an e-book

MINDFULNESS-BASED SOBRIETY
A Clinician's Treatment Guide for Addiction Recovery Using Relapse Prevention Therapy, Acceptance & Commitment Therapy, and Motivational Interviewing
ISBN: 978-1608828531 / US $49.95
Also available as an e-book

newharbingerpublications
1-800-748-6273 / newharbinger.com

 Like us on Facebook
Follow us on Twitter
@newharbinger

(VISA, MC, AMEX / prices subject to change without notice)

 Don't miss out on new books in the subjects that interest you.
Sign up for our **Book Alerts** at newharbinger.com/bookalerts

Sign up to receive **QUICK TIPS for Therapists**—
fast and free solutions to common client situations mental health professionals encounter.
Written by New Harbinger authors, some of the most prominent names in psychology today,
Quick Tips for Therapists are short, helpful emails that will help enhance your client sessions.

Sign up online at **newharbinger.com/quicktips**

Register your **new harbinger** titles for additional benefits!

When you register your **new harbinger** title—purchased in any format, from any source—you get access to benefits like the following:

- Downloadable accessories like printable worksheets and extra content
- Instructional videos and audio files
- Information about updates, corrections, and new editions

Not every title has accessories, but we're adding new material all the time.

Access free accessories in 3 easy steps:

1. Sign in at NewHarbinger.com (or **register** to create an account).

2. Click on **register a book**. Search for your title and click the **register** button when it appears.

3. Click on the **book cover or title** to go to its details page. Click on **accessories** to view and access files.

That's all there is to it!

If you need help, visit:

NewHarbinger.com/accessories